Edinburgh L

SCOTTISH ENVIRONMENTAL LAW ESSENTIALS

EDINBURGH LAW ESSENTIALS

Series Editor: Nicholas Grier, Abertay University

Scottish Administrative Law Essentials
Jean McFadden and Dale McFadzean

Medical Law Essentials
Murray Earle

Property Law Essentials
Duncan Spiers

European Law Essentials
Stephanie Switzer

Intellectual Property Law Essentials
Duncan Spiers

Media Law Essentials
Douglas Maule and Zhongdong Niu

International Law Essentials
John Grant

Employment Law Essentials
Jenifer Ross

Human Rights Law Essentials
Valerie Finch and John McGroarty

Planning Law Essentials
Anne-Michelle Slater

Company Law Essentials
Josephine Bisacre and Claire McFadzean

Jurisprudence Essentials
Duncan Spiers

Trusts Law Essentials
John Finlay

Contract Law Essential Cases
Tikus Little

Scottish Legal System Essentials
Bryan Clark and Gerard Keegan

Succession Law Essentials
Frankie McCarthy

Commercial Law Essentials
Malcolm Combe

Revenue Law Essentials
William Craig

Private International Law
David Hill

Scottish Family Law
Kenneth McK. Norrie

Scottish Contract Law Essentials
Tikus Little

Public Law Essentials
Jean McFadden and Dale McFadzean

Scottish Evidence Law Essentials
James Chalmers

Legal Method Essentials for Scots Law
Dale McFadzean and Lynn Allardyce Irvine

Delict Essentials
Francis McManus

Scottish Criminal Law Essentials
Claire McDiarmid

Roman Law Essentials
Craig Anderson

edinburghuniversitypress.com/series/ele

Edinburgh Law Essentials

SCOTTISH ENVIRONMENTAL LAW ESSENTIALS

Francis McManus, M.Litt., LL.B. (Hons), F.R.I.P.H.,
F.H.E.A., M.R.E.H.I.S., Cert. Ed.
*Honorary Professor of Law, University of Stirling and
Emeritus Professor of Law, Edinburgh Napier University*

EDINBURGH
University Press

To my students

Edinburgh University Press is one of the leading university presses in the UK. We publish academic books and journals in our selected subject areas across the humanities and social sciences, combining cutting-edge scholarship with high editorial and production values to produce academic works of lasting importance. For more information visit our website: edinburghuniversitypress.com

© Francis McManus, 2020

Edinburgh University Press Ltd
The Tun – Holyrood Road
12 (2f) Jackson's Entry
Edinburgh EH8 8PJ

Typeset in 10/13 Bembo by
IDSUK (DataConnection) Ltd, and
printed and bound by CPI Group (UK) Ltd,
Croydon, CR0 4YY

A CIP record for this book is available from the British Library

ISBN 978 1 4744 1972 7 (hardback)
ISBN 978 1 4744 1973 4 (paperback)
ISBN 978 1 4744 1974 1 (webready PDF)
ISBN 978 1 4744 1975 8 (epub)

The right of Francis McManus to be identified as author of this work has been asserted in accordance with the Copyright, Designs and Patents Act 1988 and the Copyright and Related Rights Regulations 2003 (SI No. 2498).

CONTENTS

Table of Cases vii
Table of Statutes xi
Preface xxi

1	Introduction	1
2	Common Law Controls	7
3	Statutory Nuisance	21
4	Noise	35
5	Air Pollution	55
6	Waste	77
7	Contaminated Land	101
8	Water	117
9	Integrated Pollution, Prevention and Control and Environmental Permitting	137
10	Planning and Pollution Control	153

Index 177

TABLE OF CASES

Allen v Gulf Oil Refining Ltd [1981] AC 1001 .... 16, 52
Anderson v City of Dundee Council (2000) SLT (Sh Ct) 134 29
Armistead v Bowerman (1888) 15 R 814 11
Bamford v Turnley (1862) 31 LJQB 286 .... 10, 11
Barns (NE) Ltd v Newcastle upon Tyne CC [2006] Env LR 25 31
Baxendale v MacMurray (1867) LR 2 Ch 790 17
Baxter v Camden LBC [2001] 1 AC 8, 20, 36
Belew v Cement Ltd [1948] IR 61 8
Berkeley v Secretary of State for the Environment [2001] 2 AC 603 166
Breadalbane (Earl of) v Jamieson (1877) 4R 667 18
Bridlington Relay Ltd v Yorkshire Electricity Board [1965] Ch 436 .... 11, 12
British Airports Authority v Secretary of State for Scotland 1979 SC 2000 157
Brussels Hoofstedilijk Gewest v Vlaams Gewest [2011] Env LR 26 160
Buccleuch (Duke of) v Cowan (1866) 5 M 214 118
Budd v Colchester BC [1999] Env LR 739 27
Cala Homes (South) Ltd v Secretary of State for Communities and
  Local Government [2010] EWHC 97 169
Camden LBC v Gunby [2000] 1 WLR 465 29
Camden LBC v London Underground [2000] Env LR 369 27
Central RC v Barbour European Ltd 1982 SLT (Sh Ct) 49 130
Chapman v Gosberton Farm Produce Co. Ltd [1993] Env LR 191 31
Christie v Davey [1893] 1 Ch 316 8–9
Circular Facilities (London) Ltd v Sevenoaks DC [2005] Env LR 35 108
Clydebank DC v Monaville Estates Ltd 1982 SLT (Sh Ct) 2 108
Collins v Hamilton (1837) 15 S 902 17
Colville v Middleton 27 May 1817 FC 17, 18
Commission v Spain (C-227/01); [2005] Env LR 20 160
Corby Group Litigation v Corby DC [2010] Env LR D2; [2009] EWHC 1944 .... 19, 101
Coventry CC v Cartwright [1975] 1 WLR 110 23
Coventry v Doyle [1981] 1 WLR 1325 30
Coventry v Lawrence [2015] AC 106 .... 10, 17
Cowan v Kinnaird (1865) 4 M 236 17
De Keyser's Royal Hotel Ltd v Spicer Bros Ltd (1914) 30 TLR 257 11
Dees v Hungary, ECtHR App. 2345/06, 9 November 2010 45–6
Dennis v Ministry of Defence [2003] Env LR 34 44
Dennis v Ministry of Defence [2003] Env LR 741 51
Duncan v Earl of Moray 9 June 1809 17
Environment Agency v Inglenorth [2009] Env LR 33 79
Esso Petroleum Co. Ltd v The Scottish Ministers [2015] CSOH 21 18
Esso Petroleum Co. Ltd v The Scottish Ministers [2016] CSOH 15 102
Fadeyeva v Russia, ECtHR App. 55723/00, 9 June 2005 44
Fearn v Trustees of the Tate Gallery [2019] EWHC 246 12
Fleming v Gemmill 1908 SC 340 117
Fouladi v Darout Ltd [2018] EWHC 2501 15
Friends of the Earth Ltd v Secretary of State for Housing, Communities and
  Local Government [2019] EWHC 518 171
Galer v Morrisey [1955] 1 WLR 110 24
Gateshead Metropolitan BC v Secretary of State for the Environment [1995]
  Env LR 37 .... 154, 155
Gillespie v First Secretary of State [2003] Env LR 30 163

Godfrey v Conwy County BC [2000] Env LR 38 36
Goldman v Hargrave [1967] 1 AC 645 14–15
Gomez v Spain, ECtHR App. 4143/02, 16 November 2004 45
Hammersmith and City Railway Co. v Brand (1869–70) LR 4 HL 171 16
Hatton v United Kingdom (2003) 37 EHRR 28 44
Heath v Brighton Corporation (1908) 24 TLR 414 11
Hill v Wood (1863) 1 M 360 18
Hollywood Silver Fox Farm v Emmett [1936] 2 KB 9
Hope Butuyuyu v Hammersmith and Fulham LBC [1997] Env LR D 13 30
Hopkins Development Ltd v First Secretary of State and
 North Wiltshire DC [2007] Env LR 14 155
Houlsworth v Waishaw Magistrates (1887) 14 R 920 18
Hughes v Fife Council [2019] CSOH 26 14
Hunter v Canary Wharf [1997] 2 WLR 684; [1997] Env LR 488 .... 11. 12, 18, 21
Inter-Environment Bruxelles ASBL v Région de Bruxelles-Capitale (C-567/10);
 [2012] Env LR 30 169
John Young and Co. v Bankier Distillery Co. [1893] AC 391 118
Kennaway v Thomson [1981] AC 1001 35
Kennedy v Glenbelle Ltd 1996 SC 95 .... 13, 15, 20
Kent v First Secretary of State 2005 Env LR 30 166
Kerr v Earl of Orkney (1857) 20 D 298 117
King v Advocate General for Scotland [2009] CSOH 169 51
Kintore (Earl of) v Pirie and Sons (1903) 5 F 818 .... 17, 18
Lawrence v Fen Tigers [2014] AC 822 .... 16, 17
Leakey v National Trust for Places of Historical or
 Natural Beauty [1980] QB 485 15
Liverpool Corporation v Coghill and Son [1918] 1 Ch 307 17
Logan v Wang (K) Ltd 1991 SLT 580 18
Lowe Watson v South Somerset DC [1998] Env LR 143 27
McGillivray v Stephenson [1950] 1 All ER 942 28
McKenna v O'Hare [2017] SAC (Civ) 16 101
McManus v City Link Development Co. Ltd [2015] CSOH 178 .... 19, 35
Marcic v Thames Water Utilities Ltd [2004] 2 AC 56 14
Miller v Jackson [1977] QB 966 18
Milne v Stuartfield Windpower Ltd [2019] SC ABE 25 10
Mitchell v Glasgow CC [2009] 1 AC 874 35
Montgomery v Buchanan's Trustees (1853) 15 D 853 117
Myatt v Teighnbridge DC [1995] Env LR 78 27
Network Housing Association v Westminster CC [1995] Env LR 176 .... 27, 28, 29
Network Rail Infrastructure Ltd (formerly Railtrack) v
 CJ Morris [2004] Env LR 861 11–12
Newbury DC v Secretary of State for the Environment [1981] AC 578 157
Newham LBC v White (12 March 2015, unreported) 23
North Lincolnshire CC v Act Fast North Lincolnshire (CIC)
 [2013] All ER (D) 81 27
Oakley v Birmingham CC [2001] 1 AC 617 .... 22, 34
Oluic v Croatia, ECtHR App. 61260/08, 20 May 2010 46
Pettigrew v Inverclyde Council (1999) Hous LR 31 29
Potter v Hamilton and Strathaven Railway Co. (1864) 3 M 83 117
Powys CC v Price [2017] EWCA Civ 1133 107
R v Birmingham Justices, ex p Guppy [1988] JP 159 28
R v Bolton MBC, ex p Kirkman [1998] JPL 787 155
R v Bristol CC ex p Everett [1999] 2 All ER 193 22
R v Carrick DC, ex p Shelley [1996] Env LR 273 26
R v Crown Court at Canterbury [2001] Env LR 36 27
R v Falmouth and Truro Port Health Authority, ex p South West Water Ltd
 [2001] QB 445 .... 26, 27

TABLE OF CASES

R v Fenny Stratford Justices [1976] 1 WLR 1101 27
R v Parlby (1889) 22 QBD 520 21
R v Tunbridge Wells Justices [1996] Env LR 88 28
R v W [2010] Env LR 743 81
R (Bateman) v South Cambridgeshire DC [2011] EWCA Civ 157 .... 164, 165
R (Berks, Bucks and Oxon Wildlife Trust) v Secretary of State for Transport [2019]
  EWHC 1786 170
R (Birchall Gardens LLP) v Hertfordshire CC [2017] Env LR 17 .... 164, 165
R (Blewett) v Derbyshire CC [2004] Env LR 29 166
R (Buckinghamshire CC) v Secretary of State for
  Transport [2014] 1 WLR 324 .... 168, 170
R (ClientEarth) v Secretary of State for Food, Environment and
  Rural Affairs (No. 3) [2018] EWHC 315 .... 64, 67–8
R (Cooperative Group Ltd) v Northumberland CC [2010] Env LR 40 164
R (Crest Nicholson Residential Ltd) v Secretary of State for the Environment,
  Food and Rural Affairs [2011] Env LR 1 108
R (Friends of Basildon Golf Course) v Basildon DC [2011] Env LR 16 165
R (Friends of the Earth, England, Wales and Northern Ireland Ltd) v
  Welsh Ministers [2016] Env LR 1 171
R (Jones) v Mansfield DC [2004] Env LR 21 162
R (Loader) v Secretary of State for Communities and Local Government [2012]
  Env LR 8 162
R (Malster) v Ipswich BC [2002] Env LR D7 .... 162, 163
R (National Grid Gas plc) (formerly) Transco v Environment Agency [2007]
  1 WLR 1780 .... 101, 106, 107, 115
R (OSS Group Ltd) v Environment Agency [2008] Env LR 8 .... 80, 100
R (Thakeham Village Action Ltd) v Horsham DC [2014] Env LR 21 .... 164, 165
R (Treagus) v Suffolk CC [2013] Env LR 36 163
R (Vella) v Lambeth LBC [2006] Env LR 33 36
RHM Bakeries Ltd v Strathclyde RC 1985 SC (HL) 17 .... 13, 129
Robb v Dundee CC 2002 SC 301 .... 22, 23, 28, 34
Robb v Dundee CC 2002 SC 853 .... 29, 36
Rochford Rural DC v Port of London Authority [1914] 2 KB 916 29
Rushmer v Polsue and Alfieri Ltd [1907] AC 121 9
St Albans DC v Patel [2009] Env LR 22 31
St Helens Smelting Co. v Tipping (1865) 11 HL Cas 642 9
Salford CC v McNally [1976] AC 379 22
Scottish Power Generation Ltd v Scottish Environment Protection
  Agency [2005] Env LR 38 .... 78, 100
Sedleigh-Denfield v O'Callaghan [1940] AC 880 14
Shirley v Secretary of State for Communities and Local Government, Canterbury
  CC and Corinthian Mountfield Ltd [2018] EWCA Civ 22 156
Shirley v Secretary of State for Communities and Local Government, Canterbury
  CC and Corinthian Mountfield Ltd [2019] EWCA Civ 22 157
Slater v McLellan 1924 SC 854 14
Smith v Scott [1973] Ch 314 15
Southwark LBC v Ince (1989) 21 HLR 504 22
Spurrier v Secretary of State for Transport [2019] EWHC 1070 171
Steers v Manton (1893) 57 JP 584 24
Strathclyde RC v Tudhope 1983 SLT 22 .... 27, 28, 37
Sturges v Brigman (1879) 11 Ch D 22 17
Surrey Free Inns v Gosport BC 750 [1999] Env LR 350 27
Tayside RC v Secretary of State for Scotland 1996 SLT 473 132
Tetley v Chitty [1986] 1 All ER 663 35
Tronex BV, ECJ (C-624/17) 81
Trotter v Farnie (1830) 9S 144 9
Vale of White Horse DC v Allen [1997] Env LR 212 31

Walter Lilley and Co. Ltd v Westminster CC [1994] Env LR 380 38
Waltham Forest LBC v Mitoo (unreported 26 May 2016) 30
Walton v Scottish Ministers 2013 SC (UKSC) 67 169
Watkins v Aged Seamen's Homes [2018] EWHC 2410 .... 22, 32
Watson v Croft Promo Ltd [2009] 3 All ER 249 .... 8, 18
Watt v Jamieson 1954 SC 56 .... 7, 8, 14, 20
Webster v Lord Advocate 1984 SLT 11, 12, 15, 17, 18, 36
Webster v Lord Advocate 1985 SC 173 .... 11, 36
Wellingborough BC v Gordon [1993] 1 Env LR 218 30
Wincanton Rural DC v Parsons [1914] 2 KB 34 28
Young and Hartson's Contract, Re (1885) 31 ChD 168 28
Zammit Meampel v Malta, ECtHR App 242/10, 22 November 2011 47
Zarzoso v Spain, ECtHR App. 23383/12, 16 April 2018 45
Zeb v Birmingham CC [2010] Env LR 30 164

TABLE OF STATUTES

1846	Nuisance Removal Act	3, 37
1848	Nuisance Removal Act	3, 37
1848	Public Health Act	3, 37
1849	Nuisance Removal Act	3, 37
1856	Nuisance Removal Act	3, 37
1863	Alkali Works Regulation Act	2, 55, 68
1897	Public Health (Scotland) Act	127, 133
1947	Town and Country Planning (Scotland) Act	153
1956	Clean Air Act	4, 56, 59, 61, 68, 137
1965	Gulf Oil Refining Act	16
1968	Clean Air Act	61
1968	Sewerage Act	127
	s 1	128–9
	(1)	128
	(2)	129
	(3)	129
	s 3	130
	s 3A	
	(1)	130, 134
	(2)	130, 134
	s 7	
	(1)	131
	(3)	131
	s 8	
	(1)	131
	(2)	131
	s 12	
	(1)	131
	(3)	132
	(4)	132
	(5)	132
	(8)	132
	s 14	132
	s 15	
	(1)	133
	(2)	133
	(3)	133
	(4)	133
	(5)	133
	s 16	
	(1)	130, 133
	(3)	134
	s 16A	
	(1)	134
	(2)	134
	s 17	
	(1)	134
	(4)	134
	s 24(1)	134
	s 25	135

s 29	135
(1)	135
s 31	135
s 32(1)	135
s 34	135
s 36	
(1)	135
(2)	135
(3)	135
s 37A	
(1)	136
(2)	136
s 37B	136
s 54	
(4)	135
(5)	135
s 59(1)	129, 134
1972 European Communities Act	5
1974 Control of Pollution Act	4, 37, 137
s 58(4)	30
s 60	37, 52
(1)	37
(2)	37
(3)	38
(5)	38
(7)	38
(8)	38, 39
s 61	31, 38
(4)	38
(5)	38
(7)	39
(8)	39
(9)	39
(10)	39
s 62	39
1978 Refuse Disposal (Amenity) Act	
s 1	83
(3)	84
s 2	
(1)	99
(2)	99
s 3(2)	99
s 4	99
s 5	99
s 6	99
1982 Civic Government (Scotland) Act	
s 49	53
(1)	39
(2)	39
(3)	40
s 54	53
(1)	40
(2A)	40
(2B)	40
1982 Civil Aviation Act	
s 60(3)	50
s 76(1)	50

s 77
- (1) ... 51
- (2) ... 51

1984 Roads (Scotland) Act
- s 7 ... 170

1988 Road Traffic Act
- s 41 ... 52
  - (1) ... 51, 71
  - (2) ... 51, 71
- s 42 ... 52

1989 Control of Pollution (Amendment) Act 1989 ... 95
- s 1(1) ... 95

1990 Environmental Protection Act ... 4, 68, 100, 138
- s 1
  - (1) ... 92
  - (4) ... 92
- s 23 ... 92
- s 30
  - (2) ... 93
  - (3) ... 92
- s 33
  - (1) ... 79, 81, 82–3, 83, 93, 94, 95
  - (8) ... 83
- s 34
  - (1) ... 84, 85
  - (2) ... 85
  - (2A) ... 85
  - (2B) ... 85
  - (2E) ... 85
  - (2F) ... 85
  - (2G) ... 85
- s 35
  - (1) ... 85
  - (2) ... 86
  - (3) ... 86
  - (4) ... 86
  - (5) ... 86
  - (6) ... 85, 86
  - (9) ... 86
- s 36
  - (1) ... 86
  - (2) ... 86
- s 37(1) ... 88
- s 38
  - (1) ... 88
  - (2) ... 88
  - (3) ... 88
  - (4) ... 88
  - (6) ... 88
- s 39 ... 86
  - (1) ... 88
- s 40
  - (1) ... 88
  - (2) ... 89
- s 43(1) ... 87, 88, 89
- s 45
  - (1) ... 92

(1A)	92
s 45C	
(2)	92
(5)	93
(6)	93
s 53(1)	93
s 56	93
s 59	
(1)	94
(2)	94
(3)	94
(4)	94
(5)	94
(6)	94
(7)	94
(8)	94
(9)	94
s 62(1)	96
s 63(2)	95
s 73(6)	95
s 74	
(2)	87
(3)	87
(4)	87
(7)	87
s 75	
(1)	77–8
(4)	78
s 78A	
(2)	102
(3)	104
(4)	102
(4A)	102
(5)	103
(7)	111
(9)	104
s 78AQ	
(1)	113
(2)	113
(4)	113
s 78B	
(1)	103
(2)	103
(3)	103, 104
(4)	104
s 78C	
(1)	104
(2)	104
(3)	104
(4)	105
(5)	105
(7)	104
(8)	105
s 78D	
(1)	105
(4)	105
(6)	104

s 78E
- (1) 105
- (2) 105
- (3) 105
- (4) 105–6, 110
- (5) 106, 110

s 78F 103, 105, 107
- (2) 106, 107, 108
- (3) 106
- (4) 108
- (5) 108
- (6) 108
- (7) 105
- (9) 108
- (10) 108

s 78G
- (1) 109
- (2) 109

s 78H
- (1) 110
- (3) 110
- (4) 110
- (5) 110

s 78J(7) 111

s 78K
- (1) 111
- (2) 111
- (3) 111
- (4) 112
- (5) 112

s 78L
- (1) 112
- (2) 112
- (3) 113
- (4) 113
- (5) 113

s 78M(1) 113
s 78Q(4) 104
s 78R(1) 113
s 78S 113
s 78T 113
s 78TA 113

s 78U
- (1) 114
- (2) 114

s 78V
- (1) 114
- (3) 114

s 78W(1) 114

s 79
- (1) 10, 21–5, 32, 36, 37, 52
- (1A) 103
- (1B) 103
- (2) 23
- (3) 23
- (4) 23
- (5AA) 24

(7)	28
(9)	31
(10)	25
s 79G	
(3)	109
(4)	109
s 79J	
(1)	110
(2)	110
(3)	111
(4)	111
s 79N	110
(1)	113
s 79P(1)	113
s 80	26, 29
(2)	28
(3)	30
(4)	30
(4A)	30
(5)	30
(6)	30
(7)	31
(9)	31
s 81(5)	31
s 82	39
(1)	32
(2)	32, 33
(3)	32
(4)	32
(5)	32
(6)	33
(8)	33
(9)	33
(11)	33
(12)	33
Sch 3	27
1990 Town and Country Planning Act	
s 37(1)	157
s 77	156
s 288	154, 155
1993 Clean Air Act	56, 68, 74
s 1	
(1)	56
(2)	56
(3)	56
(4)	56
s 2	
(1)	56
(2)	56
(4)	56–7
(5)	57
(6)	56
s 3(1)	56
s 4	
(1)	57
(2)	57
(3)	57

(4)	57
(5)	57
s 5	
(1)	57
(2)	57
(3)	57
(4)	57
(5)	57
s 6	
(1)	58
(5)	58
s 7	
(1)	58
(2)	58
(4)	58
(5)	58
s 8	58
s 9	
(1)	58
(2)	58
s 11	58
s 14	
(2)	59
(3)	59
(4)	59
s 15	
(1)	59
(2)	59
(3)	59
(6)	59
(7)	59
s 16	59
s 18	
(1)	60
(2)	60
(3)	60
s 19	60
s 20	60, 61
(1)	60
(2)	60
(3)	60
(4)	60
(6)	60
s 21(1)	60
s 22(1)	60
s 23	60
s 24	61
s 30(1)	61
s 33	61
s 34(1)	61
s 35(1)	61
s 41A(1)	61
s 42	61
s 51	61
s 56	61
s 60	61

1993 Radioactive Substances Act

s 1A	78
s 13	78
s 14	78
s 15(2)	78
1995 Environment Act	68, 138
s 80(1)	68
s 81	68
s 82	70
(1)	69
(2)	69
(3)	69
s 83	
(1)	69
(2)	69
s 84	
(2)	69
(4)	69
s 85	
(2)	70
(3)	70
(4)	70
(5)	66, 71
(7)	71
1997 Planning (Hazardous Substances) Act	158
s 1	159
1997 Town and Country Planning (Scotland) Act	140, 160
s 37(2)	153
1998 Scotland Act	153
1999 Pollution Prevention and Control Act	4, 78, 138, 151
s 2	25, 61
2002 Water Industry (Scotland) Act	
s 2	129
s 3	
(1)	129
(2)	129
s 4	130
2003 Waste and Emissions Trading Act	91
s 1(1)	92
s 4(2)	92
s 23	92
2003 Water Environment and Water Services (Scotland) Act	120, 136
s 5	
(2)	120
(3)	120
s 8	
(1)	120
(2)	120
s 9	
(1)	121
(7)	120
s 10(1)	121
s 11	121
s 12	121
s 13	121
s 20(6)	102
2004 Antisocial Behaviour (Scotland) Act	40, 53
s 4(1)	40

s 41
- (1) 41
- (2) 41
- (3) 41

s 42 41

s 43
- (1) 41
- (2) 42
- (3) 42
- (4) 42

s 44 42
s 45(1) 42
s 46 42
s 47 42
s 53(1) 41, 42
s 143(1) 41

2004 Civil Contingencies Act 125
2005 Environmental Assessment (Scotland) Act 172, 175
- s 1(1) 172
- s 2(1) 172
- s 4
  - (1) 172
  - (2) 172
- s 5
  - (2) 172
  - (3) 172, 173
  - (4) 172
  - (5) 172
- s 6
  - (1) 172
  - (3) 172
- s 7
  - (1) 173
  - (2) 173
  - (3) 173
  - (6) 173
- s 8
  - (1) 173
  - (2) 173
- s 9
  - (1) 173
  - (2) 173
  - (4) 174
  - (5) 174
  - (6) 174
  - (7) 174
- s 10 174
- s 14
  - (1) 174
  - (2) 174
  - (3) 174
- s 15
  - (1) 174
  - (3) 174
- s 16
  - (1) 174
  - (2) 174

　　　　s 17 175
　　　　s 18(1) 175
　　　　s 19 175
　　　　Sch 1 172
　　　　Sch 2 173
　　　　Sch 3 174
2005 Licensing (Scotland) Act 2005 43
　　　　s 27(6) 43
2007 Transport and Works (Scotland) Act
　　　　s 1 16
　　　　　　(1) 52
2014 Regulatory Reform (Scotland) Act
　　　　s 18 .... 25, 61, 151
2018 European Union (Withdrawal) Act 5

PREFACE

Never before has it been more appropriate to reiterate the oft-used, author's lachrymose observation, to the effect that there is never a good time to write a textbook! At the time of writing (March 2019), the UK is just about to leave the European Union, although the precise date of withdrawal is still shrouded in some uncertainty. EU law has had a profound influence in the shaping of environmental law and policy in the UK, since our joining the EEC (as it was then known) in 1972. Whilst UK legislation makes provision for the preservation of EU law, on our departure from the EU (which, I must quickly add, is still not a certainty) it would take the foresight of a Hebrew prophet to predict, with accuracy, what the future may bring for environmental law in Scotland. Indeed, we are living in times that are as interesting as they are uncertain.

I would like to thank the following who read and commented on various draft chapters of the book: Sarah Hendry, Jim Kerr, Greg Lloyd, Thomas Muinzer, Laura Tainsh, Lindsay Tolland and Jeremy Warner.

However, any mistakes and other shortcomings in the work rest firmly with me.

I would also like to offer my sincere thanks to the staff of the University of Stirling library, Edinburgh Napier University library, the University of Edinburgh library, the library of the Institute of Advanced Legal Studies, London and the British Library, London for their help.

Finally, I would like to thank the assistance, which has been given to me in the preparation of this work, by Edinburgh University Press.

The law is considered correct as on 21 March 2019. However, it has been possible to take account of some case law that was decided after that date at proof stage.

Francis McManus
Livingston

1 INTRODUCTION

Whereas the history of environmental law in Scotland stretches much further back than the Victorian era, it was during that august period in British history that the modern law, which is discussed in this book, owes its origins. The law really developed in the wake of the Industrial Revolution, which propelled those who were formerly employed in the country to seek work in factories, which were situated in towns. However, there was insufficient housing stock to accommodate the incoming population. The automatic response to this problem was that landlords, many of whom were also employers, either subdivided existing housing stock, or constructed jerry-built houses, in order to accommodate the labouring classes. The living conditions which were endured by the occupants of the houses were generally insanitary, and on a par with those which now exist in the poorest developing countries of the present day. The pressure which was exerted on the housing stock in Scotland was exacerbated by the influx of Irish migrants during the 1840s.

In the absence of effective regulation of the development of land by way of town and country planning, the negative impact of the rapid expansion of industrial towns also resulted in factories often being constructed in close proximity to houses, the occupants of which had to endure a relentless onslaught of smoke and malodorous fumes. Indeed, smoke was a perennial problem in urban Britain. Whereas industrial air pollution was a major problem, industry was not the sole source of the problem, with smoke from domestic chimneys also being a significant problem. The regulators, namely, local authorities, had a tendency to refrain from taking enforcement action against those who flouted the law. Often local authorities avoided taking formal proceedings, because such action would offend powerful manufacturers upon whom the prosperity of towns and cities such as Glasgow and Edinburgh depended. However, another commonly advanced reason for such a passive approach on the part of local authorities, in relation to the enforcement of the law, was that elected members of local authorities were reluctant to prosecute the occupiers of factories causing the pollution because they were often themselves the owners of the factories.

Pollution from chemical works was a notorious source of atmospheric pollution. The commercial manufacture of alkali (sodium carbonate), while of great economic benefit to the country, posed a threat to the general environment in that the by-products of the process, in the form of hydrogen sulphide and hydrogen chloride, were not only malodorous but also had a destructive effect on the environment surrounding the works.

The Alkali Works Regulation Act 1863 represented a rather bold attempt to deal with the problem of pollution from chemical works. However, the Act was confined to the regulation of alkali works, which were the largest chemical industry. Importantly, the Act allowed central government to appoint an inspectorate to regulate alkali works, in order to avoid a potential conflict of interest on the part of local authorities. Another reason why Parliament decided to entrust the task of the regulation of alkali works to an independent inspectorate was that local authority sanitary inspectors (who had a lowly status in the minds of both the public and manufacturers) did not possess the technical expertise to effectively regulate such works. The Act was a success, and it was amended in due course in order to allow other chemical processes to be regulated. The number of works and processes which were regulated expanded rapidly. In 1864, eighty-four alkali works were registered.

The rapid expansion of towns inevitably placed an unbearable strain on public utilities, in particular, water supply and drainage. As far as water supply was concerned, water companies, water trusts, or municipal authorities responsible for the public water supply, were inclined to provide only enough water to meet the immediate needs of the area. Such a myopic approach to the supply of water was commonly referred to as the 'droplet' method of water supply. The upshot of this was that there was a general shortage of water. Furthermore, until well into the nineteenth century the supply of municipal water tended to be intermittent. The fact that the water supply was intermittent also rendered the supply more prone to contamination.

A prominent and defining feature of Victorian Britain was the state of our rivers. The most infamous example of river pollution in the United Kingdom was the River Thames, which, by the mid-nineteenth century, was nothing more than an open sewer. The Clyde in Glasgow and the Water of Leith in Edinburgh were also heavily polluted. Whilst industrial effluent played a significant part in polluting our rivers, municipal authorities were also culpable. As towns grew and sewerage networks developed, WCs were replacing the notorious cesspits and middens. Though the benefits of such a transition were obvious, this resulted in more effluent being produced. The easiest and most convenient method of disposing of the effluent was simply to conduct the public sewer to the nearest watercourse, and allow it flow either down-stream or down-tide. The state of rivers would be improved only towards the end of the nineteenth century by the construction of intercepting sewers, which would receive effluent from drains and conduct the effluent to the sea. However, the problem of river pollution was not confined to towns. Rural or landward areas also suffered the consequences of the Industrial Revolution. The mining industry, shale works and paper mills were notorious polluters of streams in rural Scotland. Amongst the filthiest watercourses were the Almond, Esk and Gala. Indeed, the pollution of many of Scotland's watercourses during the nineteenth and, indeed, at least until the 1960s, provides an outstanding example of ineffective regulation.

Victorian society was afflicted by a variety of diseases such as typhus, typhoid, smallpox, scarlet fever and measles, which were all endemic and occurred cyclically. Influenza was also a major killer. However, it was cholera that was the most feared disease during the nineteenth century, affecting all ranks of society. Until 1866, cholera visited the United Kingdom in waves and had a mortality rate of around 50 per cent. Whereas cholera is spread from person to person via the faecal–oral route, during the nineteenth century it was widely believed that foul odour, or miasms, especially foul odours emanating from organic matter, spread cholera. Those who espoused the miasmatic theory of transmission of disease were known as the miasmatists.

The opposing theory to the miasmatic theory was the contagion theory. The contagionists, those who adhered to this theory, believed that disease was passed from person to person by physical contact. However, until germs were discovered by Pasteur and Lister there was no theoretical foundation to support the contagionists' beliefs. The contagion theory simply did not work. The miasmatic theory was favoured by the UK government. Any legislation which had as its purpose to strike at cholera, was therefore required to eradicate its cause. Therefore, the government passed a series of statutes, namely, the Public Health Act 1848 (which did not apply to Scotland) and the Nuisance Removal Acts 1846, 1848, 1849 and 1856 (repealed). While the miasmatic theory of transmission of disease was based on a myth, it did establish a link between the external environment and human health. Indeed, the first environmental revolution had begun.

The first half of the twentieth century saw environmental law develop slowly and piecemeal. The First World War, the Depression, the Second World War and its aftermath, all combined to ensure that priority was not given to matters environmental. However, there was some legislative activity, especially in the field of housing and planning law. In 1952, an awareness of the effects of pollution on human health was reignited. It was during the winter of that year that great volumes of smoke in London's air combined with fog to produce horrendous smog which caused hundreds of deaths. The very young and the very old were the worst affected. The disaster callously drew attention to the fact that the state of the atmosphere in Britain's towns had not substantially changed since the Victorian era. The main reason for this was that the law was heavily nuisance-based. In other words, a smoke source was required to constitute a nuisance before any enforcement action could be taken. However, this was often difficult to establish. The upshot of such a deficiency in the law meant that the urban atmosphere became more polluted with the passage of time. The Clean Air Act 1956 provided a revolutionary approach to the regulation of air pollution, in that the Act relied not on the law of nuisance, but, rather, on quantitative and qualitative standards to regulate air pollution.

General interest in the environment increased during the 1960s. In 1962, Rachel Carson's rather depressing but, at the same time, seminal *Silent Spring* drew attention to the harm that pollution was having on the external environment. Surprisingly, the environmental awareness of the 1960s did not result in immediate parliamentary intervention. However, 1974 saw the passing of the Control of Pollution Act 1974, which represented the first statute in the United Kingdom to deal with environmental pollution in a more holistic and integrated fashion by requiring regulatory authorities to take into account more than one medium when considering whether to grant a licence for certain activities, such as the disposal of waste. The momentum in favour of more integrated approach to pollution control continued with the Environmental Protection Act 1990 Act (EPA), which required a regulator who was responsible for granting a permit to take into account the effect of a polluting source on the environment as a whole. The Pollution Prevention Control Act 1999, with its wide definition of 'pollution' and 'harm' caused by such pollution, completed the move in the United Kingdom to an integrated approach to pollution control in relation to consideration by the Scottish Environmental Protection Agency (SEPA) as to whether to grant a permit for an installation that falls within the scope of the regulations made under the 1999 Act (which now supersede the provisions of the regulations made under the 1990 Act). In the context of an integrated approach to pollution control, brief mention should be made of the environmental impact assessment regime, under which regulators (mainly planning authorities) are required to assess the potential environmental impact of a proposed development etc. by taking into account a wide variety of factors. Mention should also be made of strategic environmental assessment, whereby competent authorities are required to assess the environmental impacts of plans and programmes. Whereas the former regime operates at a micro level, the latter does so at macro level.

One of the main problems with the enforcement of environmental law in Scotland is that, until comparatively recently, there were a variety of agencies responsible for enforcing environmental law. Often different agencies were responsible for regulating different forms of pollution from the same source, for example, a factory. The system of enforcement in Scotland was, in effect, transformed in 1996 with the creation of SEPA, which is a central agency responsible for the functions previously carried out by HM Industrial Pollution Inspectorate, the River Purification authorities, and certain functions of local authorities. Currently, SEPA's responsibilities include regulating activities that may pollute water, and the atmosphere, waste, radioactive substances and contaminated land.

One of the most important developments in the development of UK environmental law, post-Second World War, was the United Kingdom joining the European Economic Community (ECC, now the European Union, EU). Indeed, approximately over 80 per cent of environment-related laws are currently driven by the EU. The main areas in which environmental policy is largely, but not exclusively, EU-driven are air pollution, water and waste, and the permitting of industrial emissions. The EU has also been influential in climate change. Mention should also be made of the subject of environmental assessment, which is EU-driven.

At the time of writing (March 2019) the United Kingdom was poised to leave the EU. However, the precise departure date remains uncertain. The European Union (Withdrawal) Act 2018 (the Withdrawal Act) made provision for the repeal of the European Communities Act 1972 on 29 March 2019; this date has currently been extended to 31 October 2019. The Withdrawal Act provides for the conversion of directly applicable EU law (for example, EU regulations) into UK law. The Withdrawal Act also provides for the preservation of all the laws that have been made in the UK, in order to implement EU obligations, for example, EU directives. However, generally speaking, there will be little substantive difference in substantive UK environmental law on the day after which the UK leaves the EU.

However, the withdrawal of the United Kingdom from the EU leaves gaps in environmental governance. EU institutions, in the form of the European Commission and the Court of Justice, can hold the UK (and other member states) accountable for both the implementation of environmental law and also the environmental protection that is required by EU law. The European Environment Agency also plays an important role in the collation of environmental information and providing member states with relevant advice.

In 2018, the UK government published the draft Environmental Principles and Governance Bill, the object of which is to deal with environmental protection and governance in the United Kingdom post-Brexit. The draft Bill, *inter alia*, requires the Secretary of State to prepare a statement on environmental principles. These principles include: (1) the precautionary principle; (2) the principle of preventative action in order to prevent environmental damage; (3) the principle that environmental damage should be rectified at source; (4) the polluter pays principle; (5) and the principle of sustainable development. Furthermore, a minister of the crown is required to have regard to these principles when making, developing or revising policies that are dealt with by the statement.

Environment is a devolved function. In February 2019, the Scottish government launched a consultation paper on the subject of environmental principles and governance after Brexit. 'Environmental governance' is defined as including the scrutiny of government performance and the extent to which stated environmental objectives are being achieved. The Scottish government propose that Scottish ministers have regard to principles (1)–(4) listed above in the development of policies and legislation. Indeed, the Scottish government is committed to ensuring that these principles, which were established by the Treaty of the European Union (TFEU), remain at the heart of environmental policy and law.

By way of general conclusion, in the author's opinion, we may be on the cusp of a third environmental revolution taking place in the United Kingdom. However, in sharp contradistinction to the first and second, the third revolution (where the UK must re-examine the nature, content and sufficiency of its environmental policies and laws) is being prompted not by traumatic natural events, as were the first and second, but, rather, by the United Kingdom leaving the European Union.

2 COMMON LAW CONTROLS

In this chapter we look at the role of the common law as an instrument of environmental control. We commence with a discussion of the law of nuisance. We then briefly turn our attention to harm that is caused by negligent conduct.

THE LAW OF NUISANCE

The law of nuisance concerns itself with resolving conflicting interests in the use of land. The law of nuisance protects the occupier of land from unreasonable interference of his or her land from activities which are taking place out-with that land. In essence, the law of nuisance is concerned with the law of neighbourhood. However, the expression 'nuisance' is an amorphous concept. Indeed, one of the most outstanding and, at the same time, enduring features of the law of nuisance is that it has suffered from definitional problems. Indeed, both academics and judges have struggled to give a comprehensive definition of the expression 'nuisance'. As far as the law of Scotland is concerned, in *Watt* v *Jamieson* 1954 SC 56, which is the most frequently cited case on the law of nuisance, Lord President Cooper (who was sitting in the Outer House), whilst not attempting to define the concept, proffered a brief overview of the function of the law of nuisance. The facts of the case were simple. The pursuer, who was the proprietor of the upper floors in a flatted residence, brought an action in nuisance against the owner of the lower floors. The pursuer claimed that the effluvium from a gas water heater on the lower floors, which discharged into a flue situated on the mutual gable of the building, had caused damage to his property. By way of a defence, the defender claimed that the acts which were complained of involved only the normal, natural and familiar use of a dwelling house. In rejecting this defence, Lord Cooper stated (at [57]) that whether or not any state of affairs ranked as a nuisance depended on considerations of fact and degree. His Lordship went on to state that the critical question facing the courts was whether what the pursuer was exposed to was *plus quam tolerabile*, when due weight had been given to all surrounding circumstances of the offensive conduct and its effects. Lord Cooper added that any type of use that subjected adjoining proprietors to substantial annoyance was not a reasonable use.

UNREASONABLE CONDUCT

It is only unreasonable conduct on the part of the defender that is capable of being categorised a nuisance in law: *Watt* v *Jamieson* (above). This principle is well illustrated in the House of Lords case of *Baxter* v *Camden LBC* [2001] 1 AC 1. There, the claimants were local authority tenants. They occupied flats that had been constructed, or adapted, for multiple occupation. Unfortunately, the flats were inadequately soundproofed, the result of which was that the tenants of the flats could hear literally everything their neighbours were doing. Therefore, the tenants brought proceedings, *inter alia*, in nuisance against their local authority landlords. The House held, however, that the noise in question did not rank as a nuisance in law, since the noise emanated from the everyday normal and ordinary use of the flats.

What factors are taken into account?

Our attention now turns to the various factors which a court does, or does not, take into account when considering whether an adverse state of affairs ranks as a nuisance in law.

Social utility

The social utility (or usefulness) of the activity that causes the adverse state of affairs is taken into account. The more socially useful the relevant activity is, the less likely the court would be willing to castigate the adverse state of affairs a nuisance in law. The courts have quite readily recognised the usefulness of factories (see *Belew* v *Cement Ltd* [1948] IR 61). However, as far as other forms of activity are concerned, the courts have been less willing to take into account the social utility of the defender's activity when deciding if a nuisance exists (see, e.g., *Watson* v *Croft Promo Ltd* [2009] 3 All ER 249).

Motive of defender

If the defender simply wishes to punish, or exact retribution on the pursuer, the courts lean heavily towards the view that the adverse state of affairs, which the defender has created, ranks as a nuisance in law. The leading case is *Christie* v *Davey* [1893] 1 Ch 316. Here, the claimant's family were musically inclined. They frequently practised their musical instruments at home. This annoyed the defendant. He retaliated by banging trays on the party wall that separated his house from that of the claimant. It was held that the noise that the defendant generated, by so doing, constituted a nuisance. Again, in *Hollywood Silver Fox Farm* v *Emmett* [1936] 2 KB 468 the defendant, who was a speculative builder, had acquired land in order to build houses. However, he feared that foxes, which were bred by the claimant on land that adjoined his land, would deter potential buyers. He therefore, caused guns to be fired on the boundary that separated his premises from that of the claimant. As a result of this, the vixen on the farm became excited and devoured their young. It was held that the defendant's conduct amounted to a nuisance in law, since the conduct was motivated by spite.

Locality

In determining whether a given state of affairs ranks as a nuisance in law, the courts take into account the nature of the relevant locality (see, e.g., *Trotter* v *Farnie* (1830) 9S 144). In short, the more in keeping the adverse state of affairs is with the surrounding locality, the less likely that the state of affairs will rank as a nuisance. However, whilst the courts are less inclined to castigate as a nuisance a state of affairs that is indigenous in the area, the courts are not prepared to accord the defender carte blanche to create a nuisance. For example, in *Rushmer* v *Polsue and Alfieri Ltd* [1907] AC 121, the claimant resided in an area that was devoted to printing and allied trades. The defendants set up machinery that caused serious disturbance to the claimant and his family during the night. The House of Lords upheld an injunction restraining the defendants from causing a nuisance. Whilst the House recognised that those who resided in towns could not expect to have as pure air, or as healthy an environment, as those residing in the country, excess smoke, smell and noise in towns was capable of causing a nuisance. It was a question of degree in each case. The House added that whether the adverse state of affairs was a nuisance was a question of fact.

However, in a nuisance action the nature of the locality is only pertinent if the relevant state of affairs affects personal comfort. If the relevant state of affairs causes sensible, or physical, damage to either the heritable, or moveable, property of the pursuer, the nature of the locality is redundant. The leading case on this point is *St Helens Smelting Co.* v *Tipping* (1865) 11 HL Cas 642. Here, the vapours from the defendant's copper-smelting works, which were situated in a heavily industrialised area, damaged the trees on the claimant's estate. The House of Lords held that the nature of the locality could not be taken into account when considering whether the adverse state of affairs, which was the subject of the action, ranked as a nuisance.

Brief mention should be made of the effect, if any, of planning permission on the law of nuisance. The English courts have been grappling with this question since the early 1990s. The leading case on this issue is now the Supreme Court case of *Coventry* v *Lawrence* [2015] AC 106. Here, planning permission was granted in 1979 to construct a sports complex and stadium. At first, speedway racing took place; later banger and stock-car racing were introduced. Planning permission was subsequently granted for other motor-related sports. The claimants, who lived in close proximity to the stadium, became affected by noise from the stadium. They raised an action against the organisers of the motor sports, amongst others. At first instance, it was held that noise that emanated from the stadium constituted a nuisance in law. On appeal, the Court of Appeal held that both the grant of planning permission, coupled with the implementation of that permission, had the effect of changing the character of the area in terms of the law of nuisance. The claimants appealed.

The Supreme Court held, *inter alia*, that whereas the grant of planning permission cannot, per se, change the character of the land, or authorise a nuisance, the grant of planning permission could be accorded some import in deciding whether the relevant adverse state of affairs ranked as a nuisance in law.

There is no Scottish authority as to whether planning consent has any relevance in relation to common law nuisance. The author would suggest, however, that the development control regime has no influence on the development of the law of nuisance. In other words, planning permission for any development has no relevance as to whether the alleged adverse state of affairs that emanates from that development (which is the subject matter of the complaint) ranks as a nuisance. This is so for the simple reason that, whereas the planning regime regulates the use of land for the benefit of the public as a whole, the *raison d'être* of the law of nuisance, on the other hand, is to strike a balance between conflicting uses of land.

In the Sheriff Court case of *Milne* v *Stuartfield Windpower Ltd* [2019] SC ABE 25, the court was required to determine whether noise from a wind turbine ranked as a statutory nuisance in terms of s. 79(1)(g) of the EPA 1990. The learned sheriff was prepared to apply the learning in *Lawrence* in determining whether the noise in question ranked as a statutory nuisance.

Duration and intensity

Both the length of time over which a state of affairs exists, as well as its intensity, are taken into account when the court is deciding whether the state of affairs ranks as a nuisance (*Bamford* v *Turnley* (1862) 31 LJQB 286).

As far as noise is concerned, the nature of the noise is a relevant factor. That is to say, the more pleasant sounding the noise, the less likely it is that the noise will rank as a nuisance (*Webster* v *Lord Advocate* 1984 SLT 13; that part of the decision of the Outer House concerning the nature of the interdict which was granted to the pursuer, was overturned by the Inner House: 1985 SC 173).

Time of day

The time of day when the relevant adverse state of affairs exists may be a relevant factor. However, this factor is only relevant to noise pollution, and probably also light pollution. (See, e.g., *Bamford* v *Turnley* and *De Keyser's Royal Hotel Ltd* v *Spicer Bros Ltd* (1914) 30 TLR 257.)

Sensitivity of pursuer

As a general rule in law, the courts are unwilling to award a remedy to the oversensitive. As far as the relevance of sensitivity and the law of nuisance are concerned, the leading case is *Heath* v *Brighton Corporation* (1908) 24 TLR 414. Here, an Anglican priest complained about the noise and vibrations which came from the defendant's premises. However, the claimant failed in his action against the local authority occupier of the premises on the grounds that the sole reason why the claimant was adversely affected by the noise was that the priest had hyper-sensitive hearing.

The principle that the law will not protect the oversensitive also applies in relation to the enjoyment of property on the land of the pursuer. A good illustration of this is *Armistead* v *Bowerman* (1888) 15 R 814. Here, the defender was involved in moving timber. The timber was dragged across a stream, as a consequence of which the bed of the stream became disturbed and silt was carried downstream. As a result, ova in the pursuer's salmon hatchery was destroyed. It was held that no liability lay, in terms of the law of nuisance, since the pursuer's use of the stream was too sensitive to attract redress in terms of the law of nuisance. (See also *Bridlington Relay Ltd* v *Yorkshire Electricity Board* [1965] Ch 436.) More recently, in *Hunter* v *Canary Wharf Ltd* [1997] 2 WLR 684, the House of Lords was not prepared to rule out the possibility that the interference of the reception of television signals could never constitute an actionable nuisance.

The above cases were reviewed by the Court of Appeal in *Network Rail Infrastructure Ltd (formerly Railtrack)* v *CJ Morris* [2004] Env LR 861. In that case, it was claimed that Railtrack's signalling system had caused electromagnetic interference with electric guitars, which were being played in the claimant's recording studios. It was, however, held that amplified guitars fell into the category of extraordinary sensitive equipment, and, therefore, did not attract the protection of the law of nuisance.

The issue of the sensitive use of land, in terms of the law of nuisance, was discussed in the High Court case of *Fearn* v *Trustees of the Tate Gallery* [2019] EWHC 246. The issue that the court was required to decide was whether the claimants, who were residents of flats situated in close proximity to the Tate Modern Gallery in London, could successfully raise an action in nuisance against the defendants on the grounds that members of the public using the viewing gallery could stare into the flats. Mann J was prepared to accept the proposition that, by virtue of the claimants having chosen to reside in flats that afforded the public the opportunity to observe the residents of the flats, by virtue of the fact that the external walls of the flats were glazed, this constituted a sensitive use of property in terms of the law of nuisance.

Social utility of pursuer's activities etc.

There is some authority to the effect that, in determining whether the conduct of the defender ranks as a nuisance, the court takes into account the social utility of the use to which the pursuer's premises are put. The relevant case law is confined to the interference with television signals. In *Bridlington Relay Ltd* v *Yorkshire Electricity Board* [1965] Ch 436, it was held that the interference with the reception of television signals did not attract the protection of the law of nuisance, since television viewing was purely recreational in nature. However, in the House of Lords case of *Hunter* v *Canary Wharf Ltd* [1997] Env LR 488 at 493, Lord Goff expressed the view, *obiter*, that the function of television transcended that of mere entertainment, and that interference with such an amenity might, in certain circumstances, warrant the protection of the law of nuisance.

Could adverse state of affairs have been avoided by the pursuer?

The general rule is that the courts are unwilling to take into account the fact that the pursuer has failed to take requisite measures which would have either prevented or mitigated the effects of the adverse state of affairs in question. This principle is illustrated in the Outer House case of *Webster* v *Lord Advocate* 1984 SLT 13. A successful reclaiming motion, on the terms of the interdict that was granted to the pursuer, was made by the defender to the Inner House (see 1985 SLT 361). However, see also *Fearn* v *Board of Trustees of the Tate Gallery* (above).

Requirement of culpa

In a nuisance action in Scots law, the pursuer is required to aver and prove *culpa* (or fault) on the part of the defender. The leading case on this point is the House of Lords case of *RHM Bakeries Ltd* v *Strathclyde Regional Council* 1985 SC (HL) 17. In that case, bakery premises, which were occupied by the pursuer, were flooded as a result of the collapse of a main sewer that was vested (that is, under the control of) the defender local authority. The pursuer sued the defender, *inter alia*, in nuisance. The House of Lords held that in order to succeed, the pursuer was required to aver and prove *culpa* or fault on the part of the defender. The pursuer failed in its action, since it was unable to do so. Unfortunately, the House refrained from discussing the nature and scope of *culpa* in terms of the law of nuisance.

However, the Inner House had an opportunity to do so in the Inner House case of *Kennedy* v *Glenbelle Ltd* 1996 SC 95. There, the pursuers were the heritable proprietors of tenement properties. The first defenders, who were the tenants of a basement flat, engaged the second defenders, who were a firm of consulting engineers, to advise on, direct and also to supervise, a scheme for the removal of a section, or sections, of a load-bearing wall within the premises. The pursuer raised an action against the defenders, the former claiming that, as a result of the work which was being carried out in the basement, the pursuer's property had subsided. The basis of the action was that the carrying out of the renovation work (in such a way that the pursuer's premises were damaged) amounted to a nuisance in law, as well as an act of negligence. The court was of the view that *culpa* could be established if the pursuer could prove that the defender was negligent. However, in the view of the Inner House, the concept of *culpa* was wider than that of negligence, and included malice, reckless or deliberate conduct on the part of the pursuer. In the last analysis, the fact that the defenders knew that the deliberate removal of a section of the basement wall would result in damage to the pursuer's premises was sufficient to constitute the requisite *culpa* to ground liability in nuisance.

By way of conclusion, the concept of *culpa* is not well articulated as far as the law of nuisance is concerned. *Kennedy* v *Glenbelle* concerned physical harm which was caused by the carrying out of building works. However, the vast majority of nuisance cases concern liability for various forms of pollution, such as noise and air pollution. Therefore, it may sometimes be difficult to apply the learning in *Kennedy* to this form of nuisance.

Liability in nuisance: who may be sued?
The author of the nuisance

The person who creates the nuisance (that is to say, the author of the relevant nuisance) is liable in law (see, e.g., *Watt* v *Jamieson* 1954 SC 56). It is not necessary that the author of the nuisance has a proprietary interest in the land from which the adverse state of affairs emanates (*Slater* v *McLellan* 1924 SC 854; *Marcic* v *Thames Water Utilities Ltd* [2004] 2 AC 56). For example, the organisers of a rave, on vacant land, would be liable for excessive noise that annoys residents in the vicinity.

The occupier of land

The occupier of land from which the nuisance emanates is normally liable in law (*Sedleigh-Denfield* v *O'Callaghan* [1940] AC 880). In *Sedleigh-Denfield* a local authority trespassed on the land of the defender. The local authority then constructed a culvert on a ditch. One of the employees of the defendant knew of the existence of the culvert. Furthermore, the defendants used the culvert to get rid of water from their land. However, the culvert had not been properly constructed, the consequence of which was that it became blocked with detritus. One day, a heavy thunderstorm caused the ditch to flood. The claimant's land became flooded as a consequence. The House of Lords held the defendant liable in nuisance on the basis that the defender had both continued and adopted the nuisance. The nuisance had been adopted by virtue of the defendant using the culvert for its own purposes. The nuisance had also been continued because the defendant had failed to take the relevant remedial measures after becoming aware (through one of its employee) of the existence of the nuisance. (See also *Hughes* v *Fife Council* [2019] CSOH 26.)

Whereas in *Sedleigh-Denfield* the adverse state of affairs, which harmed the claimant's property, was foist upon the occupier by an act of man, in contrast in *Goldman* v *Hargrave*[1967] 1 AC 645, the adverse state of affairs was created by an act of nature. In this case, a tall gum tree, which was situated on the defendant's land, was struck by lightning. The tree caught fire. The defendant cut the tree down the following day. However, he did not take further steps to prevent the fire from spreading, preferring simply to let it burn itself out. Several days later the weather changed. The wind became stronger and the air temperature also increased. This caused the fire to revive. It spread to the claimant's land, which was damaged. On appeal from the High Court of Australia, the Privy Council held that the defendant was liable for the harm which was caused, on the basis that he had failed to remove the nuisance from his land. Furthermore, no distinction fell to be made between liability in terms of the law of nuisance and that in negligence. However, in determining whether the defendant had failed to reach the standard of care which was demanded of the defendant, one was required to adopt a subjective approach. That is to say, one was required to take into account both the defendant's physical and also financial resources.

The Court of Appeal was required to consider whether the learning in *Goldman* applied to the law of England in *Leakey v National Trust for Places of Historical or Natural Beauty* [1980] QB 485. In that case, the claimants owned houses, which were situated at the base of a steep conical hill bearing the illustrious name the 'Burrow Mump'. Part of the hill, which adjoined the claimants' land, had become unstable. The condition of the hill had been made known to the defendants by the claimants. However, the defendants took no remedial action. After a few weeks, there was a substantial fall of earth and a few tree stumps on to the land of the claimant. The Court of Appeal held the defendants liable in nuisance. In so doing, the court did not distinguish between a nuisance that had been foist on the defendant by man-made activities and a state of affairs that arose by the operation of nature.

It is suggested that the above trilogy of cases apply to the law of Scotland. It should be mentioned, however, that given the breadth of the concept of *culpa*, as expressed in *Kennedy v Glenbelle Ltd*, the degree of fault that is required to ground liability in terms of the law of nuisance, a Scottish court would have no need to avail itself of the learning in these cases when determining whether an occupier of land is liable for harm that has been caused as a consequence of a failure to remove a nuisance from his or her land.

The landlord

A landlord is not liable for every nuisance emanating from the property that he or she has leased (see, e.g., *Smith v Scott* [1973] Ch 314 and *Fouladi v Darout Ltd* [2018] EWHC 2501). For example, a landlord is not liable in nuisance for noise that is made by his or her tenants. However, a landlord is liable for any nuisance that he or she has authorised the tenant to create, or for a nuisance that is either the certain, or highly probable, result of the tenant's occupation of the leased premises: *Smith v Scott* [1973] Ch 314.

The licensor of the nuisance

If the defender authorises the creation of the nuisance, especially if he or she makes no attempt to either abate or remove the nuisance, the defender is liable for the nuisance: *Webster v Lord Advocate* 1984 SLT 13.

Defences

We now briefly discuss defences that are specifically relevant to nuisance. However, it should be stressed that other defences that apply in the law of delict are also relevant (Francis McManus, *Delict Essentials*, 3rd edn, 2017, ch. 11).

Statutory authority

If Parliament has sanctioned, or approved, the very state of affairs which constitutes the relevant nuisance, this provides a complete defence to an action in nuisance. However, the defence is confined to sanction or approval by Acts of Parliament. The defence does not apply to operations, activities, premises, etc. which have been granted planning permission: *Lawrence* v *Fen Tigers* [2014] AC 833; aka *Coventry* v *Lawrence* (see above). The leading case on the defence of statutory authority is the House of Lords case of *Allen* v *Gulf Oil Refining Ltd* [1981] AC 1001. In that case, a private Act of Parliament, namely, the Gulf Oil Refining Act 1965, authorised the defendants, a multinational oil company, to acquire land in order to construct an oil refinery. However, soon after the refinery commenced operations, certain residents who lived in the vicinity of the refinery began to complain about the smell, noise and vibration emanating from the plant. The residents raised an action in nuisance against the defendants. The defendants, in turn, invoked the defence of statutory authority. The House of Lords held that the Act had authorised, either by express or necessary implication, both the construction and the operation of the refinery. The inevitable consequence of this was the creation of the nuisance in question. The claimants, therefore, failed in their action. However, the defence of statutory authority does not apply if the activities which are the subject matter of the nuisance action are being carried out negligently.

However, if the relevant statute authorises the relevant activity to be carried out without causing a nuisance, the defence of statutory authority is inapplicable if the activity is carried on in such a manner as to cause a nuisance: *Hammersmith and City Railway Co.* v *Brand* (1869–70) LR 4 HL 171.

Whilst there is no authority on the point, it is the view of the author that that which is authorised by an order which has been made by Scottish ministers under s. 1 of the Transport and Works (Scotland) Act 2007, would be immune from successful challenge in terms of the law of nuisance, under the defence of statutory authority.

Prescription

The law will not provide a remedy to a pursuer who has failed to complain in the face of a nuisance for twenty years or more: *Duncan v Earl of Moray* 9 June 1809. In order that the defence can succeed, it is necessary that the nuisance has remained substantially the same over the prescriptive period: *Webster v Lord Advocate* 1984 SLT 13. For the defence to succeed, it is also necessary that the nuisance has been actionable over the prescriptive period: *Sturges v Bridgman* (1879) 11 Ch D 22. Therefore, since liability in nuisance is prefaced on *culpa* there must also be a convergence of fault on the part of the defender, and the manifestation of the nuisance for the defence to succeed. However, the nuisance need not have been in uninterrupted existence over the prescriptive period. It simply suffices that the nuisance manifests itself, on a frequent basis, during that period: *Sturges v Bridgman*; *Webster v Lord Advocate*; *Lawrence v Fen Tigers* [2014] AC 822. For the defence to succeed, the pursuer must have had either actual or constructive knowledge of the nuisance: *Liverpool Corporation v Coghill and Son* [1918] 1 Ch 307. The prescriptive period commences when the pursuer could have successfully raised a successful action against the defender (*Liverpool Corporation v Coghill and Son*). Finally, if the defender does acquire a prescriptive right to continue a nuisance, he or she does not, thereby, acquire the right either to create another nuisance or increase its intensity (*Baxendale v MacMurray* (1867) LR 2 Ch 790).

Acquiescence

Scots law recognises the defence of acquiescence in relation to a nuisance action. This defence is quite separate from that of prescription: *Collins v Hamilton* (1837) 15 S 902. The defence of acquiescence must be specifically pled: *Colville v Middleton* 27 May 1817 FC. For the defence to succeed, it is required to be a clear, unequivocal and also positive act on the part of the pursuer, which indicates that he or she has consented to being adversely affected by the relevant nuisance. The person who is alleged to have acquiesced in the face of the nuisance is required to have had full knowledge of the nuisance, and also possessed the power to abate, or stop, the thing of which it is complained: *Earl of Kintore v Pirie and Sons* (1903) 5 F 818. Furthermore, mere silence, or passiveness, in the face of the nuisance is insufficient to ground the defence: *Cowan v Kinnaird* (1865) 4 M 236. However, the occupation of the land that is affected by the nuisance, coupled with the knowledge of the existence of the nuisance, is capable of raising the presumption that the pursuer has acquiesced to its continuance: *Colville* v *Middleton* 27 May 1817 FC. Furthermore, the longer the pursuer remains impassive in the face of the nuisance, the stronger is the presumption that the pursuer has acquiesced. However, in *Colville* it was held that twenty-two years of passive inaction on the part of the pursuer was insufficient to ground the defence. Since the defence is based on implied consent, the defence of acquiescence is redundant if the pursuer objects timeously to the nuisance: *Hill* v *Wood* (1863) 1 M 360. Furthermore, the pursuer can only acquiesce in the face of the effects of a nuisance, in contradistinction to the creation of the adverse state of affairs from which the nuisance arises: *Earl of Kintore* v *Pirie* (1903) 5 F 818. The act of acquiescence can be inferred from circumstances of the case: *Houldsworth* v *Wishaw Magistrates* (1887) 14 R 920. The defence does not apply if the nuisance differs, either in nature or intensity, from that which has been consented to by the pursuer: *Colville* v *Middleton* 27 May 1817 FC 9; *Houldsworth* v *Wishaw Magistrates* (1887) 14 R 920.

The fact that the pursuer has 'come to' the nuisance that is the subject matter of the action, is not a defence in a nuisance action: *Webster* v *Lord Advocate* 1984 SLT 13 (over-ruled by Inner House 1985 SC 173 in relation to the terms of interdict which the Lord Ordinary granted). See also *Miller* v *Jackson* [1977] QB 966; *Watson* v *Croft Promo Sport Ltd* [2009] 3 All ER 249.

Remedies

In order to raise a successful action in nuisance, it is necessary that the pursuer is required to have a proprietary interest in the land which is affected by the relevant nuisance: *Hunter* v *Canary Wharf Ltd* [1997] Env LR 488. The remedies of damages, interdict and declarator, which apply generally in Scots law, are applicable in nuisance actions.

As far as the remedy of interdict is concerned, there is some weak authority to the effect that if the pursuer raises an action for an interdict in relation to a nuisance, he does not require to aver and prove *culpa*, or fault, on the part of the defender: *Logan* v *Wang (K) Ltd* 1991 SLT 580; *Esso Petroleum Co. Ltd* v *The Scottish Ministers* [2015] CSOH 21. However, in the view of the author, one is, indeed, required to prove *culpa*. This is the case simply because an interdict is a preventative proceeding in order to prevent a wrong being done: *Earl of Breadalbane* v *Jamieson* (1877) 4R 667 at 671 (*per* Lord President Inglis). The grant of an interdict must, therefore, be prefaced on the existence of either a wrong or a threatened wrong. There can be no separation of the concept of 'wrong' and that of 'fault' (or *culpa*) in terms of any state of affairs that constitutes a nuisance. That is to say, the concept of fault is inextricably enmeshed in the very activity that generates the adverse state of affairs that is the subject matter of the action. Therefore, before any state of affairs can rank as a nuisance, which falls to be interdicted, the adverse state of affairs is required to be caused by *culpa*, or fault, on the part of the defender.

Negligence

Brief mention can only be made in a book of this nature of the role of the law of negligence in terms of environmental law. There are a variety of circumstances, ranging from harm caused by the negligent release of fumes from industrial premises, to harm caused by the occupier of a factory negligently allowing effluvium to escape from his or her premises and then polluting an adjoining stream. A tragic example of the law of negligence being invoked to secure redress for harm is seen in *Corby Group Litigation* v *Corby DC* [2010] Env LR D2. Here, the claimants had been born with serious birth defects. The claimants claimed that their mothers had been exposed to certain contaminants during pregnancy, which they attributed to the clean-up of contaminated land by the defendant in the area where they resided. It was held that the defendant had breached its duty of care to the claimants, in that it had failed to prevent the escape of mud and dust containing contaminants from the sites which it owned and operated. (See also *McManus* v *City Link Development Co. Ltd* [2015] CSOH 178.)

Essential Facts

- The law of nuisance protects the enjoyment of the occupier of land from interference of that land by unreasonable conduct which takes place out-with that land.
- The courts take a variety of factors into account in determining whether any adverse state of affairs ranks as a nuisance, namely, the social utility of the defender's conduct, the motive of the defender, the nature of the locality, the duration and intensity of the state of affairs, the time of day, the sensitivity of the pursuer and the social utility of activity of premises affected by adverse state of affairs.
- A nuisance normally requires some form of emanation from the premises of the defender.

- The pursuer is required to prove *culpa*, or fault, on the part of the defender.
- The creator, or author, of the nuisance is liable.
- The licensor of the nuisance may be liable.
- A landlord is not liable for every nuisance that emanates from premises that he or she has leased.
- If Parliament has sanctioned the state of affairs that constitute the nuisance, this is a complete defence.
- The law will not give a remedy if the pursuer has failed to complain for twenty years, or more, in the face of a nuisance.
- The pursuer may also lose his or her right to raise an action if he or she acquiesces in the face of it.
- In order to raise an action, the pursuer is required to have a proprietary interest in the land which is affected by the nuisance.
- The relevant remedies are interdict, damages and declarator.

Essential Cases

Watt v Jamieson (1954): the law must strike a balance between the right of a proprietor of land to do as he or she pleases on his or her own land and the similar right of a neighbour. Whether the state of affairs complained of ranks as a nuisance is a question of fact and degree. One approaches the issue from the viewpoint of the pursuer.

Baxter v Camden LBC (2001): it is only conduct that is unreasonable that can rank as a nuisance.

Kennedy v Glenbelle Ltd (1996): the pursuer must prove *culpa*, or fault, on the part of the defender.

3 STATUTORY NUISANCE

INTRODUCTION

In the last chapter we looked at how a private individual can invoke the common law to secure redress against the defender whose conduct unreasonably interferes with the former's enjoyment of land. However, the common law has its limitations. For one thing, to raise an action in nuisance is expensive. We have also seen, in *Hunter* v *Canary Wharf Ltd* ([1997] Env LR 488), that the pursuer requires a proprietary interest in the land that is affected by the conduct of the defender, in order to raise an action in nuisance.

In this chapter we look at the subject of statutory nuisance which, as we have seen (p. 3, above), has its origins in the mid-nineteenth century. Currently, the law relating to statutory nuisance is found in ss. 79–82 of the EPA 1990, to which we now turn our attention.

STATUTORY NUISANCES

Section 79(1) of the EPA designates a variety of adverse environmental circumstances as a nuisance. We now look at each in turn.

Premises

Under s. 79(1)(a) 'any premises in such a state as to be prejudicial to health or a nuisance' rank as a statutory nuisance and, therefore, fall to be dealt with in terms of the EPA. The subsection comprises two quite separate limbs, namely:

(a) premises that are prejudicial to health; and

(b) premises that are a nuisance.

Therefore, in order to rank as a statutory nuisance the relevant premises must either be prejudicial to health or a nuisance, or both.

'Prejudicial to health'

In order for premises to be prejudicial to health, in terms of the EPA, the physical state of the premises must be prejudicial to health, in contrast to the use to which the premises are put (see, e.g., *R* v *Parlby* (1889) 22 QBD 520). Furthermore, it is not sufficient that the relevant state of affairs simply interferes with human comfort. Rather, the premises must affect human health: *Salford City Council* v *McNally* [1976] AC 379. The mischief at which the EPA is striking at is risk to human health, excluding such risk, by way of an accident which is posed by the state of the premises: *R* v *Bristol City Council ex p Everett* [1999] 2 All ER 193. Therefore, in *Everett* premises that contained a steep staircase, which posed a risk of falling, to either occupants or visitors, could not be described as prejudicial to health. In *Watkins* v *Aged Seamen's Homes* [2018] EWHC 2410, it was held that it is a question of fact and degree whether the relevant premises are prejudicial to health.

Premises can be rendered prejudicial to health by a state of affairs (for example, noise) that exists outside the premises: *Southwark LBC* v *Ince* (1989) 21 HLR 504. However, for premises to be prejudicial to health the premises must contain some intrinsic feature, or attribute, that renders the premises prejudicial to health. It is not sufficient that the physical layout of the premises is conducive to insanitary practices on the part of those who reside in the premises. The leading case on this requirement is the House of Lords case of *Oakley* v *Birmingham City Council* [2001] 1 AC 617. In that case, the ground floor of a house included a bathroom with a washbasin. The bathroom was situated next to a kitchen which had a sink. On the side of the kitchen, which was situated opposite the bathroom, was a door which led to a lavatory. There was no washbasin in the lavatory. Furthermore, there was no room to install a washbasin. The local authority served an abatement notice on the owner of the premises, the local authority being of the opinion that the premises were prejudicial to health in terms of s. 79(1)(a) of the EPA. However, the House of Lords held that the premises were not prejudicial to health, in terms of the EPA, on the grounds that it was not sufficient that the physical layout of the premises was conducive to unhygienic practices on the part of those who resided in the house. Rather, in order to come within the scope of the section, the relevant risk was required to emanate from some source of infection, or disease or illness, which derived from dampness, mould, dirt, evil-smelling accumulations or the presence of rats.

Finally, the question as to whether premises pose a risk to human health is required to be judged objectively: *Robb* v *Dundee City Council* 2002 SC 301. That is to say, one is required to decide whether the premises would pose a risk to the health of an ordinary person, in contrast to the health of the residents of the premises.

'Nuisance'

As we have already observed (p. 14, above) in order to constitute a nuisance at common law, it is essential that the adverse state of affairs exists outside the premises that is affected by that state of affairs. However, there is no similar requirement as far as the expression 'nuisance' in s.79(1)(a) is concerned, that is to say, that the relevant adverse state of affairs can emanate from within the premises that is affected by the nuisance: *Robb v Dundee City Council* 2002 SC 301. However, *Robb* is authority for the proposition that the impact of the relevant adverse state of affairs must be of a similar nature as a state of affairs that would rank as a nuisance at common law: see also *Newham LBC v White* (12 March 2015, unreported); *Milne v Stuartfield Windpower Ltd* [2019] SC ABE 25.

Smoke

Under s. 79(1)(b) smoke emitted from premises so as to be prejudicial to health, or a nuisance, ranks as a statutory nuisance under the EPA. However, this requirement is subject to certain exceptions: s. 79(2)(3).

Fumes

Under s. 79(1)(c) fumes or gases emitted from premises so as to be prejudicial to health, or a nuisance, rank as a statutory nuisance. However, the subsection does not apply to premises other than private dwellings: s. 79(4).

Dust, steam etc.

Under s. 79(1)(d) any dust, steam, smell or other effluvia arising from industrial, trade or business premises which is prejudicial to health, or a nuisance, ranks as a statutory nuisance.

'Accumulation, deposits, etc.'

Under s. 79(1)(c) any accumulation or deposit that is prejudicial to health or a nuisance, ranks as a statutory nuisance. Whereas the accumulation or deposit must pose the threat of disease or vermin, etc., it is insufficient that people could be injured walking on the accumulation or deposit: *Coventry City Council v Cartwright* [1975] 1 WLR 110.

Water

Under s. 79(1)(ea) 'any water covering land which is covering water, which is in such a state as to be prejudicial to health or a nuisance' ranks as a statutory nuisance. The paragraph would cover smell nuisance from stagnant water and, also, water which escapes from a pond to adjoining land.

Animals

Under s. 79(1)(f) 'any animal kept in such a place, or in such a manner, as to be prejudicial to health, or a nuisance' ranks as a statutory nuisance. It requires to be shown that either the place, or the manner of keeping the animal, either prejudices health, or is a nuisance. The keeping of the animal may be only for a relatively short time in order to come within the scope of the EPA: *Steers* v *Manton* (1893) 57 JP 584. In *Galer* v *Morrisey* [1955] 1 WLR 110, it was held, *obiter*, that it was the manner of keeping the animal that fell within the scope of the then English equivalent to the subsection. Therefore, the subsection did not cover noisy animals at all. The paragraph would also cover a situation in which zoonotic diseases could be transmitted to humans, by virtue of either the place, or the manner, in which animals are kept.

Insects

Under s. 79(1)(faa) 'any insects' (subject to certain exceptions provided by s. 79(5AA)) emanating from premises (certain premises are exempt under s. 79(1)(5AB)) and being prejudicial to health or a nuisance, ranks as a statutory nuisance in terms of the EPA. The paragraph would cover a range of situations, including one in which insects have bred in stagnant pools.

Artificial light

In recent years, light pollution has become a serious problem. Powerful lamps are increasingly being used to illuminate the exteriors of premises, for both reasons of security and also for decorative purposes. Furthermore, outdoor all-weather tennis courts and football pitches are often artificially illuminated, sometimes to the annoyance of those who live in the vicinity.

Noise

Under s. 79(1)(g) 'noise emitted from premises, so as to be prejudicial to health or a nuisance' ranks as a statutory nuisance. Furthermore, under s. 79(1)(ga) noise that is prejudicial to health or a nuisance and is emitted from or caused by a vehicle in a road, also ranks as a nuisance.

The above provisions are discussed below (see p. 36).

Other statutory nuisances

Under s. 79(1)(h) 'any other matter declared by any enactment to be a statutory nuisance', ranks as a statutory nuisance. Therefore, any nuisance provision that is contained in any public general, or private, Act of Parliament would come within the scope of the paragraph, as would similar nuisance provisions which are contained in local authority bye-laws. Generally, this provision would allow the court to impose a more severe penalty for failure to comply with an abatement notice.

The Scottish ministers may amend s. 79(1) in order to add to the above list of statutory nuisances, or they may vary the description of any matter that constitutes a statutory nuisance: s. 79(1ZA).

STATUTORY NUISANCE AND CONTAMINATED LAND

The EPA makes special provision for land that is in a contaminated state (see Ch. 7, below). Therefore, in order to avoid any overlap between the statutory nuisance regime that has just been discussed, and that which governs contaminated land, the Act provides that no matter constitutes a statutory nuisance to the extent that it consists of, or is caused by, any land being in a contaminated state (s. 79(1A)). The expression, 'land in a contaminated state' is defined as 'land by reason of substances in', or under land that:

(a) significant harm is being caused or there is a possibility of such harm being caused, or
(b) significant pollution of the water environment is being caused or there is a significant possibility of such pollution being caused (s. 79(1B)).

STATUTORY NUISANCE AND THE POLLUTION PREVENTION AND CONTROL ACT 1999

A local authority may not institute proceedings for statutory nuisance under Part III of the EPA in terms of s. 79(1)(b), (d), (e), (g) or (ga) under s. 79(1) if proceedings could be instituted under regulations which are made under s. 2 of the Pollution Prevention and Control Act 1999 (see the Pollution Prevention and Control (Scotland) Regulations 2012 (SSI 2012 No. 360) (see Ch. 9, below) or s. 18 of the Regulatory Reform (Scotland) Act 2014: s. 79(1)(10)). The rationale for this provision is to avoid regulatory duplication, in that SEPA regulates the range of installations which fall within the scope of the regulations (see Ch. 9, below).

Duty of local authority to inspect area

A local authority is under a mandatory duty to inspect its area from time to time in order to detect any statutory nuisances, which ought to be dealt with under s. 80 of the EPA. Where a complaint of a statutory nuisance is made to a local authority by a person who lives in its area, it is required to take such steps, as are reasonably practicable to investigate the complaint. However, in actual practice a local authority does not systematically, or constantly, inspect its area in order to ascertain the presence of nuisances. Rather, local authorities simply react to complaints from members of the public. Indeed, the statutory nuisance regime serves, in the author's view, as an outstanding example of a regulatory regime that is complaints-driven. It should be added that the EPA does not specify what steps a local authority is required to take to investigate a complaint. Therefore, the local authority need not visit the relevant *locus*, or communicate in any way with the complainant, or the alleged (if any) author of the reputed nuisance. Furthermore, the EPA does not specify the form that the complaint should take. Therefore, a relevant complaint could be made by means of email, phone call, fax, letter or verbally.

Summary proceedings for statutory nuisance

The procedure relating to the removal of statutory nuisances has changed little in substance since the inception of the statutory nuisance in the mid-nineteenth century.

Where a local authority is satisfied that a nuisance exists, or is likely to occur or recur, in the area of the local authority, it is required to serve an abatement notice which imposes all, or any, of the following requirements:

(a) the abatement of the nuisance, or the prohibition of, or restricting its occurrence or recurrence;

(b) the execution of such works, and the taking of such other steps as may be necessary for any of those purposes: s. 80(1).

The notice is also required to specify the time, or times, within which there must be compliance with the notice. When the local authority has decided that a nuisance exists, the local authority automatically comes under a mandatory duty to serve the notice (*R v Carrick DC ex p Shelley* [1996] Env LR 273). Furthermore, there is no requirement that the local authority should consult with the perpetrator of the nuisance prior to serving the abatement notice (*R v Falmouth and Truro Port Health Authority ex p South West Water Ltd* [2001] QB 445).

Content of abatement notice

The EPA does not prescribe the precise content of the abatement notice. However, the notice is required to contain a statement to the effect that an appeal lies against the notice to the sheriff (Sch. 3). Furthermore, the terms of the notice must be precise, practical, reasonable and certain: *Strathclyde RC v Tudhope* 1983 SLT 22; *Network Housing Association v Westminster City Council* [1995] Env LR 176. The abatement notice can be worded to take immediate effect: *Strathclyde Regional Council v Tudhope* 1983 SLT 22. The notice must make clear to the person on whom it is served, what is wrong: *Myatt v Teignbridge DC* [1995] Env LR 78. However, in determining whether the notice is sufficiently clear, one can take external factors into account. For example, the content of an accompanying letter can be taken into account: *London Borough of Camden v London Underground* [2000] Env LR 369. Furthermore, the abatement notice need not specify whether that which is the subject matter of the notice is either prejudicial to health or a nuisance: *Lowe Watson v South Somerset DC* [1998] Env LR 143. Rather, it suffices that the person on whom the notice is served knows what is required to be done in order to abate the nuisance.

The local authority can simply require the recipient of the abatement notice to abate the nuisance. That is to say, the former need not specify the measures that are required to be taken to abate the nuisance: *Budd v Colchester BC* [1999] Env LR 739; *R v Crown Court at Canterbury* [2001] Env LR 36; *North Lincolnshire County Council v Act Fast North Lincolnshire (CIC)* [2013] All ER (D) 81. In other words, the local authority can simply leave it up to the perpetrator of the nuisance to choose the mode of abatement of the nuisance. However, it was stated, *obiter*, in *Budd* that there were certain circumstances in which it would be unreasonable for a local authority to refrain from specify the steps which are required to abate the nuisance. If the relevant notice requires works or other steps to be carried out, the relevant measures must be specified: *Surrey Free Inns v Gosport BC* 750 [1999] Env LR 350; *R v Falmouth and Truro Health Authority ex p South West Water Services* [2001] QB 445.

If the abatement notice concerns noise nuisance, the local authority need not specify an acceptable maximum noise level. The abatement notice can simply impose a requirement for the perpetrator of the noise nuisance to abate the noise: *R v Fenny Stratford Justices* [1976] 1 WLR 1101. However, if the local authority chooses to specify the levels of noise which must not be exceeded, the method of ascertaining (or measuring) whether such levels are being exceeded, and where the relevant noise readings should be taken, must be stipulated.

Finally, in order to ascertain the validity of an abatement notice, one should look objectively at its substance: *McGillivray* v *Stephenson* [1950] 1 All ER 942.

Time for compliance

The abatement notice can be framed in such a way that it has immediate effect: *Strathclyde Regional Council* v *Tudhope* 1983 SLT(Notes) 22. Furthermore, if the abatement notice simply prohibits the recurrence of the nuisance, the notice is not required to specify the period of time at the end of which the notice expires. In other words, the local authority need not insert a time limit into the abatement notice. The notice continues indefinitely: *R* v *Birmingham Justices ex p Guppy* (1988) JP 159; *R* v *Tunbridge Wells Justices* [1996] Env LR 88.

Person on whom notice is served

The abatement notice is required to be served on the person responsible (as defined in s. 79(7)) for the nuisance, unless the nuisance arises from any defect of a structural character, in which case the notice must be served on the owner of the premises: s. 80(2). The abatement notice must also be served on the owner of the premises, if the person responsible for the nuisance cannot be found, or the nuisance has not yet occurred. The EPA defines the person responsible as the person through whose act, default or sufferance the nuisance is attributable (s. 79(7)). The words, 'act', 'default' and 'sufferance' have tended to be construed conjunctively by the courts, that is to say, that the courts have attributed the same meaning to each word: *Robb* v *Dundee City Council* 2002 SC 301; *Network Housing Association* v *Westminster City Council* [1995] Env LR 176 However, the words, 'act', 'default' and 'sufferance' have separate and distinct meanings. The word 'act' bears its everyday meaning. The words, 'default' and 'sufferance' are now briefly discussed.

'Default'

The word 'default' simply means one not doing what it is reasonable to do in the circumstances: *Re Young and Hartson's Contract* (1885) 31 ChD 168. One can be in default in terms of the EPA, notwithstanding the fact that the relevant adverse state of affairs has arisen wholly, or partly, due to a third party being wholly, or partly, in default of his or her legal obligations, including statutory obligations: *Wincanton Rural District Council* v *Parsons* [1914] 2 KB 34.

'Sufferance'

One suffers an adverse state of affairs if one is a position in which one can both physically, and legally, put an end to the state of affairs that constitutes the nuisance but, nonetheless, one fails to do so: *Rochford Rural District Council* v *Port of London Authority* [1914] 2 KB 916. For one to suffer a nuisance, one is required to either have actual or constructive knowledge of its existence: *Network Housing Association* v *Westminster City Council* [1995] Env LR 176.

Defect of a structural character

We have already noted (p. 28, above) that if the nuisance arises from a defect of a structural character, the abatement notice is required to be served on the owner of the relevant premises.

In the Sheriff Court case of *Pettigrew* v *Inverclyde Council* (1999 Hous LR 31), it was held that defects in the sound insulation of a house could rank as defects of a structural character in terms of the EPA.

In the Sheriff Court case of *Anderson* v *City of Dundee Council* (2000 SLT (Sh Ct) 134), it was held that the expression 'defect of a structural character' implied that the existing state of the building should be different from what was originally designed. However, the fact that the building in its present form did not suit its purpose in the way it did thirty years ago, did not mean that it was structurally defective. In deciding the building's original purpose, one took into account the relevant building standards of the time.

The Inner House had the opportunity to discuss the meaning of 'defect of a structural character' in *Robb* v *Dundee City Council* 2002 SLT 853. Lord Johnson (at 865) was of the opinion that whereas lack of insulation was part of the structure of a building, it did not rank as a structural defect in terms of the EPA. In her dissenting judgment, Lady Paton (at 867) was of the opinion that the expression 'defect of a structural character' could cover situations where there existed a defect which did not threaten the structural integrity of a building but, nevertheless, arose from the manner in which, or the materials from which, the premises were built.

Owner

The expression 'owner' is not defined in the EPA. However, in *Camden LBC* v *Gunby* [2000] 1 WLR 465, it was held that the expression 'owner' of the premises, in terms of s. 80 of the EPA, was the person who received the rack-rent of the premises, regardless of whether that person was acting as an agent.

Appeals against notice

A person who is served with an abatement notice can appeal against the notice to the sheriff within a period of twenty-one days, beginning from the date on which the notice was served (s. 80(3)). The Statutory Nuisance (Appeals) (Scotland) Regulations 1996 (SI 1996 No. 1076) specify, *inter alia*, the grounds on which an appeal may be made.

Failure to comply with abatement notice

It is an offence for the person on whom an abatement notice is served to fail to comply with the notice: s. 80(4). In *Wellingborough BC* v *Gordon* [1993] 1 Env LR 218, it was held that having a birthday party did not provide a reasonable excuse for the defendant's breach of a noise reduction notice, which had been served under the now repealed s. 58(4) of the Control of Pollution Act 1974. However, in *Hope Butuyuyu* v *Hammersmith and Fulham LBC* [1997] Env LR D 13, it was held that it was not possible to provide a comprehensive definition of what matters either were, or were not, capable of amounting to a reasonable excuse for one failing to comply with an abatement notice. The relevant circumstances would vary from case to case. In *Hope* the court considered it relevant to take into account the illnesses of both the defendant and her son. *Hope*, therefore, is authority for the proposition that the court can take subjective factors into account when determining what circumstances constitute a reasonable excuse in terms of s. 80(3) of the EPA. In the Divisional Court case of *Waltham Forest LBC* v *Mitoo* (unreported 26 May 2016), it was held that the creation of noise nuisance by the person on whom an abatement notice had been served, had created the nuisance in order to drown out noise which had been caused by construction works, did not rank as a reasonable excuse.

The relevant date, in relation to which one determines whether the abatement notice has been complied with, is the date on which the relevant local authority commences formal court proceedings, as opposed to the date of the relevant trial: *Coventry* v *Doyle* [1981] 1 WLR 1325.

The EPA makes provision for fixed penalty notices. Where a local authority has reason to believe that a person has committed an offence by failing to comply with an abatement notice, the local authority may give him or her the opportunity to discharge any liability in terms of the EPA by paying a fixed penalty: s. 80(4A). The EPA also makes provision for fines for such failure: s. 80(5)(6).

Defence of best practicable means

The EPA makes provision for the defence of best practicable means (as defined in s. 79(9)) in relation to proceedings by a local authority for failure to comply with an abatement notice. Subject to certain exceptions, it is a defence to prove that the best practicable means were used either to prevent or to counteract the effects of the nuisance: s. 80(7). The onus of establishing the defence is on the defender. The standard to which the defender is required to establish the defence is on the balance of probability: *Chapman* v *Gosberton Farm Produce Co. Ltd* [1993] Env LR 191. The financial implications of complying with an abatement notice may be relevant in certain circumstances as to whether the statutory defence applies. For example, it has been held that the court is entitled to take into account the fact that a public house, without a beer garden (which has given rise to noise complaints from residents nearby) would not be financially viable: *St Albans DC* v *Patel* [2009] Env LR 22.

Noise nuisance – construction sites

As far as proceedings concerning noise from construction site are concerned, it is a defence to prove that the alleged offence was covered by a notice that had been served under s. 61 of the Control of Pollution Act 1974: s. 80(9).

Proceedings by local authorities

If a local authority is of the opinion that the abatement proceedings under the EPA would afford an inadequate remedy in the case of any statutory nuisance, the authority may take proceedings in order to abate the nuisance, in any court of competent jurisdiction, for the purpose of securing the abatement, prohibition or restriction of the nuisance: s. 81(5). The local authority need not have suffered any damage from the nuisance. In Scotland, the relevant proceedings would normally take the form of an interdict. Before taking such proceedings, the local authority is required to conclude that the statutory nuisance proceedings would afford an inadequate, as opposed to a less convenient, remedy in the circumstances: *Vale of White Horse District Council* v *Allen* [1997] Env LR 212. Furthermore, in reaching that conclusion, the local authority is required to address the statutory procedure for dealing with a statutory nuisance, which comprises both consecutive and distinctive steps: *Barns (NE) Ltd* v *Newcastle upon Tyne City Council* [2006] Env LR 25. First, the service of an abatement notice by the local authority is required. Secondly, if there is no compliance with the notice, either prosecution, or self-help, must be attempted by the local authority in order to secure redress. Only as a last resort may the local authority take proceedings in a court of competent jurisdiction.

Powers of enforcement

The EPA makes provision for the enforcement of various nuisance abatement provisions, such as powers of entry to premises.

SUMMARY PROCEEDINGS BY PRIVATE INDIVIDUALS

The EPA allows a person who is aggrieved by the existence of a nuisance to take summary action in the Sheriff Court for the abatement of the nuisance: s. 82(1). In *Watkins* v *Aged Merchants Seamen's Homes* [2018] EWHC 2410, it was held that it was normally, although not necessarily, sufficient in every case for the individual who raises an action under s. 82 to be in occupation of the premises, whether or not that occupation was lawful. If the sheriff is satisfied that (1) the alleged nuisance exists, or (2) although abated, the nuisance is likely to recur on the same premises, or, in the case of a nuisance that falls within s. 79(1)(ga), in the same road, the sheriff is required to make an order for either, or both, of the following purposes. That is to say: (1) requiring the defender to abate the nuisance within the time specified in the order, to execute any work that is necessary for that purpose; and (2) prohibiting the recurrence of the nuisance, and requiring the defender to abate, within a time specified in the order, to execute any works that are in order to prevent recurrence of the nuisance: s. 82(2). If the sheriff is satisfied that the alleged nuisance exists and renders premises unfit for human habitation, the sheriff may prohibit the use of the premises for human habitation until the premises are rendered fit for that purpose: s. 82(3).

Subject to certain exceptions, proceedings require to be brought against the person who is responsible for the nuisance: s. 82(4). Where more than one person is responsible for a nuisance that falls within the scope of s. 82, liability under the section is both joint and several, irrespective of whether or not the adverse state of affairs that has been created by any one person would, of itself, have constituted a nuisance: s. 82(5). Prior to instituting proceedings for an order under s. 82(2) of the EPA, the person who is aggrieved by the nuisance is required to give the person responsible for the nuisance notice in writing of his or her intention to bring the relevant proceedings: s. 82(6). The notice is required to state the subject matter of the complaint. It is an offence, without reasonable excuse, to contravene any requirement or prohibition that is imposed by an order made under s. 82(2).

As is the case in respect of an abatement notice that is served by a local authority, subject to certain exceptions, the defence of best practicable means applies in relation to proceedings that are brought by private individuals: s. 82(9). If a person is convicted of an offence under s. 82(8) the sheriff may, after giving the relevant local authority the opportunity of being heard, direct the local authority to do anything, which the person who was convicted of the offence was required to do, under the order to which the conviction relates: s. 82(11). Where it is proved that the nuisance existed at the date on which the summary application was made, the sheriff has the power to compensate the person who brought the proceedings: s. 82(12). If the person who is responsible for the nuisance cannot be found, the sheriff may, after giving the local authority the opportunity of being heard, direct the local authority to do anything that the sheriff would have ordered that person to do.

Essential Facts

- The EPA 1990 places a local authority under a duty to inspect its area in order to detect statutory nuisances.
- If a local authority receives a complaint that concerns a statutory nuisance, the local authority is required to take reasonable steps to investigate the complaint.
- If a local authority is satisfied that a statutory nuisance exists, the local authority is required to serve an abatement notice on the person who is responsible for the statutory nuisance.
- It is an offence for a person, without reasonable excuse, to either contravene or fail to comply with an abatement notice.
- The EPA makes provision for fixed penalties as an alternative to prosecution for contravention of an abatement notice.
- The EPA makes provision for a private individual to take proceedings in the Sheriff Court in order to abate a statutory nuisance.

Essential Cases

Oakley v Birmingham City Council (2001): layout of premises which poses potential health risk to occupants does not constitute statutory nuisance.

Robb v Dundee City Council (2002): in order to rank as 'prejudicial to health' in terms of s. 79(1)(a) of the EPA the statutory nuisance must be of such a nature that it would pose a risk to the health of a normal individual, as opposed to the occupant of the relevant premises.

4 NOISE

INTRODUCTION

In this chapter we look at the subject of noise. Noise is now recognised as a pollutant that can have profound effects on human health. Indeed, the World Health Organization (WHO) has observed that environmental noise is an important public health issue, which features amongst the top environmental risks to health: WHO *Environmental Noise Guidelines for the European Region* (2018), p. xiii. The WHO has also calculated that at least 1 million healthy life years are lost every year in western European countries because of environmental noise, with cardiovascular disease contributing to the vast majority of these deaths, especially from high blood pressure, heart attacks and coronary heart disease.

Interestingly, noise is the only pollutant in respect of which people are prepared to commit murder (see, e.g., *Mitchell* v *Glasgow City Council* [2009] 1 AC 874). However, over the years, noise is not a subject that has captured the public imagination. Unlike many other forms of pollution, noise is not an emotive topic, unless one is the victim of the relevant noise pollution. Until comparatively recently, noise was not a subject that had commanded the attention of the government. Indeed, in 1994, the author described noise as the 'Cinderella' pollutant. This is largely due to the very nature of the pollutant. Noise, of course, is invisible. It leaves no residue and, thus, does not have the fallout factor associated with other pollutants, such as, for example, health problems that could arise from contaminated land (see, e.g., *McManus* v *City Link* [2015] CSOH 178). Somewhat surprisingly, there was no national legislation dealing with noise until 1960, with the passing of the Noise Abatement Act 1960 (repealed), which made noise a statutory nuisance.

Noise pollution can be dealt with, either at common law, in terms of the law of nuisance, or under statute.

NOISE AND COMMON LAW

Individuals who are affected by noise can invoke the law of nuisance in order to secure redress. Indeed, a wide range of noise sources have been held to constitute a nuisance at common law. These include noise from power boats (*Kennaway* v *Thomson* [1981] AC 1001), a go-cart track (*Tetley* v *Chitty* [1986] 1 All ER 663), and the performance of a military tattoo (*Webster* v *Lord Advocate* 1984 SLT 13; the decision of the Outer House, over-ruled by the Inner House, as to the nature of the interdict, which was granted to the pursuer 1985 SC 173).

STATUTORY CONTROLS OVER NOISE

The statutory control over noise is fragmented. Arguably, this represents the most fragmented branch of environmental law.

Neighbourhood noise

The Environmental Protection Act 1990

As far as the control of neighbourhood noise is concerned, the most important statute is the EPA 1990. Under s. 79(1)(g), noise which is emitted from premises as to be prejudicial to health or a nuisance is a statutory nuisance, which falls to be dealt with under the provisions of the EPA. The courts give the expression 'noise nuisance' the same meaning as that under common law: *Godfrey* v *Conwy County BC* [2000] Env LR 38. In order to constitute a noise nuisance under the EPA, the noise in question would be required to be of such intensity, duration, etc. as to constitute a nuisance at common law: *Robb* v *Dundee City Council* 2002 SLT 853.

The occupants of flats in tenement property are, obviously, potentially prone to noise that is created by neighbours. This problem can be compounded by poor sound insulation of the walls and ceilings of such property. As we saw in the leading case of *Baxter* v *Camden LBC* [2001] 1 AC 1 (see p. 8, above), which concerned an action for common law nuisance by tenants of council flats against their landlords. The tenants claimed that their flats were so inadequately insulated against the transmission of noise that they could hear literally everything that their neighbours were doing. The House of Lords held that, since the noise in question was everyday noise which people make in their houses, and, therefore, not unreasonable, the noise did not rank as a nuisance at common law.

In *R (Vella)* v *Lambeth LBC* [2006] Env LR 33, an action was brought by the tenant of a housing association against his local authority landlord. The claimant, V, resided in a flat. He claimed that the sound insulation in the flat was so poor that he could hear almost everything that his neighbour, who lived upstairs, was doing. V claimed that the noise was materially contributing to a depressive condition of which he was suffering. V, therefore, claimed that the premises in question was prejudicial to health in terms of s. 79(1)(a) of the EPA. He complained to the defendant local authority, which refused to serve an abatement notice under s. 80 of the EPA, either on V's neighbour or the housing association. V, therefore, raised an action against the local authority by way of judicial review. However, the court held that the premises were not prejudicial to health, in terms of s. 79(1)(a), on the grounds that the statutory nuisance provisions, which were contained in the predecessors to the EPA (the so-called 'sanitary statutes' of the nineteenth century, such as the Nuisance Removal Acts and the Public Health Acts), were aimed at suppressing disease from insanitary, filthy or verminous premises. In the last analysis, lack of adequate sound insulation in premises did not render the premises prejudicial to health in terms of s. 79(1)(a) of the EPA.

Construction site noise

Noise from construction sites presents a particular problem on account of the nature of noise associated with such sites. Such noise tends to be intermittent, and also varies in nature and, therefore, more likely to annoy. Furthermore, occupants of premises who live in close proximity to such sites have not had sufficient time to become habituated to the noise and, therefore, are more likely to become annoyed by the noise. Since 1974, construction site noise has merited a special form of regulatory control in terms of the Control of Pollution Act 1974 (COPA).

Section 60 of COPA 1974 gives local authorities extensive powers to deal with noise from construction sites. The section applies to:

(a) the erection, construction, alteration, repair or maintenance of buildings, structures or roads;
(b) breaking up, opening or boring under any road, or adjacent land, in connection with the construction, inspection, maintenance or removal of works;
(c) demolition or dredging work; and
(d) whether or not comprised in paragraph (a), (b) or (c), any work of engineering construction (s. 60(1)).

Section 60(2) empowers a local authority to serve a notice, which imposes requirements as to the way in which the works are either being carried out, or are going to be carried out. Importantly, there is no requirement that the relevant works are causing either a nuisance at common law, or under s. 79(1)(g) of the EPA 1990, before such notice can be served. The terms of the notice are required to be practical and also precise: *Strathclyde Regional Council* v *Tudhope* 1983 SLT 22. The notice is required to relate to, and also to specify, the works that are either being carried out, or will be carried out in the future. If the notice relates to works that are currently being carried out, the notice is ineffective in relation to noise that emanates from future works that, at the time of the service of the notice, were not within the contemplation of the local authority: *Walter Lilley and Co. Ltd* v *Westminster City Council* [1994] Env LR 380.

Under s. 60(3) the relevant notice may, in particular:

(a) specify the plant or machinery that can or cannot to be used;
(b) specify the hours during which works may be carried out;
(c) specify the level of noise that may be emitted from the premises in question, or at any specified point on those premises, or that may be so emitted during specified hours; and
(d) provide for any change of circumstances.

The notice must be served on the person who appears to the local authority either to be carrying out the works, or about to carry out the works: s. 60(5). The notice may also be served on the person who appears to the local authority either to be responsible for, or to have control over the carrying out of the works, as the local authority thinks fit. The person who is served with a notice under s. 60, may appeal to the sheriff within twenty-one days from the service of the notice: s. 60(7). If a person on whom a notice is served contravenes, without reasonable excuse, any requirement of the notice, he or she commits an offence under Part 3 of COPA 1974: s. 60(8).

The prospect of a local authority serving a notice under s.60 poses a constant threat to a builder, since he or she needs to know, before the start of the relevant construction operations, how long the building operations will last. The builder also requires to know the type of machinery, and also the plant, which will be used on the site. Section 61, therefore, allows a person who intends to carry out building works to apply to the local authority for consent. The local authority is required to give its approval to the application if it considers that the application contains sufficient information for the purpose, that if the works are carried out in accordance with the application, the local authority would not serve a notice under s. 60 of COPA in relation to such works: s. 61(4). The local authority also has the power to attach any condition to the consent, limit or qualify, the consent to allow for a change of circumstances, and also limit the duration of the consent: s. 61(5). It is made an offence for any person to carry out work, or permit work to be carried out, in contravention of any conditions that are attached to the consent.

The applicant can appeal to the sheriff against the decision of the local authority to refuse consent or against any condition, or qualification, that is attached to a consent (s. 61(7)). In any proceedings for an offence under s. 60(8), it is a defence to prove that the alleged contravention amounted to the carrying out of works that are in accordance with a consent that has been given under the section: s. 61(8). However, the relevant consent is required to contain a statement to the effect that consent does not, of itself, constitute any ground of defence against proceedings that are instituted under s. 82 of the EPA 1990 (see p. 32, above): s. 61(9). Where consent has been given under s. 61, and the works are carried out by a person (for example, a subcontractor, where consent has been given to the main contractor) the former is required to take all reasonable steps to bring the consent to the notice of that other person: s. 61(10). A penalty is imposed for failure to do so.

Loudspeakers in roads

Loudspeakers in vehicles have been a problem for a number of years. However, the problem has worsened in recent years by virtue of certain antisocial individuals (mainly, but not exclusively, young people) who use loudspeakers in their cars, such loudspeakers being capable of generating great volumes of noise, to the discomfort of members of the public. At present the problem of noise from loudspeakers in vehicles is dealt with under COPA 1974. Section 62 makes it an offence, subject to certain exemptions, for a person to use a loudspeaker in a road during certain periods of the day.

Noise from creatures and musical instruments, etc.

Noise from creatures

We have already observed that, in certain circumstances, noise from animals can constitute a statutory nuisance and also a nuisance at common law (Chs 2 and 3, above). The Civic Government (Scotland) Act 1982 makes special provision in relation to creatures. Under s. 49(1) any person who suffers, or permits, any creature in his or her charge to cause danger or injury to any other person who is in a public place, or to give such person reasonable cause for alarm or annoyance, is guilty of an offence and liable, on summary conviction, to a fine. Under s. 49(2) a district court may, if satisfied that any creature that is kept in the vicinity of any place where a person resides, is giving that person while in that place, reasonable cause for annoyance, make an order requiring the person who is keeping the creature, to take within such period as is specified in the order such steps (short of destruction of the creature) to prevent the continuance of the annoyance, as may be so specified. An application to a district court can be made by any person (s. 49(3)). It is made an offence, subject to a penalty, for any person to fail to comply with the relevant order (s. 49(4)).

Musical instruments

Noise from televisions, radios and record players is a perennial problem in the United Kingdom. Excessive noise from such devices can rank either or both as a nuisance or statutory nuisance (see Chapters 2 and 3). It should also be observed that many street buskers are employing powerful amplifiers and loudspeakers while performing. Under s. 54(1) of the Civic Government (Scotland) Act 1982, any person who sounds or plays any musical instrument, sings or performs, or operates any radio or television receiver, record player, tape recorder or other sound-producing device so as to give reasonable cause for annoyance, and fails to desist on being required to do so by a constable in uniform, commits an offence under the Act, and is liable to a fine. Importantly, where a constable reasonably suspects that an offence has been committed in relation to a musical instrument, or in relation to a radio, television receiver, record player or other sound-producing device, the constable may enter the premises on which he or she reasonably suspects that instrument or device to be, and seize any such instrument, or device, that he or she finds there (s. 54(2A)). The constable may use reasonable force in entering the premises and in seizing the equipment (s. 54(2B)). Whereas no empirical research has been carried out, it seems that the section works well in practice.

Antisocial behaviour and noise

The Antisocial Behaviour etc. (Scotland) Act 2004 (ABSA) makes provision for various forms of antisocial behaviour, amongst which is noise. Under Part 2 of the ABSA, a sheriff, on the application of a relevant authority (that is, a local authority or a registered social landlord), can make an antisocial behaviour order if certain conditions are met (s. 4(1)). The conditions are:

(a) that the specified person is at least twelve years of age;
(b) that the specified person has engaged in antisocial behaviour towards a relevant person; and
(c) that an antisocial behaviour order is necessary for the purpose of protecting relevant persons from further antisocial behaviour by the specified person.

The expression 'antisocial behaviour' is term of art (technical term) and is defined as such if the relevant person:

(a) acts in a manner that causes or is likely to cause alarm or distress; or
(b) pursues a course of conduct that causes or is likely to cause alarm or distress to at least one person who is not of the same household as that person (s. 143(1)).

The expression 'conduct' includes speech; and a course of conduct must involve conduct on at least two occasions (s. 143(1)). It can be seen, therefore, that antisocial behaviour includes conduct that generates noise. The expressions 'alarm' and 'distress' are not defined in the ABSA and should, therefore, be given their everyday meaning. Any form of neighbourhood noise that causes reasonable annoyance on the part of the receiver could, therefore, fall within the scope of Part 2. It will be a question of fact and degree whether the conduct in question has caused alarm or distress.

Noise nuisance

Part 5 of the ABSA makes special provision for the control of neighbourhood noise. However, the relevant provisions are simply adoptive and, therefore, apply to the relevant area of a local authority only if the local authority has so resolved (s. 41(1)). The resolution is required to state, *inter alia*, the periods of the week during which noise is to be controlled under the ASBSA (the 'noise control period': s. 41(2)(b)). A local authority that has resolved to adopt the ABSA, is given degree of flexibility as to the periods of the week and also times during which the provisions of the ABSA should apply (s. 41(2)(3)). The local authority could, for example, opt to make the noise control period applicable during the whole week, or the local authority could confine the relevant noise control period to certain periods of the week. Furthermore, different noise control periods can be set for different areas, and for different times of the year. The relevant resolution can either be repealed or amended by the local authority (s. 42).

Investigations of excessive noise

Where a local authority receives a complaint from an individual that excessive noise (the expression 'excessive noise' is not defined in the Act) is being emitted from relevant property (as defined in s. 53(1)) during a noise control period, the local authority is required to ensure that an officer of the authority investigates the matter (s. 43(1)). The expression 'investigates' is not defined in the ASBA. There is, therefore, no statutory requirement, for example, that any officer of the local authority should visit the alleged offender's premises or the complainant. The complaint can be made by any means (s. 43(2)). If, in consequence of such an investigation, the local authority is satisfied that noise is being emitted from a relevant property (the offending property) and the noise, if it was measured from the relevant place (as defined in s. 53(1)) would or might exceed the permitted level (as defined in s. 48) the officer may serve a notice about the noise under s. 44 (s. 43(3)). It is a matter for the discretion of the relevant officer to decide: first, whether any noise, if it was measured from the relevant place, might exceed the permitted level; secondly, to decide from what place to assess the relevant noise; and, thirdly, to decide whether to use any device for measuring the noise (s. 43(4)).

Warning notices, offences, and fixed penalty and seizure of equipment

The ABSA makes provision for the service of warning notices by an officer of the local authority on the person responsible for the noise if the former considers that the noise exceeds, or may exceed, the permitted level (s. 44). It is made an offence, subject to a penalty, for a person on whom a warning notice has been served to exceed the permitted level (s. 45(1)). The ABSA also makes provision for the service of fixed penalty notices by a relevant officer of the local authority, or a constable, on a person whom he or she suspects of either committing, or having committed, an offence under s. 45 (s. 46). The notice gives the person, on whom it is served, the opportunity of discharging any liability to conviction by payment of a fixed fine (s. 46).

An important feature of the regime constituted by the ABSA is that it makes provision for the seizure of equipment that is used to create noise. Section 47 gives either an officer of the local authority, or someone authorised by the authority, power to seize and remove any equipment that appears to the officer is being used, or has been used, in the emission of noise. The equipment can be seized and removed if a warning notice has been served in respect of the noise that has been emitted from the relevant property, and an officer of the local authority, in whose area the relevant property is situated, has reason to believe that at any time during the period specified in the notice, noise that was emitted from the premises exceeded the permitted level, as measured from the relevant place. Power is also given to a sheriff, or justice of the peace, to authorise the entry of an officer of the local authority (or a person authorised by the local authority) into the relevant premises, in the event of the officer, or person authorised, being refused entry to the premises (or where such refusal is apprehended) or where a request by an officer of the authority would defeat the object of entry.

LICENSING (SCOTLAND) ACT 2005

Licensed premises have increasingly provided entertainment, in the form of live music, karaoke and discotheques, for their customers. As far as Scotland is concerned, the Licensing (Scotland) Act 2005 allows a licensing board to impose conditions in a premises licence, as the board considers necessary, or expedient, for the purposes of securing any of the licensing objectives: s. 27(6). One such objective is the prevention of 'public nuisances'. Whereas the concept of public nuisance does not exist in Scots law, the phrase, as used in the section, would cover the emission of noise from licensed premises. Many licensing boards have imposed conditions in licences to the effect that no noise can be discernible at the perimeter of the relevant premises.

TOWN AND COUNTRY PLANNING

The law relating to noise which we have been looking at thus far in the chapter permits the appropriate authority to take remedial action only after the relevant noise has come into existence. In other words, the law is reactive in nature. However, it is preferable that the law should be able to prevent any adverse situation coming into existence at the very outset, rather than providing machinery by means of which the relevant adverse state of affairs can be abated afterwards. The law of town and country planning, therefore, has an important role to play as far as the prophylactic control of noise is concerned. This subject is covered in another book in the series.

NOISE AND HUMAN RIGHTS

Human rights law has an important role to play in relation to the control of noise. Under Article 8 of the European Convention of Human Rights (ECHR) and Article 1 of Protocol No. 1 to the ECHR (which guarantee respect for family life and home, as well as the right to peaceful enjoyment of property and possessions). We now consider the development of noise law in terms of the ECHR.

UK cases

Almost all of the UK cases on the subject of noise have related to noise from aviation. In *Dennis* v *Ministry of Defence* [2003] Env LR 34, Buckley J was prepared to hold that the noise from military aircraft infringed both Article 8 and Article 1 of Protocol No. 1 to the ECHR, and also ranked as a nuisance at common law by being sufficiently loud and, secondly, by dint of the effect on the market value of the property of the claimant. The noise in question was also held to be a nuisance. However, the damages which fell to be awarded under each head of action would be satisfied by an award of damages in terms of the law of nuisance.

In *Hatton* v *United Kingdom* (2003) 37 EHRR 28, a group of residents who lived near Heathrow airport, brought against the UK government in terms of Article 8 and Article 1 of Protocol No. 1. It was claimed that noise, which was caused by night-time flying, contravened the rights of the residents, in terms of Article 8 of the ECHR. The Grand Chamber of the European Court on Human Rights (ECtHR) was prepared to hold that where an individual was both 'directly and seriously affected' by noise or other pollution, Article 8 could be 'engaged'. The court went on to hold that Article 8 could be contravened, either by a positive act on behalf of the state or by its failure to protect its citizens from environmental pollution. However, in either case, the state enjoyed a wide margin of appreciation in determining whether it had taken sufficient measures to secure compliance with the ECHR. In the last analysis, the court decided that the UK government had not overstepped its margin of appreciation by failing to strike a fair balance between the rights of those who were affected by the noise, and the economic interests of the country as a whole by its policy in relation to night flying.

The issue of pollution, including noise pollution, came before the ECtHR in *Fadeyeva* v *Russia* (App. 55723/00, judgment, 9 June 2005). Ms Fadeyeva resided in a steel-making town in Russia. She alleged the level of pollution (which included noise emanating from a steel plant) at her place of residence had seriously affected her health. The court held that in order to engage Article 8 of the ECHR, the adverse effects of the environmental pollution are required to attain a minimum level in order to fall within the scope of Article 8. The assessment of that level was, however, relative, and depended on all the circumstances of the case, such as the intensity and duration of the nuisance, and also the physical and mental effects of the relevant pollution. The general context of the environment was also required to be taken into account. Furthermore, there would be no claim under Article 8 if the detriment which was complained of, was negligible in comparison with the environmental hazards which were inherent to life in every modern city.

The subject of noise, and its engagement with Article 8, was considered again in *Gomez* v *Spain* (App. No. 4143/02, judgment, 16 November 2004). Ms Gomez (G) lived in a flat that was situated in a residential quarter of Valencia. Since 1974, Valencia City Council (VCC) had allowed licensed premises, such as bars, pubs and discotheques, to open in the vicinity of her home, making it impossible for those who lived in the vicinity to sleep. G claimed that this adverse state of affairs amounted to a breach of her rights under Article 8 on the grounds that, whereas VCC had not caused the noise that was complained of directly, VCC had caused the adverse state of affairs to come into existence by issuing an unlimited number of licences without taking the requisite measures to reduce the noise. G further claimed that the level of noise that was caused by more than 127 nightclubs infringed her right to health, in accordance with the relevant WHO guidelines.

The court accepted the fact that a breach of Article 8 could take place by virtue of the intrusion of noise into the home. Furthermore, a serious breach of Article 8 could take place if the adverse state of affairs prevented a person from enjoying the amenities of his or her home. The court went on to reiterate the point that had been made in *Hatton*, to the effect that, whereas the prime object of Article 8 is to protect the individual against arbitrary interference by public authorities, Article 8 may also place an affirmative duty on the state to take measures to ensure that the rights enshrined in Article 8 are not flouted by the conduct of private individuals. However, in both contexts, one was required to have regard to the fair balance that had to be struck between the competing interests of the individual and the community as a whole. In the last analysis, as far as the issue as to whether the noise that was the subject matter of the action flouted Article 8 was concerned, it sufficed that the relevant maximum permitted noise levels had been exceeded for a number of years. In reaching its decision to the effect that Article 8 had been breached, the court set store by the fact that VCC had failed to implement the rules contained in the very bye-laws which it had made. (See also *Zarzoso* v *Spain* (App. No. 23383/12, judgment, 16 April 2018).)

The subject of traffic noise pollution and its interaction with Article 8 of the ECHR fell to be considered in *Dees* v *Hungary* (App. No. 2345/06, 9 November 2010). Here, the applicant, D, claimed that by virtue of the increase in the volume of traffic on the road outside his home, it had become almost uninhabitable by virtue of the noise, pollution and smell which emanated from the traffic. D claimed that, as a consequence of this, his rights under Article 8 had been infringed. In deciding in favour of D, the court recognised that an individual has a right to respect for his home. Such a right did not mean simply the individual's right to the actual physical area of his home, but also the quiet enjoyment within reasonable limits of that home. Furthermore, breaches of Article 8 were not confined to concrete breaches, such as unauthorised entry into a person's home, but also breaches which were more diffuse, such as noise, emissions or smell, or other similar forms of interference. After recognising the now well-established principle that the state enjoys a certain margin of appreciation in its attempts to balance the rights of the individual and the rights of other road users when one was considering whether the state had taken sufficient measures to protect the individual's rights under Article 8, the court was of the view that, in the instant case, a disproportionate burden fell on D. D's rights under Article 8 had, therefore, been breached.

In *Oluic* v *Croatia* (App. No. 61260/08, 20 May 2010), the applicant (O) owned a house. She lived in part of the house with her family. The other part of the house consisted of a bar. She complained to the local County Sanitary Inspection (CSI), which was a public authority responsible for noise nuisance abatement in the area where O lived, that she had been constantly exposed to excessive noise (which largely consisted of music) from the bar, which was open from 7 am until midnight. The CSI accepted the fact that the noise from the bar exceeded permitted noise levels, and duly took enforcement action against the company that owned the bar, ordering the owner of the bar to reduce the noise levels from the bar. The decision by the CSI to take enforcement action was, however, quashed on appeal by the bar owner. About a year later the CSI ordered the bar owner to provide suitable sound insulation to the bar. However, O continued to be affected by the noise. She, therefore, brought an action before the ECtHR, on the basis that the state had failed to protect her from the excessive noise that emanated from the bar.

The ECtHR held that before one could take a case before the Court, one was required to make use of normal domestic remedies which are effective, sufficient and accessible. If there were a number of domestic remedies, an individual could make use of any of such remedies which addressed his or her grievance. In other words, when one remedy had been pursued, there was no need for the applicant to pursue another remedy that had the same objective. In the instant case, the statutory remedies, which O had invoked, were aimed at securing the same objective as the appropriate civil proceedings, namely, the abatement of the noise nuisance from O's premises. Therefore, O was not required, at the same time, to bring a civil action, or to use any other remedy, before she could enlist the aid of the Court.

The Court went on to decide that a serious breach of Article 8 had taken place if one was prevented from enjoying the amenities of one's home. Furthermore, a breach of Article 8 could take place by virtue of the state failing to take appropriate measures to prevent a violation of the Article, by third parties. The Court went on to observe that, in deciding if Article 8 had been violated, one was required to take into account all the circumstances of the case, including the intensity and duration of the nuisance, and its physical and mental effects. The levels of noise to which O had been subjected exceeded the maximum permitted domestic levels, and also exceeded the international standards by the WHO. In view of the volume of noise, and the fact that it continued over a number of years and nightly, the state was required to implement measures to protect the applicant from such noise.

In *Zammit Meampel* v *Malta* (App. No. 24203/10, 22 November 2011), the applicants alleged that every year, on the occasion of certain village feasts, firework displays were set up in the fields situated close to the applicant's (Z) residence. The applicants claimed that each time fireworks were let off from the area, they were exposed to risk and peril to their life, physical health and personal security. The applicants further claimed that the state had failed to take the requisite measures to protect a violation of their rights in terms of Article 8 of the ECHR. The key issue in this case was whether the state had struck the correct balance in weighing the competing interests of the individuals who were affected by the disturbance and the community as a whole. The Court noted that in this respect, the state was allowed a wide margin of appreciation. In reaching its judgment in favour of the state, the Court took into account that the damage that had occurred to the property of Z was minimal, and reversible. Furthermore, Z could have taken action against the authors of the fireworks nuisance by way of civil proceedings. Whereas the repeated letting-off of fireworks at noise levels that exceeded at least 120 decibels for two weeks each year, even though intermittently, created considerable inconvenience for Z, such inconvenience was required to be balanced against the interests of the community. Importantly, the authorities were, in identifying distances from where third parties could perform relevant displays, required to take into account 'the geographical situation' (i.e., relatively small and compact nature) of Malta and its population density. Moreover, the state had put in place a certain degree of protection. Also the various fireworks displays, which were the subject matter of the action, were monitored by the police and by the fire service.

Significantly, the court set store by the fact that Z were fully aware of the very state of affairs of which they complained before they moved into the affected property. In the last analysis, the state had not overstepped its margin of appreciation in striking a balance between the rights of the individuals who were affected by the noise etc. from the fireworks and those of the community as a whole. In the last analysis, there had been no violation of Article 8 by the state.

Conclusions on noise and human rights law

By way of conclusion on the subject of the impact of human rights law and noise, one can briefly summarise the current law by stating that, in determining whether noise flouts Article 8 of the Convention, the court is required to take into account a variety of factors, including whether the noise in question is of such a level that it contravenes domestic law; appropriate WHO standards; whether the claimant has come to the nuisance; and also, whether the noise in question is typical of modern life. It seems almost certain that in order to contravene Article 8, the level(s) of noise is required to be at least as loud, if not louder, than that which would be deemed a nuisance at common law.

EUROPEAN NOISE LAW

In this section we turn our attention to how the European Union has addressed the subject of noise pollution. It is recognised that noise pollution remains a major environmental health problem in Europe: EEA Briefing 01/2017. Road traffic is the dominant source of noise, both inside and out of urban areas. Indeed, around 100 million people are exposed to road traffic noise above 55 dB Lden in the EEA-33 member countries. Of these, 32 million are exposed to very high levels above 65 dB Lden. Railways are the noise source with the second highest number of people exposed: 19 million people exposed above the 55 dB Lden level. Aircraft noise is the third main noise source, with more than 4.1 million people exposed above 55dB Lden level. Industrial noise is the fourth main noise source, with approximately 1.0 million people exposed above the 55db Lden level.

The earliest measures used by the EU to deal with noise were harmonisation measures, which were aimed at specific products, such as vehicles, in order to eliminate barriers to trade and also to facilitate the free movement of goods within the community. In reality, there was no EU noise policy as such. However, the growing awareness that noise could have a detrimental effect on human health saw a change in the direction of EU noise policy. The EU's Fifth Action Programme, which dealt with the subject of urban noise, recognised the fact that noise has a detrimental effect on human health. Under this programme a general objective was established, to the effect that no person should be exposed to noise levels that endanger health and also the quality of life. The EC Green Paper, titled *Future Noise Policy*, was published in 1996. That Paper again recognised the negative impact of noise on human health. Importantly, the Sixth Environmental Action Programme of 2001 recognised that noise affected both the health and the quality of life of at least 25 per cent of the EU population. This action programme set targets for the systematic reduction of the numbers of those who were affected by noise. This policy prompted the EU Directive on the assessment and management of noise, which is commonly referred to as the END Directive (Directive 2002/49/EC), which is now briefly discussed.

The END Directive

The END Directive's main objective is to establish a common EU framework for the assessment and management of exposure to environmental noise (by noise mapping) by using common methods of noise measurement and, furthermore, and importantly, by ensuring that member states make such information available to the public (Art. 1). The END focuses mainly on noise from major sources, such as road and railway traffic, as well as noise from aircraft and also industrial noise. The scope of the END is wide-ranging and applies to environmental noise to which humans are exposed, particularly in built-up areas, in public parks or other quiet areas in an agglomeration (i.e., an area containing more than 100,000 persons, Art. 3), in quiet areas in open country, and near schools, hospitals and other noise-sensitive buildings and areas (Art. 2). Overall responsibility for implementing the END Directive lies with member states (Art. 4). Member states are required to ensure that both strategic noise maps, and action plans, are made available and also disseminated to members of the public (Art. 9). Importantly, the information is required to be clear, comprehensible and also accessible. In Scotland, the END is implemented by the Environmental Noise (Scotland) Regulations 2006 (SSI 2006 No. 465).

NOISE FROM AIRCRAFT

Noise from aircraft can pose a particular problem. With an expected increase in the number of aircraft flying over our skies, the problem is set to worsen.

Civil aircraft

Civil aircraft can pose noise problems for the community, either when the aircraft is taking off, when it is landing at an airport, or when it is in flight. The relevant statutory controls that govern aircraft noise, therefore, can be roughly divided into controls that relate to the flight (or navigation) of aircraft, and controls that are aimed at noise from aerodromes.

Flight noise

The flight paths of civil aircraft are often directly over houses and other occupied property. The noise that aircraft generate can, therefore, cause considerable annoyance to those who live beneath such flight paths. However, s. 76(1) of the Civil Aviation Act 1982 provides that no action in trespass or nuisance may lie, by reason only of the flight of an aircraft over any property, at a height above the ground which, having regard to wind, and all the circumstances of the case, is reasonable, or is the ordinary incidents of the flight, provided that the provisions of any Air Navigation Order have been complied with. Section 60(3) allows Air Navigation Orders to be made, *inter alia*, in order to regulate the conditions and, in particular, the aerodromes to and from which aircraft either entering or leaving the United Kingdom may fly, and also the conditions under which aircraft may fly from one part of the UK to another part.

It is of the utmost importance that noise be reduced at source, that is to say, from the aircraft itself. The most important, but not exclusive, legal instrument for reducing such noise is by way of noise certification which ensures that aircraft meet minimum environmental standards. The Chicago Convention on International Civil Aviation (which deals with aviation generally, and was signed in 1944) makes specific provision for noise certification under Annex 16. The International Civil Aviation Organisation (ICAO), which was established under that Convention, has the responsibility of ensuring that the provisions of the Annex are implemented by countries that are signatories to the Convention. As far as the United Kingdom is concerned, the Civil Aviation Authority (CAA) is responsible for issuing noise certificates in terms of its requirements under Annex 16.

As far as European Aviation Safety Agency (EASA) aircraft are concerned, noise certificates are issued under EU Regulation No. 2016/2008, Art. 6. This Article makes provision for compliance within the EU of environmental protection standards, which are placed on the state by Annex 16 to the Convention. (See also EU Regulation No. 748/2012, which, *inter alia*, makes further provision for noise certification.) As far as non-EASA aircraft are concerned, the CAA issue noise certificates in terms of the provisions of the Aircraft Noise Regulations 1999 (SI 1999 No. 1452, as amended). The Air Navigation (Environmental Standards for Non-EASA Aircraft) Order 2008 (SI 2008 No. 3133) makes further provision for the noise certification of non-EASA aircraft.

Airport noise

Noise from aircraft poses a particular problem in the vicinity of aerodromes. Under s. 77(1) of the Civil Aviation Act 1982, provision may be made by an Air Navigation Order for regulating the conditions under which noise and vibration may be caused by aircraft on an aerodrome. Such an Order may provide that s. 77(2) applies to such noise and vibration. Section 77(2) provides that no action may lie, in respect of the law of nuisance, by reason only of the noise and vibration of aircraft on an aerodrome, provided that the provisions of the Order are complied with. Article 218 of the Air Navigation Order 2016 provides that s. 77(2) applies, *inter alia*, to government aerodromes, national licensed aerodromes and EASA certified aerodromes.

Finally, mention should be made of the Aerodrome (Noise Restrictions) (Rules and Procedures) Regulations 2003 (SI 2003 No. 1742). As far as Scotland is concerned, the Regulations apply only to civil airports that have more than 50,000 take-offs or landings of civil subsonic jet aeroplanes per calendar year (Reg. 3). The competent authority is the airport operator. The airport operator is required to adopt a balanced and proportionate approach when dealing with noise problems (Reg. 5). When considering whether to apply operating restrictions at a relevant airport, the competent authority is required to take into account matters that are specified in the Regulations (Reg. 6).

Military aircraft

Generally, the legal controls which apply to civil aircraft do not apply to noise from military aircraft. However, the Crown can be sued in relation to noise which contravenes Article 8 of the ECHR, and also noise which ranks as a nuisance (see, e.g., *Dennis* v *MoD* [2003] Env LR 741; *King* v *The Advocate General for Scotland* [2009] CSOH 169).

ROAD TRAFFIC NOISE

Section 41(1)(2) of the Road Traffic Act 1988 allows the Scottish ministers to make regulations which govern, *inter alia*, the construction and equipment in motor vehicles, and the conditions under which they may be used. Provision can be made for the regulation of noise from vehicles. Section 42 makes it an offence for a person to fail to comply with regulations that are made under s. 41. The main regulations governing the construction and use etc. of vehicles are the Road Vehicles (Construction and Use) Regulations 1986 (SI 1986 No. 1078) (as amended). Under Reg. 54(1)(2), every vehicle that is propelled by an internal combustion engine is required to be fitted with an exhaust system, including a silencer, both of which are required to be kept in good working order. Importantly, Regs 55–57 make provision for noise limits, which may not be exceeded. Furthermore, Reg. 97 provides that no motor vehicle may be used in such a manner as to cause excessive noise, which could have been avoided by the exercise of reasonable care on the part of the driver.

Railway noise

Noise from trains can be problematic. The vast majority of railway lines in Scotland were constructed during the nineteenth century under the authority of a private Act of Parliament. The defence of statutory authority is, therefore, potentially applicable if an action for private nuisance were brought against the relevant train operator, provided that the noise in question was the inevitable consequence of that which was authorised by the relevant Act: see, e.g., *Allen* v *Gulf Oil Refining Ltd* [1981] AC 1001. As far as new railway lines are concerned, the Transport and Works (Scotland) Act 2007, s. 1(1), allows the Scottish ministers to make provision, by way of an order, which authorises the construction and operation of a railway line that starts, ends and remains in Scotland. There is no authority on whether the defence of statutory authority would be applicable in relation to noise from trains that are running on railway lines that are authorised under such an order. However, it is the author's view that the defence of statutory authority could apply in such circumstances.

Essential Facts

- Section 79(1)(g) of the Environmental Protection Act 1990 allows local authorities to abate noise that is prejudicial to health or a nuisance.
- Section 60 of the Control of Pollution Act 1974 gives local authority power to control noise from building sites.

- Sections 49 and 54 of the Civic Government (Scotland) Act 1982 makes special provision in relation to noise that is caused by creatures and musical instruments, respectively.
- The Antisocial Behaviour etc. (Scotland) Act 2004, Part 2, makes provision for the control of forms of antisocial behaviour, including noise. Part 5 of the Act gives a local authority power to control neighbourhood noise.
- Excessive noise can constitute an infringement of Article 8 and Article 1 of the European Convention of Human Rights (ECHR).
- In determining whether the ECHR has been infringed, the court takes into account a variety of factors, including whether the level of the relevant noise contravenes domestic law, appropriate WHO standards, whether the complainant has come to the noise in question, and whether the noise in question is typical of modern life.
- The Environmental Noise Directive (Directive 2002/49/EC) makes provision for the preparation of strategic noise maps and action plans, both of which require to be made available to members of the public.
- The most important legal instrument for controlling noise from aircraft is by way of noise certification.
- The Road Vehicles (Construction and Use) Regulations 1986 (as amended) set limits for noise from vehicles.

5 AIR POLLUTION

INTRODUCTION

In 2018, a European Court of Auditors report concluded that air pollution is now the biggest environmental risk to public health in the European Union. Each year air pollution causes about 400,000 premature deaths, and hundreds of billions of euros in health-related external costs. People in urban areas are particularly exposed to air pollution. Particulate matter, nitrogen dioxide and ground level ozone are the air pollutants responsible for most of these early deaths: *Air Pollution: Our Health Still Insufficiently Protected* (at p. 6).

Indeed, poor air quality has been recognised as the largest environmental risk to public health risk in the United Kingdom, with high NO_2 levels exacerbating the impact of pre-existing health conditions, especially for the elderly and children: *Tackling Nitrogen Dioxide in Our Towns and Cities* (*UK Government: A Consultation*, May 2017, at p. 4). Again, the Clean Air Strategy 2019 stated that air pollution presents one of the UK's biggest public health challenges (Executive Summary).

However, poor air quality also has a wider environmental impact. Poor air quality can harm sensitive habitats, as well as ecosystems and agriculture. Poor air quality also has a detrimental effect on the economy. Air pollution derives from a number of sources, such as industry, farming, transport, energy generation and the heating of homes.

The modern law relating to air pollution has its origins in the nineteenth century, which was a period during which the Industrial Revolution was in full swing when factories would belch out smoke and fumes. However, the legislation which local authorities could employ to tackle the problem was largely nuisance-based. This had its limitations as far as the regulation of air pollution was concerned. One of the main disadvantages of nuisance-based law was the difficulty in establishing a causal link between any smoke source, such as a factory chimney, and either physical injury to property or personal discomfort to individuals. It was, therefore, often difficult to prove that a nuisance existed. However, not only was the law defective in substance, it tended to be under-enforced. Indeed, there was a general lack of confidence in the ability of local authorities to regulate air pollution effectively. It was partly due to this reason that an independent inspectorate, namely, the Alkali Inspectorate, was instituted in 1863 by the Alkali Act of that year. Whereas the original function of the Alkali Inspectorate was to simply regulate pollution from alkali works (which exacted a devastating toll on the surrounding environment), the remit of the Inspectorate was subsequently extended to include other industries. The modern successor of the Alkali Inspectorate in Scotland is SEPA.

The substantive law relating to air pollution remained, largely, nuisance-based until the inadequacy of the law was cruelly exposed by the London Smog disaster of 1952. This prompted the passing of the Clean Air Act 1956 (amended in 1968). The 1956 Act was repealed and replaced by the Clean Air Act 1993, to which we now turn our attention.

CLEAN AIR ACT 1993

In post-war Britain, pollution, largely, but not exclusively, took the form of smoke pollution which, essentially, came from two sources, namely, industry and domestic sources. In framing the 1956 Act, Parliament adopted a sectoral approach to address the problem, that is to say, it attempted to control pollution from specific sources.

Clean Air Act 1993
Dark smoke

Whereas smoke from industry played no small part in causing the London Smog disaster, the main culprit was smoke from domestic sources. Section 1(1) of the Clean Air Act 1993 (the Act) makes it an offence for dark smoke (as defined in s. 3(1)) to be emitted from the chimney of any building. Section 1(2) makes similar provision in relation to smoke from boilers and industrial plant. Because it is neither practical, nor possible, for a boiler or plant to be operated without emitting dark smoke, s. 1(3) allows the Scottish ministers to make regulations which permit dark smoke to be emitted from such sources for limited periods (see the Dark Smoke (Permitted Periods) Regulations 1958 (SI 1958 No. 498). Section 1(4) makes provision for defences in certain circumstances.

Since the emission of dark smoke, of course, is not confined to smoke emission from chimneys, s. 2(1) of the Act makes it an offence for an occupier of any industrial or trade premises (as defined in s. 2(6)) to either cause, or permit, the emission of dark smoke from the premises. Section 2(1) does not apply to the emission of dark smoke from a chimney to which s. 1 applies (s. 2(2)). Section 2(4) provides that it is a defence to prove that the alleged emission was inadvertent, and also that all practicable steps had been taken to prevent or minimise the emission of dark smoke. A person who is guilty of an offence under s. 2 is liable to a fine: s. 2(5).

Furnace smoke

Furnaces, of course, have the potential to pollute the atmosphere. The Act, therefore, makes provision to reduce pollution from this source. No furnace may be installed in any building, or in any fixed boiler or industrial plant, unless notice of the proposal to install the furnace has been given to the local authority: s. 4(1). The Act goes on to provide that no furnace may be installed in a building, or any fixed boiler, or industrial plant, unless the furnace is capable, so far as practicable, of being operated continuously, without emitting smoke, when burning fuel which is of a type for which the furnace was designed to burn: s. 4(2). However, any furnace that has been installed in accordance with plans and specifications that have been submitted to, and approved for the purposes of the Act, by the local authority, is deemed to have complied with that requirement: s. 4(3)). The Act makes provision for penalties in relation to furnaces which have been installed in contravention of the Act: s. 4(4). Finally, the Act does not apply to the installation of domestic furnaces: s. 4(5).

Grit and dust

The presence of grit and dust in the atmosphere was recognised as a serious problem by Parliament when it drafted the original Clean Air Act 1956. At that time, the main source of the grit and dust was industrial boilers. The Act, therefore, allows the Scottish ministers to make regulations which prescribe limits on the rates of emission of grit and dust from such furnaces: s. 5(2) (see the Clean Air (Emission of Grit and Dust from Furnaces)(Scotland) Regulations 1971 (SI 1971 No. 626)). The Act does not apply to domestic furnaces: s. 5(1). If the emissions from a furnace chimney exceed those limits, the occupier of the building in which the furnace is situated is guilty of an offence: s. 5(3). However, the Act makes provision for the defence of the use of best practicable means for minimising the alleged emission: s. 5(4). If there is no prescribed limit applicable to a furnace that is served by a chimney, and the occupier fails to use any practicable means which there may be for minimising the emission of grit and dust from the chimney, he or she commits an offence: s. 5(5).

Grit arrestment plant

It is advantageous to address the problem of grit and dust emissions from factories by preventing emissions at source. Under s. 6(1) of the Act, a furnace (other than a domestic furnace) may not be used in a building:

(a) to burn pulverised fuel; or

(b) to burn at a rate of 45.4 kg or more any other solid matter; or

(c) to burn at a rate equivalent to 366.4 kW or more any liquid or gaseous matter, unless the furnace is provided with plant for arresting grit and dust which has been approved by the local authority, or which has been installed in accordance with plans approved by the local authority, or which has been installed in accordance with plans and specifications approved by the local authority, and that plant is properly maintained and used.

Under s. 6(5) it is an offence to contravene the Act.

Under s. 7(1) of the Act, the Scottish ministers have power to make regulations to exempt furnaces from the requirement to have grit arrestment plant (see the Clean Air (Arrestment Plant)(Exemption) Regulations 1969 (SI 1969 No. 1262)). The Act also gives a local authority, on the application of the occupier of a building, power to exempt a furnace from the requirement to have grit and dust arrestment plant if the local authority is satisfied that the furnace will not be prejudicial to health, or a nuisance: s. 7(2). In the face of refusal of such an application, the occupier can appeal to the Scottish ministers: s. 7(4). It is made an offence for the occupier of any building to use a furnace, other than for a purpose prescribed in the relevant regulations, or, as the case may be, for a purpose that has been sanctioned by the local authority under s. 7(2), or the Scottish Ministers under s. 7(5). The Act also makes provision for the of arrestment plant in domestic premises: s. 8.

Where a local authority determines an application for approval of grit arrestment plant under either s. 6 or s. 8, the local authority is required to give written notification of its decision: s. 9(1). If the local authority decides to refuse to grant approval, then reasons are required to be given. Appeal against refusal lies to the Scottish ministers, who have complete powers of review: s. 9(2).

In order to allow enforcing authorities to accurately ascertain the quantity of grit and dust that is being emitted from industrial plant, the Act makes provision for the measurement of grit dust and fumes by the occupier of relevant buildings: s. 10, and also measurement by local authorities: s. 11.

Chimneys

It is important that a chimney is of sufficient height to permit the dispersal in the atmosphere of emissions from the furnace which the chimney serves. The Act, therefore, gives a local authority power to regulate the height of chimneys which serve furnaces within its area. Section 14(2)(3) of the Act makes it an offence for the occupier of a building in which a furnace is served by a chimney to knowingly cause or permit the furnace to be used to burn:

(a) pulverised fuel;

(b) at a rate of 45.4 kg or more an hour, any solid matter; or

(c) at a rate equivalent to 45.4 kg or more, any liquid or gaseous matter, unless the height of the chimney serving the furnace has been approved by the local authority, and any conditions subject to which the approval was granted are complied with.

Fixed boilers and industrial plant are required to meet the same requirements: s. 14(4).

Under s. 15(1)(2) a local authority may not approve the height of a chimney under s. 14, unless it is satisfied that it will be sufficient to prevent, so far as practicable, the smoke, grit and dust, gases or fumes emitted from the chimney from becoming prejudicial to health or a nuisance, having regard to:

(a) the purpose of the chimney;

(b) the position and descriptions of the buildings near it;

(c) the levels of the neighbouring ground; and

(d) any other matters requiring consideration in the circumstances.

The local authority may grant approval, without qualification, or subject to conditions, as to the rate or quality of emissions from the chimney: s. 15(3). Appeal lies to the Scottish ministers against the decision of the local authority: s. 15(6). The Scottish ministers have complete powers of review: s. 15(7). The Act also makes provision for local authority control of chimneys other than those which serve furnaces: s. 16.

Domestic provisions

One of the most innovative provisions of the original Clean Air Act 1956 (repealed) was the institution of smoke control areas. The implementation of the smoke control legislation, which we now discuss, greatly improved the quality of the atmosphere in the United Kingdom.

The Act empowers a local authority to declare either the whole, or part, of its area a smoke control area, by a smoke control order: s. 18(1). A local authority is given wide scope, as to the form that the order can take. The order may make different provision for different parts of the smoke control area, and the order may also limit the operation of s. 20 of the Act (prohibition of emissions of smoke) to specified classes of buildings in the area: s. 18(2). The order may also exempt specified buildings or classes of buildings, or specified fireplaces or classes of fireplaces in the area from the operation of s. 20, upon such conditions as may be specified in the order. A smoke control order can be either revoked, or varied, by a subsequent order: s. 18(3). SEPA is given default powers to require a local authority to establish a smoke control area: s. 19.

Section 20(1) of the Act provides that, if, on any day, smoke is emitted from the chimney of any building that is situated in a smoke control area, the occupier of the building is guilty of an offence. Similarly, if, on any day, smoke is emitted from a chimney (not being the chimney of a building) that serves the furnace of any fixed boiler, or industrial plant, within a smoke control area, the person having possession of the boiler, or plant, is guilty of an offence: s. 20(2). However, no offence is committed if the smoke emission is covered by an exemption that is in force under the Act: s. 20(3). In any case, in proceedings for an offence under s. 20, it is a defence to prove that the alleged emission was not caused by the use of any fuel, other than an authorised fuel: s. 20(4). An authorised fuel is one which has been authorised by the Scottish ministers under s. 20(6) of the Act.

The automatic result of a smoke control area coming into effect, is that an occupier of premises is required either to adopt another means of heating or, alternatively, to adapt to an existing fireplace in order to burn an authorised fuel. However, there are fires which are capable of burning fuels, other than authorised fuels, without emitting smoke in significant quantities. The Scottish ministers are, therefore, empowered to exempt any class of fireplace from the provisions of s. 20 if they are satisfied that such fireplaces can be used for burning fuel, other than authorised fuels, without producing any smoke or a substantial quantity of smoke: s. 21(1). The Scottish ministers have also the power, by order, to suspend, or relax, the operation of s. 20 (prohibition of smoke in smoke control areas) in relation to either the whole, or part, of a smoke control area: s. 22(1). In order to ensure that the aforementioned provisions are complied with, the Act makes it an offence, subject to certain exceptions, to acquire, or sell, any fuel, other than an authorised fuel, in a smoke control area: s. 23.

Finally, the Act gives a local authority power to compel either the owner, or occupier, of a building to carry out works on the relevant building in order to avoid contravention of s. 20: s. 24.

Control of other forms pollution

The Scottish ministers are given the power to make regulations which impose requirements as to the composition and contents of any fuel of a kind that is used in motor vehicles: s. 30(1).

Other provisions

The main remaining provisions of the Act can only be mentioned in brief here.

The Act makes it an offence (subject to certain exceptions) for a person to burn insulation from a cable with a view to recovering metal from the cable: s. 33.

The Act empowers a local authority to either undertake or to contribute towards the cost of investigation and research which relates to pollution: s. 34(1). The Act allows a local authority to obtain information (subject to certain exceptions) about the emission of pollutants and other substances into the air: s. 35(1).

In order to avoid overlap between respective regulatory regimes, the Act precludes the application of Parts I–III to an activity that is subject to regulations made under s. 2 of the Pollution Prevention and Control Act 1999, or s. 18 of the Regulatory Reform(Scotland) Act 2014: s. 41A(1).

The Act makes provision, *inter alia*, for controlling the emission of smoke and fumes from colliery spoil-banks: s. 42.

The Act makes provision for the notification of offences: s. 51; the rights of inspection on the part of local authorities: s. 56; and the default powers (subject to certain exceptions) of the Scottish ministers, in the face of a local authority's failure to perform any function which it ought to have performed in terms of the Act: s. 60.

Conclusions on the Clean Air Acts

The Clean Air Act 1956 can, rightly, be regarded as a world, 'first'. Both the 1956 and 1968 Clean Air Acts prevented many thousands of deaths from bronchial illness, and also made cities both cleaner and better places in which to live. Indeed, the Clean Air Act concept was adopted by many other countries, and laid the basis for air quality standards which were set by the European Union.

AMBIENT AIR QUALITY

We have seen, above, how Parliament attempted to address the problem of atmospheric pollution, in post-war UK, by concentrating mainly on pollution from industry and domestic sources, which were the main culprits of the London Smog disaster. However, currently, the sources of atmospheric pollution are more diverse, and include a wide range of sources and activities, such as industrial processes, farming, transport, energy generation and heating homes: *Tackling Nitrogen Dioxide in Our Towns and Cities: A Consultation* (UK Government, May 2017), at p. 4.

We first look at the role the European Union (EU) (which, to date, has been the main driver of UK ambient air pollution policy) has played in dealing with ambient air pollution, and then, we turn our attention to Scotland.

EU ambient air quality policy and legislation

Currently, the main components of EU air quality policy and legislation consist of:

>2005 EU Thematic Strategy on Air Pollution;
>
>2001 National Emission Ceilings Directive (NECD);
>
>Ambient Air Quality Directive;
>
>source-specific legislation.

2005 EU Thematic Strategy on Air Pollution (COM (2005) 446)

The European commission recognised in its 2005 Thematic Strategy on Air Pollution that air pollution is both a local and a transboundary pollutant, which either alone or in conjunction with chemical reactions leads to negative health and environmental impacts. The strategy sets health and environmental objectives, and emission reduction targets for the main pollutants, namely, O_3 (ground level ozone), SO_2 (sulphur dioxide), NO_x (nitrogen oxides), VOCs (volatile organic compounds), NH_3 (ammonia), and primary PM2.5 (particles which are emitted directly into the air). The strategy also sets specific long-term objectives for the year 2020. The European Commission reviewed the policy, which was set out in the 2005 Thematic Strategy, in its Clean Air Programme for Europe: COM/2013/0918. The new strategy, which is contained in the programme, sets out new interim objectives for health and environmental impacts up to 2030.

2016 National Emission Ceilings Directive

The National Emissions Ceilings Directive (Directive 2016/2284/EU) sets national emission ceilings for four pollutants, namely, sulphur dioxide (SO_2), nitrogen oxides (NO_x) non-methane volatile organic compounds (NMVOCs), ammonia (NH_3), and fine particulate matter (PM2.5) for each member state: Art. 1. Member states are obligated to draw up national air pollution control programmes, and also that emissions of those pollutants, and those pollutants which are referred to in Annex 1, as well as their impacts, be monitored and also reported. Member states are required to limit the annual emission of these pollutants in accordance with the national emission reduction commitments applicable from 2020 to 2029 and from 2030 onwards, as laid down in Annex II: Art. 4.

The Directive is implemented in the UK by the National Emissions Ceilings Regulations 2018 (SI 2018 No. 129).

Ambient Air Quality Directive

In accordance with the aims of the Thematic Strategy, EU air quality legislation has been streamlined by the Directive on Ambient Air Quality and cleaner air for Europe (Directive 2008/50/EC). The Directive makes provision for defining, and also establishing, objectives for ambient air quality which are designed to avoid, prevent or reduce the harmful effects on human health, and also the environment as a whole; assessing the ambient air quality in member states, on the basis of common methods and criteria; obtaining information on ambient air quality in order to help combat air pollution and nuisance, and to monitor long-term trends and improvements resulting from national and community measures; ensuring that such information on ambient air quality is made available to the public; maintaining air quality where it is good, and improving it in other cases; and promoting increased cooperation between member states in reducing air pollution: Art. 1. The Directive also makes provision for the establishment of zones and agglomerations (the terms which are defined in Art. 2) where air quality assessment and air quality management is to be carried out: Art. 4. An assessment regime is established in relation to sulphur dioxide, nitrogen dioxide and oxides of nitrogen, particulate matter (PM10 and PM2.5), lead benzene and carbon monoxide. Member states are required to assess ambient air quality, in relation to the aforementioned pollutants, in accordance with the criteria which are laid down in the Directive: Art. 6. In zones and agglomerations where the levels for the aforementioned pollutants are below the appropriate limit values (defined in Art. 2) specified in the Directive (Annexes

XI and XII), member states are required to maintain the levels of these pollutants below those limit values in order to preserve the best ambient air quality which is compatible with sustainable development: Art. 12. Member states are also required to ensure that throughout the relevant zones and agglomerations, the levels of SO_2 and PM10, lead and CO_2 in the ambient air do not exceed the limit values laid down in the Directive: Art. 13. Member states are required to ensure compliance with the critical levels (as defined in Art. 2) in accordance with the Directive: Art. 14. A national exposure reduction target (as defined in Art. 2) and also target value and limit value (as defined in Art. 2) are set for PM2.5: Arts 15 and 16. Member states are required to take all necessary measures, which do not entail excessive cost, to achieve the relevant target and target value. The Directive also provides that the target values, and long-term objectives for ozone are attained: Art. 17. Where, in any zones or agglomerations, the levels of pollutants in the ambient air exceed any limit or target value, plus any relevant margin of tolerance (as defined in Art. 2), a member state is placed under an obligation to ensure that air quality plans are established for those zones and agglomerations, in order to achieve the related limit value or target value that is specified in the Directive: Art. 23.

Finally, the Directive makes provision for member states to draw up short-term action plans if, in a given zone or agglomeration, there is a risk that the levels of pollutants will exceed one, or more, of the alert thresholds specified in the Directive: Art. 24.

The Directive is implemented in Scotland by the Air Quality Standards (Scotland) Regulations 2010 (SSI 2010 No. 204).

However, the UK's implementation of the provisions of the 2008 Directive has not been uncontroversial, and on three occasions has recently been the subject of challenge by an environmental pressure group, namely, ClientEarth. In the most recent, *R (ClientEarth) v Secretary of State for Food, Environment and Rural Affairs (No. 3)* [2018] EWHC 315, the court was required to decide whether the Secretary of State had legally implemented the UK's duties in terms of the Directive.

The UK government's national air quality plan (AQP) was adopted in 2017, after earlier plans were held not to comply with the 2008 Directive and also the English Air Quality Standards Regulations 2010 (SI 2010 No. 1001). ClientEarth (the claimants) challenged the adequacy of the 2017 AQP.

As far as the legislative scheme was concerned (as stated above), Art. 13 of Directive 2008/50/EC (the 2008 Directive) imposes limit values and alert thresholds for the protection of human health. It provides that member states are required to ensure that, throughout their zones and agglomerations, the levels of sulphur dioxide, PM10, lead and carbon monoxide in the ambient air do not exceed the values laid down in Annex X1. In relation to nitrogen dioxide and benzene, the limit values specified in Annex XI may not be exceeded from the date specified therein.

Shortly after the November 2016 judgment, DEFRA set about the task of preparing a new AQP. A long list of potential policy options to tackle nitrogen dioxide emissions was identified. Among these options, was a wider deployment of clean air zones (CAZ) than that contemplated by the 2015 AQP (which had been held by the court to be defective). However, CAZs were divided into two categories. The first comprised 'non-charging' CAZs. These comprised defined geographical areas, which were used as a focus for action to improve air quality. The second category comprised Charging Clean Air Zones (CCAZ). These were zones where, in addition to the requirements which were contained in the former category, vehicle owners were required, *inter alia*, to pay a fee to enter, or move, within a zone if they were driving a vehicle of a specific type. The UK government finally opted for CCAZs.

As stated above, under Art. 23 of the 2008 Directive, where, in given zones or agglomerations, the levels of pollutants in the ambient air exceed any limit value, member states are required to ensure that air quality plans are established for those zones and agglomerations in order to achieve the related limit value specified in Annexes XI and XIV to the Directive. Article 23 further provides that, in the event of exceedances of these values, for which deadlines have already expired, the air quality plan is required to set out appropriate measures so that the exceedance period is kept as short as possible.

The 2008 Directive was transposed into UK domestic law by four sets of regulations for the home nations. Regulation 26 of the English Regulations (Air Quality Standards Regulations 2010 (SI 2010 No. 1001) requires the Secretary of State, when the levels of NO_2 (among other pollutants) exceed any limit value, to draw up and implement an AQP in order to achieve that limit value. Regulation 26 provides that the AQP must include measures which are intended to ensure compliance with any relevant limit value, within the shortest possible time.

The UK government published its new AQP in July 2017. The AQP explained that the United Kingdom is divided into forty-three zones for the purposes of air quality reporting. In all but two of these zones, the UK was achieving the statutory hourly mean limit value for NO_2. However, in thirty-seven zones the statutory annual mean limit value for NO_2 was exceeded.

However, the various zones were not coterminal with local authority areas. Indeed, many zones incorporated more than one local authority area. However, the AQP of 2017 was directed at local authorities, which were regarded as having a central role to play in bringing the AQP into effect.

The AQP explained that in 2017 the UK government had published thirty-seven individual zone plans for each non-compliant zone in the UK. The degree of non-compliance varied greatly. The AQP, therefore, adopted different approaches, which depended on the degree of non-compliance which was forecast.

First, there were twenty-three local authorities which represented areas with the greatest problem, that is, those with exceedances which were projected beyond the next 3–4 years. Secondly, there were five cities which were previously the focus of the 2015 AQP. Thirdly, there were forty-five local authorities which currently had air quality exceedances, but, at the same time, were expected to achieve compliance with the NO_2 limit values by 2021.

Whereas, the AQP adopted different measures for each of the above groups, the AQP identified CAZs (which included charging CCAZs) as the means by which the United Kingdom would meet its NO_2 limit values in the shortest possible time. Therefore, this measure was to be used by the government as the benchmark for assessing locally-led solutions to the pollution problem.

For the first group, under the AQP, local authorities were required to develop local plans in order to achieve NO_2 limit values within the shortest possible time. The AQP explained that if the local authorities adopted a CCAZ model, they could achieve statutory NO_2 limit values by 2021. However, given the potential impact on individuals and businesses etc., if any local authority did adopt such a model, the AQP allowed that local authority to use alternative measures to achieve the NO_2 limit values if the authority could show that its plan would cause NO_2 levels in the area to attain legal compliance within the shortest possible time. By a Direction under s. 85(5) of the of the Environment Act 1995 (EA) local authorities were placed under a legal duty to develop and implement such plans.

As far as the second group was concerned, the AQP anticipated that the five cities would be mandated to implement CCAZs which would achieve compliance by 2020. In December 2017, new Directions were issued to each of the five cities under the EA 1995, which required each local authority to prepare, as part of its feasibility study, a full business case for its area for approval by the Secretary of State.

As far as the third group was concerned, the AQP proceeded on the basis that the local authorities would not be required to develop further local plans or undertake a feasibility study which was benchmarked, in terms of effectiveness, against a CCAZ.

In delivering his judgment, Garnham J held that the 2017 AQP was flawed (and seriously flawed at that) in its application of the three-year benchmark to the forty-five local authority areas where compliance with the Directive was anticipated within three years in any event. According to Garnham J, whereas it would be pointless to require these local authorities to embark on establishing a CCAZ in an area where compliance would be achieved within the same period without a CCAZ, the government could not substitute the application of its CCAZ benchmark, for the requirements of the Directive and the Regulations, in areas where it was not. Garnham J pointed out that the obligation, which was imposed by Art. 23 of the Directive, was specific to each and every zone or agglomeration. That obligation applied where, in given zones or agglomerations, the levels of pollutants in the ambient air exceeded any limit value. When the obligation arose, member states were required to ensure that AQP's were established for those zones.

His Lordship emphasised that under Art. 23, a threefold obligation was imposed on the Secretary of State. First, he was required to secure compliance with the Directive by the earliest possible date. Secondly, the Secretary of State was required to choose a route to achieve that objective, which reduced pollution as quickly as possible. Thirdly, the Secretary of State was required to take steps to ensure that meeting the relevant limit values was not just possible but was likely. It, therefore, followed that the Secretary of State was required to ensure that there was in place an AQP that met this threefold obligation. His Lordship added that, given the fact that the obligation which was imposed on the Secretary of State was zone-specific, it was quite irrelevant that each of the local authority areas would achieve compliance with the provisions of the 2008 Directive by 2021. That is to say, that the Secretary of State was required to ensure that in each of the forty-five areas, steps were taken to achieve compliance as soon as possible, by the quickest route possible, and also by means which made that outcome likely. The CCAZ benchmark could not be used as a means of watering down those obligations. Furthermore, there were no means of enforcing local air quality plans under the AQP. Article 23 of the Directive had obligated the Secretary of State to ensure that local air quality plans are established. Therefore, polite letters from the government to local authorities, which simply urged additional steps on the part of local authorities to secure compliance, were not enough. It, therefore, followed that the AQP, in its application to the forty-five local authority areas, did not ensure compliance with the 2008 Directive or the English Regulations.

Finally, the court held that the AQP did not contain sufficient information, as was required by Annex XV of the Directive or Schedule 8 of the English Regulations.

In the last analysis, Garnham J held the AQP to be unlawful. A mandatory order was, therefore, granted to compel the government to provide a Supplement to the 2017 AQP in order to remedy the relevant defects identified by his Lordship. Finally, his Lordship directed that the 2017 AQP should remain in force while the Supplement was being prepared.

AIR QUALITY STRATEGY FOR ENGLAND, SCOTLAND, WALES AND NORTHERN IRELAND

The traditional approach taken by the United Kingdom to address the problem of air pollution was to adopt a sectoral approach, that is to say, Parliament simply focused on regulating pollution from specific sources, such as smoke from chimneys, air pollution from certain industries which posed a perceived problem. The Alkali Acts, the Clean Air Acts and the Environmental Protection Act 1990 serve as good examples of such a form of regulation. However, during the 1990s it was becoming increasingly clear that that a more holistic approach was required in order to deal with air pollution. The Environment Act 1995, therefore, places the Scottish ministers under a duty to prepare, and publish, a statement (or strategy) containing policies with respect to the assessment, or management, of air quality: s. 80(1). The first United Kingdom Air Quality Strategy was published in 1997: Cmnd. 3587 (HMSO, 1997). That strategy was revised and replaced in 2000, and re-named the Air Quality Strategy for England, Scotland and Wales and Northern Ireland, to reflect the devolution of air quality policy: The Air Quality Strategy for England, Scotland, Wales and Northern Ireland, Cmnd. No. 4548, SE 2000/3 (HMSO, 2000). The most recent version of the strategy was published in 2007: The Air Quality Strategy for England, Scotland, Wales and Northern Ireland, Cmnd. 7169 (HMSO, 2007). Whereas the strategy does not have the force of law, SEPA is required to have regard to the strategy in discharging its pollution control functions: s. 81.

LOCAL AUTHORITY REVIEW OF AIR QUALITY

The responsibility for implementing the strategy rests with local authorities. A local authority is required to conduct a review of air quality in its area for time being, and also for the future: s. 82(1). In conducting such a review, the local authority is required to assess whether air quality standards and objectives are being achieved within the relevant period, within the local authority's area: s. 82(2). The relevant air quality objectives, which are contained in the strategy, are prescribed in the Air Quality (Scotland) Regulations 2000: SSI 2000 No. 97 (as amended). The Regulations set air quality objectives for eight pollutants, namely, benzene, 1,3-butadiene, carbon monoxide, lead, nitrogen dioxide, PM2.5, PM10 and sulphur dioxide. The regulations also make provision for the relevant period, within which the relevant air quality objective is to be achieved.

If, after carrying out a review, a local authority is of the opinion that any air quality standard or objective either is not being achieved or is not likely to be achieved within the relevant period, the local authority is required to identify any parts of its area in which it appears that those objectives are not likely to be achieved, within the relevant period: s. 82(3). If, after having conducted such a review within its area, it appears to a local authority that any air quality standards or objectives either are not being achieved, or are not likely to be achieved within the relevant period, the local authority is required to designate, by order, an air quality management area: s. 83(1). As a result of a subsequent air quality review, any order which is made, may, if it appears on such a review, that the air quality standards or objectives are being achieved (and likely to be achieved throughout the relevant period) within the designated area, the relevant order may be varied or revoked by a subsequent order: s. 83(2).

DUTIES OF LOCAL AUTHORITIES IN DESIGNATED AREAS

When an order which is made under s. 83(1) comes into operation, the local authority is required to prepare an action plan in order to achieve the requisite air quality standards and objectives within the relevant area, by means of the exercise of its powers by the local authority: s. 84(2). The action plan may be revised from time to time: s. 84(4).

Reserve powers of SEPA

SEPA (acting with the approval of the Scottish ministers) may either itself conduct or make, or cause to be conducted, or made:

(a) a review of the quality of the air for the time being and the likely future air quality within the relevant period, within the area of any local authority;

(b) an assessment of whether air quality standards and objectives are being achieved, or are likely to be achieved, within the relevant period within the area of the local authority;

(c) an identification of any parts of the area of a local authority in which it appears that those standards are not likely to be achieved, within the relevant period;

(d) an assessment of the respects (if any) in which it appears that air quality standards are not being achieved, or are not likely to achieved, within the relevant period within the area of a local authority or within a designated area: s. 85(2).

SEPA is empowered to give directions to give a local authority if it appears that:

(a) air quality standards or objectives are not being achieved, or are not likely to be achieved, within the relevant period within the area of the local authority;

(b) a local authority has failed to discharge any duty which is imposed on it under Part IV of the Act;

(c) the actions or the proposed actions by a local authority in relation to the proposed discharge of its responsibilities under Part IV of the Act, is concerned, are inappropriate; or

(d) developments in science or technology, or material changes in circumstances have rendered inappropriate either the actions, or the proposed actions, of a local authority in pursuance of its responsibilities under Part IV of the Act: s. 85(3).

SEPA possesses wide powers in respect of giving directions to local authorities in relation to the latter's powers and duties under the Act. For example, SEPA may require a local authority to conduct an air quality review under s. 82, or designate an air quality management area, or prepare an action plan for such area: s. 85(4). Finally, the Scottish ministers have the power to give directions to local authorities, as the former considers appropriate, for the implementation of any of the UK obligations under the EU treaties, or any international agreement to which the UK is, for the time being, a party in relation to air quality: s. 85(5). The relevant local authority is under a duty to comply with any direction which is given to the local authority under Part IV of the Act: s. 85(7).

TRANSPORT

Transport is a major contributor to air quality pollutant emissions. Indeed, in 2013, transport emissions, which included international aviation and shipping, made up just under a quarter of Scotland's total emissions. More than two-thirds of such emissions came from road transport. Transport, including international maritime and aviation-related emissions, was responsible for all EU greenhouse gas (GHG) emissions in 2009: European Environment Agency 2016. Whilst the most important legislative control of pollution from transport takes the form of regulating emissions at source, town and country planning has an important role to play.

Road vehicle emissions

As far as Scotland is concerned, under the Road Traffic Act 1988 the Scottish ministers are empowered to make regulations as to the use of motor vehicles and trailers on roads, their construction and equipment, and also the conditions under which vehicles may be used: s. 41(1). In particular, the regulations may make provision, *inter alia*, for the emission, or consumption of smoke, fumes or vapour, and the emission of sparks, ashes and grit: s. 41(2). The Road Vehicles (Construction and Use) Regulations 1986 (SI 1986 No. 1078) (as amended) were made under the Act. The main purpose of the regulations is to ensure that vehicles are manufactured to high standards, and also to ensure that such standards are maintained while vehicles are still in use. The Regulations have been substantially amended over the years to implement EU legislation on emissions.

The Secretary of State is empowered under the 1988 Act to make regulations which require the type approval of vehicles, with regard to, *inter alia*, their design, construction and equipment: s. 54(1). The Motor Vehicles (Type Approval) (Great Britain) Regulations 1984: (SI 1984 No. 981 (as amended)), were made under the Act. Goods vehicles are subject to the Motor Vehicles (Type Approval for Goods Vehicles) (Great Britain) Regulations 1982 (SI 1982 No. 1271 (as amended)).

In 2011, the UK government announced its intention to end the sale of conventional car and vans by 2040. The government also announced its intention that every car and van on the road to be a zero emission vehicle by 2050.

In July 2017, the UK government published its plan for tackling roadside nitrogen dioxide concentrations: see *UK Plan for Tackling Roadside Nitrogen Dioxide Concentrations* (2017). The government recognised that the risk from nitrogen dioxide (NO_2) was a local problem in that concentrations of the gas were focused in particular places. Remedial intervention, therefore, was required to be focused on problem areas. The government identified NO_2 pollution from road vehicles as the main cause of pollution. Indeed, this source contributed 80 per cent of the problem at the roadside. The growth in the number of diesel cars had exacerbated the problem. Since this form of air pollution was a local problem, local authorities were required to assume a major role. However, the government stated that it would financially assist local authorities in tackling air pollution.

As far as Scotland is concerned, the Transport (Scotland) Bill was introduced in the Scottish Parliament in 2018. The Bill provides, *inter alia*, for the introduction of the concept of low emission zones, which are set up under low emissions schemes. A low emissions scheme is a scheme under which individuals driving vehicles which fail to meet specific emissions standards are prohibited from driving vehicles in contravention of the scheme within a designated geographical area. The duty of putting in place such schemes falls to local authorities which have a discretion as to whether such schemes should be introduced.

Aircraft emissions

The Air Navigation (Environmental Standards for Non-EASA Aircraft) Order 2008 (SI 2008 No. 3133) sets out environmental standards with which specified categories of UK-registered aircraft which are not subject to the Basic EASA (European Aviation Safety Agency) Regulation (OJ No. L240 of 7.09.2002, p1) must comply. Such aircraft are state aircraft and those coming within one of the categories which are listed in Annex II to that Regulation. Aircraft and aeroplanes are prohibited from taking-off or landing at UK airports unless they comply with the fuel-venting requirements, for which the Order makes provision, and are also fitted with engines which are specified in the emissions certificate to comply with emissions requirements for smoke, unburned hydrocarbons, carbon monoxide and nitrogen. UK registered aircraft which are subject to the Basic EASA Regulation must, instead, comply with the environmental standards which are provided for in that Regulation and also in Commission Regulation (EC) No. 1702/2003).

Emissions certificates for aircraft that are registered in the United Kingdom are issued by the Civil Aviation Authority (CAA). For aircraft registered elsewhere, certificates are issued by the competent authority of the relevant state.

Shipping

Emissions from maritime vessels pose a significant problem as far as atmospheric pollution and GHGs are concerned. In 2013, the European Environment Agency concluded that emissions of CO_2, NO_x, SO_2 and PM2.5 from shipping in European waters can contribute up to 10–20 per cent of worldwide shipping emissions (European Technical Report No. 4/2013 (European Environment Agency, 2013), at p. 5. Emissions from shipping can also contribute to local air quality problems.

The Merchant Shipping (Prevention of Air Pollution from Ships) Regulations 2008 (SI 2009 No. 2924) include provisions which regulate the deliberate emission of ozone-depleting substances from ships, shipboard incineration and fuel oil quality.

OZONE DEPLETION

The ozone layer is situated 15–20 km above the Earth's surface. The ozone layer forms part of the stratosphere: it absorbs some of the sun's ultraviolet radiation, and so acts as a protective layer. Increased ultraviolet light, which results from ozone-depletion, can have an adverse effect on health and can also harm aquatic systems and crops. The 1987 Montreal Protocol (as amended) to the 1985 Vienna Convention for the Protection of the Ozone Layer, made provision for the reduction, and gradual phasing out, of certain ozone-depleting substances (ODS) such as chlorofluorocarbons (CFCs) and halons. The EU ratified the Protocol in 1988 (Council Decision 88/540/EEC). The provisions of the Protocol are currently implemented in the EU by Regulation 1005/2009 (as amended) on substances which deplete the ozone layer. The main provisions of the Regulation include a general ban on the production, marketing and use of ozone-depleting substances, subject to certain exemptions and derogations. As far as the enforcement of the EU Regulation 1005/2009 is concerned, the Ozone-Depleting Substances Regulations 2015 (SI 2015 No, 168, Reg. 3) make the Secretary of State the competent authority for the purposes of the EU Regulation. The enforcement of the EU Regulation in Scotland is divided between SEPA and local authorities (SI 2015 No. 168, Reg. 12). The UK regulations make provision for offences (Regs 8 and 9) and penalties (Reg. 10).

Essential Facts

- In response to the London Smog disaster of 1952 the Clean Air Act 1956 was passed. The 1956 Act was amended in 1968 and consolidated by the Clean Air Act 1993.
- The Clean Air Act 1993 makes provision for the regulation of smoke, grit and dust from premises.
- The Act makes provision for the establishment of smoke control areas by local authorities.
- The National Emissions Ceiling Regulations 2002 (SI 2002 No. 3118) set UK maximum limits in the ambient air for SO_2, NO_x, VOCs and ammonia.
- The Air Quality Standards (Scotland) Regulations 2010 (SSI 2010 No. 204) set ambient air quality standards and make provision for the monitoring of the ambient air.
- The Air Quality (Scotland) Regulations 2000 (SSI 2000 No. 97) set air quality objectives for certain pollutants and also make provision for the relevant period within which the relevant air quality is to be achieved.
- The Montreal Protocol on ozone depletion is implemented in the EU by Regulation 1005/2009. The enforcement of the Regulation is divided between SEPA and local authorities.

Further Reading

F. McManus, *Environmental Law in Scotland* (Edinburgh University Press, 2016).

F. McManus (ed.), *Environmental Law in Scotland* (SULI/W. Green) (looseleaf).

J. Houghton, *Global Warming*, 4th edn (Cambridge University Press, 2009).

Low Carbon Scotland, Meeting our Emissions Reductions Targets 2013–2027, 2nd Report on Proposals and Policies (Scottish Government, 2013), available at: www.gov.scot/Resource/0042/00426134.pdf.

Climate Ready Scotland: Scottish Climate Change Adaption Programme (Scottish Government, 2014) (SG/2014/83), available at: www.gov.scot/Resource/0045/00451392.pdf.

Our Climate Challenge (SEPA, 2014), available at: www.sepa.org.uk/media/40789/our_climate_challenge-2014_2015.pdf, last accessed 21 July 2017.

6 WASTE

INTRODUCTION

In this chapter we look at the important and, at times, complex subject of the regulation of waste in Scotland. Currently, more than 20 million tonnes of waste are produced each year in Scotland. Traditionally, waste was largely regarded as something to be disposed of as quickly, and effectively, as possible. However, the current approach is, rather, to treat waste as a resource that can be utilised for the benefit of the economy. Furthermore, a greater responsibility is now being placed on the producers of waste to ensure there is an effective disposal route for waste by those who are commissioned to dispose of waste materials. This so-called 'top-down' approach is mirrored by the obligation being placed on manufacturers of certain products, such as cars and electrical equipment, to ensure that the product is satisfactorily disposed of when it is no longer fit for use. SEPA, which is Scotland's main environmental regulator, is responsible for the regulation of waste treatment and disposal in Scotland. In turn, local authorities are responsible for the collection and disposal of domestic waste (and some commercial waste) which it collects.

As far as national waste policy is concerned, the Zero Waste Plan (ZWP) for Scotland was published in 2010 by the Scottish government. The ZWP covers a ten-year period. The mission statement in the ZWP is to facilitate the achievement of zero waste, which involves more efficient use of resources in the country by minimising the use of primary resources, and maximising the re-use, recycling and recovery of resources, instead of treating them as waste. The ZWP places emphasis on the prevention of the creation of waste, and also its re-use, recycling and recovery.

THE REGULATION OF WASTE

The Environmental Protection Act 1990 (EPA) makes provision, *inter alia*, for the unlawful deposit of waste, and places individuals under a duty of care in relation to waste. The expression 'waste' is a term of art, or technical term, and is defined in s. 75(1) of the EPA as:

(a) anything that is waste within the meaning of Art. 3(1) of the Waste Framework Directive 2008/98/EC (WFD) as read with Arts 5 and 6 of thereof, and which is not excluded from the scope of the WFD by Art. 2(1)(2) or (3);

(b) radioactive waste within the meaning of s. 1A of the Radioactive Substances Act 1993 which is exempt from the requirement for authorisation under ss. 13 or 14 of that Act by virtue of an order made or having effect as made under s. 15(2) of that Act;

(c) where land is undergoing on-site remediation, that land, including unexcavated contaminated soil and any contaminated buildings permanently connected with that land.

Under s. 75(4) of the EPA, 'controlled waste' is defined as household, industrial or commercial waste, or any such waste. The definition of waste is important, because the precise classification of substances as waste is necessary for the clear formulation of waste management policy, as well as the effective regulation of substances which fall to be so classified. The expression, 'waste' derives, in effect, from the WFD.

The meaning of waste was considered in the Outer House case of *Scottish Power Generation Ltd* v *Scottish Environment Protection Agency* [2005] Env LR 38. In that case, the pursuers, Scottish Power (SP) used certain waste-derived products (WDP) to produce electricity in a power station which they operated. The fuel was produced from sewage by SMW Ltd (SMW), the sludge having been taken from a waste water treatment works. The power station originally operated under an integrated pollution control authorisation, in terms of the EPA, and subsequently, under the Pollution Prevention and Control Act 1999 regime. However, SEPA sought to apply the provisions of the Waste Incineration (Scotland) Regulations 2003 (2003 SSI 170) (which set more rigorous controls over waste plants compared with the controls which were applied to the normal operation of a power station) by means of a variation notice. SP, therefore, challenged the notice by means of judicial review. SP argued that the sludge did not rank as waste in terms, *inter alia*, of the Waste Framework Directive (Directive 75/442/EC: see now the WFD). However, in the opinion of Lord Reed, the sludge remained waste. This was so, since the processing of the sludge did not constitute a complete recovery operation, whereby a substance which was originally waste, ceased to be waste, in terms of the WFD. In reaching his decision, His Lordship (who reviewed the relevant EU law) expressed the view that the word, 'waste' derived its meaning from the word 'discard' as used in the WFD. In this context, the word 'discard' had a special meaning: [2005] Env LR 38, at 65. In short, the word was a term of art. It, therefore, followed from this, that the fact that a processor of a substance derived economic benefit from processing the substance, did not prevent the substance from being categorised as waste. In his Lordship's opinion, indicators of the fact that either a substance is being discarded, or that the holder of the substance had an intention to discard the substance included the following:

(a) was the substance undergoing, or intended to undergo, a disposal operation or a recovery operation that was set out in the WFD;
(b) was the use of the substance, as fuel, a common method of recovering waste; and
(c) was the substance commonly regarded as waste?

Importantly, Lord Reed emphasised (at para. 136) that in determining whether a substance had been discarded, one was required to take into account the general aims of the WFD, foremost amongst which was the protection of health, and the protection of the environment. In the last analysis, the WDF could not be used under the same conditions of environmental protection as the coal that would otherwise be used at SP's power station, or without any greater danger of harm to human health or the environment (at para. 139).

The meaning of waste in terms of s. 33(1) of the EPA was considered in the Divisional Court case of *Environment Agency* v *Inglenorth* [2009] Env LR 33. Here, the defendant company was involved in the transportation, disposal and recycling of waste. The defendant had been contracted to collect materials, which had been created by the demolition of a greenhouse at one garden centre, and then take the materials to another garden centre. The owner of both garden centres told the defendant that he wanted to use the materials for the construction of a car park. The defendant collected some of the material from the first garden centre, and left the material at the other site. However, the owner of the garden centre did not have a waste management licence. The defendant was subsequently charged by the Environment Agency (EA) with the unlawful deposit of controlled waste, contrary to s. 33(1) of the EPA. However, the magistrates dismissed the information, on the basis that on the date when the waste was delivered at the second site, the owner of the garden centre intended to use the material as part of the construction of a car park. Accordingly, there was no necessary intention to discard the material. Therefore, it was not waste in terms of the WFD. On appeal, the Queen's Bench Divisional Court upheld the decision of the magistrates. Sir Anthony May, who gave the leading judgment, decided that the sole question that was required to be answered by the court was the status of the material, at the time of its deposit, at the second garden centre (at [13]). Therefore, it did not matter where the material came from. His Lordship drew the distinction between depositing the material for storage, pending re-use, and, on the other hand, depositing it for use, more or less, straight away without the material being, in any sense of the word, stored (at [33]). Sir Anthony May went on to state that, depending always on the facts, hardcore that was going to be used the following week for current building operations was not being stored in terms of the Act. In the instant case, therefore, the material in question was not waste (at [38]).

The meaning of waste in terms of the WFD was considered again in *R (on the application of the OSS Group Ltd) v Environment Agency* [2008] Env LR 8. Here, two companies sold waste-derived products, which were marketed on the basis that they had been recovered and, therefore, had ceased to be waste. The first claimant (SRM) operated a solvent recovery process, whereby contaminated solvents were collected and recovered to produce product grade distillates (PGD). Following the implementation of Directive 2000/76/EC on waste incineration (WID), the respondent, the EA, classified the PGD as waste, the consequence of which was that the burning of the PGD was subject to the WID. The second claimants, OSS, operated a business of collecting, recycling and processing used oils, and selling the product as recycled fuel oil. Following the implementation of the WID, OSS invested in new and improved processes, in order to facilitate the production of higher quality clean fuel oil (CFO). However, the EA took the view that the CFO ranked as waste, which meant that any purchaser of the CFO who wished to burn that product would be required to comply with the WID. The practical effect of this was that the market for CFO, so categorised, would be lost. Both SRM and OSS, therefore, sought judicial review of the EA's decision to classify both the PGD and the CFO as waste. The main questions which fell to be answered by the Court were, first, in what circumstances did waste cease to be such if it was to be burnt as fuel? Secondly, whether the waste ceased to be waste when a prior process was carried out for rendering it safe to be burned as fuel, or whether it could cease to be waste only when it was actually burnt? However, the High Court rejected the OSS's application for judicial review. OSS then appealed to the Court of Appeal, solely on the issue as to whether lubricating oil that was not originally used as fuel and then became waste could, thereafter, be burnt as anything other than waste. The Court allowed the appeal.

Carnwath LJ (as he then was), after reviewing EU law, provided a useful summary of the definition of waste (at [14]). The main points of his Lordship's judgment include the following points:

1. The concept of waste could not be interpreted restrictively.
2. According to its ordinary meaning, waste is what falls away when one processes a material, or object, and is not the end product which the manufacturing process directly seeks to produce.

3. The term 'discard' 'covers' or 'includes' disposal or recovery within the terms of Annex 11A of the WFD. However, the fact that an article is treated by one of the methods described in the Annexes of the WFD does not lead to the necessary inference that it is waste.

4. The term 'discard' must be interpreted in the light of both the WFD and also Article 174(2) of the Treaty, respectively, that is to say, the protection of human health and the environment against the harmful effects caused by the collection, transport, treatment, storage and tipping of waste; and Community policy on the environment, which aims at a high level of protection, and is based on the precautionary principle, and the principle that preventative action should be taken.

5. Waste includes a substance that has been discarded by its owner, even if the waste is capable of economic re-utilisation, or has a commercial value and is collected on a commercial basis for recycling, reclamation or re-use.

6. In deciding whether the use of a substance for burning is to be regarded as 'discarding', it is irrelevant that the substance may be recovered as fuel in an environmentally responsible manner and without substantial treatment.

However, His Lordship stated (at [55]), somewhat laconically, that a search for coherence in the EU as to the definition of waste was probably doomed to failure. See also *Tronex BV* (C-624/17).

The question as to whether excavated material ranked as waste was considered again in the Court of Appeal case of *R v W* [2010] Env LR 743. In that case, the first respondent (W) was the manager of a construction site upon which a new hotel was to be constructed. The second and third respondents (C) were the owners of a farm that adjoined the construction site. The farm was situated in a Special Area of Conservation, as designated under the Habitat Directive (Directive 92/43/EC). W agreed to deposit large quantities of materials, which had been excavated from the site, on C's land for the purpose of creating an area of hard-standing. All three respondents were charged with knowingly permitting the deposit of controlled waste, and also with keeping controlled waste, contrary to s. 33(1) of the EPA. However, the trial judge acquitted the defendants. On appeal, the Court held that the question of immediate re-use of any material could not be entirely determinative of its status, regardless of other considerations. In the opinion of the Court, the trial judge had erred in concentrating entirely on the intentions of the respondents to put the material to immediate re-use. Excavated soil that had to be discarded would be capable of being waste and, ordinarily, would be waste. Having become waste, it remained so, until something happened to alter its status. Furthermore, whether such a thing had happened was a question for the jury. The possibility of some re-use, at some indefinite future time, did not alter its status. However, actual re-use might do so, but only if consistent with the aims and objectives of both the Act and the Directive, which were the avoidance of harm to either persons or the environment. The trial judge had been in error in assessing the status of the materials entirely by reference to the respondents as holders. It was open to the jury to find that the material had been waste, from the moment of its excavation at the neighbouring farm, before C and W became holders. Furthermore, the additional question of whether the materials had ceased to be waste, either because of the intended, or actual, use by the respondents, as the new holders of the material, was also a question of fact for the jury.

By way of conclusion on the meaning of 'waste', in terms of the WFD, the courts have found the task of defining waste fiendishly difficult, if not impossible. The problem is particularly difficult when we a dealing with the transfer of material from one person to another. As we can see from the case law above, the concept of 'discard' seems a rather impotent tool in assisting in determining the status of material upon its transfer to a third party and in the possession of the third party. Indeed, the problem of defining waste can, arguably, be regarded as representing one, if not the most complex, issue in domestic environmental law.

PROHIBITION OF FLY-TIPPING ETC. OF WASTE

The unauthorised dumping of waste is a perennial problem. One of the most important provisions of the EPA, as far as the regulation of waste is concerned, is the prohibition of the fly-tipping (a term that is in common use, but, at the same time, is not a term of art or a technical term) of waste, that is to say, the disposal of waste in any manner other than that which is authorised by the EPA. Section 33(1) of the EPA provides that a person may not:

(a) deposit controlled waste, or knowingly cause or knowingly permit controlled waste to be deposited in, or on, land, unless a waste management licence authorising the deposit is in force, and the deposit is in accordance with the licence;

(b) treat, keep or dispose of controlled waste, or knowingly cause or knowingly permit controlled waste to be treated, kept or disposed of:

(i) in or an any land, or

(ii) by means of any mobile plant, except under, and in accordance with a waste management licence;

(c) keep or manage controlled waste in a manner likely to cause pollution of the environment or harm to human health.

However, the EPA makes provision for a defence in relation to a person who is charged with an offence under s. 33, namely:

(a) to prove that he or she took all reasonable precautions, and exercised all due diligence to avoid the commission of the offence; or

(b) that he or she acted under the instructions from his or her employer, and that the person neither knew, nor had reason to suppose that acts done by him or her constituted a contravention of subsection (1) above; or

(c) that the acts alleged to constitute the contravention were done in an emergency in order to avoid danger to human health, in a case where:

(i) he or she took all such steps as were reasonably practicable in the circumstances for minimising pollution of the environment and harm to human health, and

(ii) particulars of the acts were furnished to the waste regulation authority as soon as reasonably practicable after they were done.

The EPA makes provision for penalties for offences which are committed under the section: s. 33(8), and also for fixed penalties in relation to contraventions of s. 33(1)(a) and (c): s. 33A. The Environmental Regulation (Enforcement Measures) Regulations 2015 (SSI 2015 No. 383) give SEPA powers to enforce civil enforcement measures in relation to offences which are committed under s. 33(1) of the EPA.

The reader's attention should, however, be drawn to the Waste Management Licensing (Scotland) Regulations 2011 (SSI 2011 No. 228) which exempt certain activities from the requirement for the relevant person to possess a waste management licence: Regs 17–18.

In the context of fly-tipping, mention should be made of the Refuse Disposal (Amenity) Act 1978, s. 1, which places a duty on a local authority to provide places where refuse (which includes any matter whatsoever, whether inorganic or organic) other than commercial waste, may be disposed of, free of charge, by residents who are situated in the area of the local authority. However, a local authority is entitled to charge others for the use of the facility. As far as the deposit of commercial waste is concerned, a local authority may, on such terms as it sees fit, provide places where such waste may be dumped: s. 1(3). Furthermore, the local authority may provide plant and apparatus for the treatment and disposal of such waste. The local authority may sell, or otherwise dispose, of such waste.

THE DUTY OF CARE

Since the mid-nineteenth century, legislation has attempted to control waste by regulating the deposit of waste in terms of so-called 'command and control' enforcement. That is to say, statute or local authority byelaws would proscribe the deposit of waste in certain places on pain of a penalty. With the possible exception of potential delictual liability for subsequent harm caused by the relevant waste, a person who produced waste ceased to have any legal responsibility for the manner in which the waste was dealt with after it had left his or her possession. However, the EPA introduces an entirely new concept in the regulation of waste, by imposing an on-going obligation (in essence, a non-delegable duty) on those who have any control over waste to ensure that the waste is disposed of lawfully. The intention is to encourage, in effect, self-regulation. Those who produce waste are now under a stronger incentive than formerly to monitor the activities of those whom the former have commissioned to dispose of the waste. Section 34(1) of the EPA provides that:

(1) Subject to subsection (2) below, it shall be the duty of any person who imports, produces, keeps or manages controlled waste, or as a broker or dealer, has control of such waste, to take all such measures applicable to him in that capacity, as are reasonable in the circumstances:

  (a) to prevent any contravention by any other person of s. 33 above;

   (aa) to prevent any contravention by any other person of regulation 11 of the Pollution Prevention and Control (Scotland) Regulations 2012, or of a condition, or permit, granted under those Regulations;

   (ab) to prevent any contravention by any other person of subsection (2A)(2E)(2F)(2I) or (2K);

  (b) to prevent the escape of the waste from his control, or that of any other person;

   (ba) on the transfer of any waste oil, to ensure that it is collected separately from other types of waste so as to facilitate a specific treatment where technically feasible.

The subsection also requires that on the transfer of waste, the transfer is only to an authorised person, or to a person who is authorised for transport purposes. Furthermore, on the transfer of the waste, such a transfer must be accompanied by an appropriate written description of the waste.

As far as occupiers of domestic property are concerned, under s. 34(2) such occupiers are only under a duty to take reasonable steps to ensure that the transfer of waste is to an authorised person, or to a person for authorised transport purposes. Otherwise, occupiers of domestic property are not under any duty to comply with the provisions of s. 34(1). Importantly (subject to certain exceptions), a duty is placed on any person who produces, keeps or manages controlled waste, or as a broker or dealer, has control of such waste, to take all such measures as are reasonable in the circumstances, to apply the waste hierarchy set out in Article 4(1) of the WFD which makes provision for a hierarchy in terms of waste management. The preferred option is (a) prevention, (b) preparation for re-use, (c) recycling and (d) recovery, and (e) disposal: s. 34(2A)(2B). A duty is placed on any person who produces controlled waste (other than an occupier of domestic property in relation to household waste which is produced on that property) to take all reasonable steps to ensure the separate collection of dry recyclable waste: s. 34(2E). Subject to certain exceptions, a duty is placed on a person who controls or manages a food business that produces controlled waste to ensure the separate collection of food waste produced by that business: s. 34(2F)(2G). Section 35(6) makes provision for offences which are committed for breach of s. 34(1). See also the Environmental Regulation (Environmental Enforcement) Regulations 2015 (SSI 2015 No. 383), which make provision for civil enforcement measures by SEPA for an offence committed under s. 34(1).

WASTE MANAGEMENT LICENCES

Unless premises which produce waste are regulated, potential problems can arise. Waste, which is not effectively disposed of, can potentially pose risks to public health and also impact negatively on the environment. As far as Scotland is concerned, Part II of the EPA makes provision for the regulation of waste. Essentially, the EPA allows SEPA to regulate waste treatment facilities, by means of a licensing system. Under s. 35(1) of the EPA a waste management licence is defined as:

> a licence granted by a waste regulation authority, authorising the treatment, keeping, or disposal, of any specified description of controlled waste in, or on, specified land, or the treatment, or disposal, of any specified description of controlled waste, by means of specified plant.

A licence which relates to the treatment, keeping or disposal of waste in, or on land, is required to be granted to the person who is in occupation of the land, whereas, in the case of a licence relating to treatment or disposal of waste by means of a mobile plant, to the person who operates the plant: s. 35(2). SEPA, in effect, regulates waste treatment facilities by attaching conditions to a licence. SEPA has wide powers in this respect. Under s. 35(3) a licence is required to be granted on such terms, and subject to such conditions, as appear to SEPA to be appropriate: s. 35(3). The relevant conditions may relate to the activities which the licence authorises, the relevant precautions which are required to be taken, either in connection with, or in consequence of, those activities, and also to the location of the boundaries of the specified land. Importantly, conditions may be imposed in the licence to the effect that they are required to be complied with before the activities which the licence authorises have begun, or after such activities have ceased. Furthermore, s. 35(4) provides that relevant conditions may be imposed which require the holder of a licence to carry out works, or do other things, notwithstanding that the holder is not entitled to carry out the works, for example, a condition could make provision for access to the relevant site over land that is not owned by the licence-holder. In turn, any person whose consent would be required is placed under a duty either to grant, or to join in granting, the holder of the licence such rights as will allow the holder of the licence to comply with the requirements which are imposed on him or her by the licence. The EPA makes provision for compensation in relation to the granting of such rights.

Furthermore, conditions may relate to where waste, other than controlled waste, is to be treated, kept or disposed of, and to the treatment, keeping or disposal of that other waste: s. 35(5). The Scottish ministers are empowered to make regulations which govern the conditions which are, or are not, to be included in a licence: s. 35(6). Finally, a licence may not be surrendered except in accordance with the provisions of the EPA, s. 39: s. 35(9).

GRANT OF LICENCE

An application for a site licence must be made to SEPA: s. 36(1). An application for a mobile plant licence must to be made to the waste regulation authority in whose area the operator of the plant has his or her principal place of business. However, a licence may not be granted unless planning permission is in force in relation to that land: s. 36(2). Subject to this condition, SEPA may not reject an application for a licence if it is satisfied that the applicant is a fit and proper person, unless SEPA is satisfied that the rejection of the licence is necessary for the purpose of preventing:

(a) pollution of the environment;

(b) harm to human health; or

(c) serious detriment to the amenities of the locality.

However, (c) is inapplicable where planning permission is in force in relation to the use of the land which will be put under the licence: s. 36(3).

Whether a person is a person is a 'fit and proper person' is to be determined by reference to the carrying on by him or her of the activities which are to be authorised by the licence, and fulfilment of the requirements of the licence: s. 74(2). Currently, a person is required to be treated as not being a fit and proper person if it appears to SEPA that:

(a) he, or another relevant person, has been convicted of a relevant offence (the WML, Reg. 3 lists the relevant offences);

(b) the management of the activities which are to be authorised by the licence are not, or will not be, in the hands of a technically competent person; or

(c) the person who holds, or is to hold, the licence has not made, and either has no intention of making, or is in no position to make, financial provision adequate to discharge the obligations arising from the licence: s. 74(3).

However, SEPA may, if it considers it proper to do so in a particular case, treat a person as a fit and proper person, notwithstanding that either he, or another relevant person, has been convicted of a relevant offence: s. 74(4). Section 74(7) lists a variety of circumstances where another relevant person is to be treated in relation to the licence-holder, or proposed licence-holder, as having been convicted of the relevant offence.

An appeal lies to the Scottish ministers if the relevant application for a licence is rejected, or in relation to the conditions which SEPA attach to the relevant licence: s. 43(1).

VARIATION, REVOCATION, SUSPENSION, SURRENDER AND TRANSFER OF LICENCES

Variation of licence

The EPA makes provision for the variation of a licence that has been granted. While a licence that SEPA has granted is in force, SEPA may, on its own initiative, modify the conditions of the licence to any extent that, in the opinion of SEPA, is desirable and is unlikely to require unreasonable expense on the part of the holder: s. 37(1). SEPA may also modify a licence on the application of the relevant licence-holder.

Revocation and suspension of licences

The EPA may revoke a licence, either entirely or partially, if it appears that the licence-holder has ceased to be a fit and proper person by reason of his or her having been convicted of a relevant offence, or that the continuation of the activities which are authorised by the licence would cause pollution of the environment, or harm to human health, or would be seriously detrimental to the amenities of the locality that is affected, and that the pollution, harm or detriment cannot be avoided by modifying the conditions of the licence: s. 38(1)(3) and (4). Furthermore, SEPA has the power to suspend (in whole or in part) or revoke a licence (either entirely or partially) if it appears to SEPA that the holder of a licence has ceased to be a fit and proper person, by reason of the management of the activities which are authorised by the licence having ceased to be in the hands of a technically competent person: s. 38(2)(6).

The licence can also be suspended, either in whole or in part, if it appears that serious pollution of the environment or serious harm to human health either has resulted from, or is about to be caused by, the activities to which the licence relates, or the happening, or threatened happening, of an event affecting these activities, and that the continuation of all, or any, of those activities may cause serious pollution of the environment or harm to human health: s. 38(6).

An appeal lies to the Scottish ministers against both the revocation and the suspension of a licence: s. 43(1).

Surrender and transfer of licences

A licence may also be transferred by its holder to SEPA, but in the case of a site licence, only if SEPA accepts the surrender of the licence: s. 39(1). An appeal lies to the Scottish ministers against the decision by SEPA to reject an application for the surrender of a licence: s. 43(1).

A licence may be transferred to another person, whether or not the licence is either partly revoked or suspended in terms of the EPA: s. 40(1). Where the holder of a site licence wishes the licence to be transferred to another person – that is, the transferee – both the licence-holder and the proposed transferee are required to jointly make an application to SEPA: s. 40(2). An appeal lies to the Scottish ministers against the decision of SEPA to reject an application for the transfer of a licence: s. 43(1).

LANDFILL

Whilst the disposal of waste to landfill comprises both the oldest, as well as the most widely practised, method of disposing of waste, landfill sites can pose a variety of environmental problems, including the production of leachate (a liquid formed when waste is broken down by bacteria) which can cause contamination of groundwater. Furthermore, other environmental problems are also associated with landfill, including rodent infestation, the production of methane gas and carbon dioxide. However, on a more positive note, landfill gas can be used as a valuable source of renewable energy. However, the disposal of waste by means of landfill comprises the least acceptable form of the disposal of waste in terms of the WFD, Art. 4. More specifically, this policy is expressed in the Landfill Directive (Directive 1999/31/EC). That Directive is implemented in Scotland by the Landfill (Scotland) Regulations 2003 (SSI 2003 No. 235) (the 2003 Regulations). Subject to certain exceptions, a landfill is defined as a waste disposal site for the deposit of waste onto or into land: Reg. 3(2).

Classification of landfills

Before granting a permit, SEPA is required to classify the relevant landfill as a:

(a) landfill for hazardous waste (defined as any waste which is to be considered hazardous under Arts 3(2) and 7 of the WFD): Reg. 2(1);

(b) landfill for non-hazardous waste (defined as waste which is non-hazardous waste): Reg. 2(1); or

(c) landfill for inert waste (defined as waste which (i) does not undergo any significant physical, chemical or biological transformations; (ii) does not dissolve, burn or otherwise physically or chemically react, biodegrade or adversely affect other matter with which it comes into contact in a way likely to give rise to environmental pollution or harm to human health; and (iii) has insignificant total leachability and does not endanger the quality of any surface water or groundwater: Reg. 2(1).

Conditions to be included in landfill permit and prohibitions of certain wastes

SEPA can effectively regulate the day-to-day operation of a landfill site by including appropriate conditions in the relevant permit. A landfill permit is required to include conditions which specify the list of defined types, and also the total quantity of waste, which is authorised to be deposited in the landfill: Reg. 10(1). The permit is also required to include certain other conditions, including those which specify the requirements for the preparations for the landfill, the carrying out of landfilling operations, and also conditions which specify monitoring and control procedures, including contingency plans: Reg. 10(2). The Regulations also prohibit the acceptance of certain types of wastes at landfills by the operator of a landfill: Reg. 11(1).

Waste which may be accepted in the different classes of landfill

An important feature of the Landfill Directive is that only waste that has been subject to pre-treatment may be landfilled: Directive 99/31/EC, Art. 6. The intention of the Directive is to minimise the harmful effects of waste before it is sent to landfill. The 2003 Regulations require the operator of a landfill to ensure that the landfill is only used for landfilling waste that is subject to prior treatment, unless

(a) it is inert waste for which treatment is not technically feasible; or
(b) it is waste, other than inert waste and treatment would not reduce its quantity or the hazards which it poses to human health or the environment: Reg. 12(1).

In turn, the operator of a landfill for hazardous waste (hazardous waste is defined as waste which is described as such under Articles 3(2) and 7 of the WFD; Landfill (Scotland) Regulations 2003, Reg. 2(1)) is required to ensure that only waste which fulfils the waste-acceptance criteria contained in the 2003 Regulations (Reg. 12(2), Sch. 2) is accepted at the landfill: Reg. 12(2).

The operator of a landfill for non-hazardous waste ('non-hazardous waste' is defined as waste which is not hazardous waste: Reg. 2(1)) is required to ensure that the landfill is only used for landfilling:

(a) municipal waste ('municipal waste' is defined as waste from households as well as other waste, which, because of its nature or other composition, is similar to waste from households: Reg. 2(1));

(b) non-hazardous waste of any other origin which fulfils the waste-acceptance criteria contained in the 2003 Regulations: Reg. 12(2), Sch. 2;

(c) stable, non-reactive hazardous waste which fulfils the waste-acceptance criteria contained in the 2003 Regulations: Reg. 12(3).

Offences

The 2003 Regulations make it an offence for a landfill operator to contravene provisions of the Regulations which relate to the acceptance of waste on a landfill: Reg. 19(1). A person who commits an offence is liable to a statutory penalty: Reg. 19(2). When an offence is committed by a body corporate, and the offence is committed with the consent or connivance of, or is attributable to any neglect on the part of, a person who

(a) is a director, or secretary of the body corporate; or

(b) or who purports to act in any such capacity; or

(c) the offence is committed by a Scottish partnership and the offence is committed with the consent or connivance of, or is attributable to any neglect on the part of a person who is a partner or purports to act in that capacity, that person, as well as the body corporate, or Scottish partnership, is guilty of an offence, and is liable to be proceeded against and punished accordingly: Reg. 19(3).

It should also be noted that the disposal of waste to landfills to which the 2003 Regulations apply, also ranks as a Part A process in terms of the Pollution Prevention and Control (Scotland) Regulations 2012 (SSI 2012 No. 360, Sch. 1) and, therefore, the operator of the relevant landfill requires a permit under the latter regulations.

LANDFILL ALLOWANCE TRADING SCHEME

One of the main aims of the Landfill Directive 1999 (Directive 1999/31/EC, Art. 5) is to limit the amount of biodegradable waste that is disposed to landfill. Part 1 of the Waste and Emissions Trading Act 2003 gives legal effect to the general obligations which are imposed by the Directive. The Secretary of State is empowered to make regulations which specify the maximum amounts which may be sent to landfills from each country of the United Kingdom in each scheme year which is a target year ('scheme year' and 'target year' are defined s. 23): s. 1(1). The Secretary of State is required to consult the Scottish ministers before setting limits for Scotland: s. 1(4). The Scottish ministers are required to ensure that the total amount of waste which is authorised to be sent to landfills by the allowances which the Scottish ministers allocate does not exceed the amount which is allowed for Scotland: s. 4(2). The Landfill Allowances Scheme (Scotland) Regulations 2005 (SSI 2005 No. 157) give legal effect in Scotland to the provisions of the Act. The Regulations make detailed provision for both the monitoring and enforcement of the landfill allowances which are allocated to waste disposal authorities. SEPA is the relevant monitoring authority for Scotland: Reg. 10.

COLLECTION OF CONTROLLED WASTE

For centuries local authorities and other municipal bodies (for example, Police Commissions) have been responsible for the collection of waste in their areas. Indeed, the collection of waste must rank amongst one the oldest functions which these bodies exercised. Currently, the EPA places a duty (subject to certain exceptions) on each waste collection authority in Scotland (namely, the relevant local authority: s. 30(3)) to arrange for the collection of household waste in its area: s. 45(1). The authority has also a duty to arrange for the collection of commercial waste from premises, if requested by the occupier of premises in its area. Furthermore, the authority also has a duty to arrange for the collection of dry recyclable waste, or food waste, if so requested by the occupier of premises in its area. However, such a duty does not extend to the collection of either dry recyclable waste or food waste which is household waste, or food waste from premises which is situated in a rural area: s. 45(1A).

Separate collection of dry recyclable waste and food waste

Traditionally, waste, with some exceptions, was simply regarded as something to dispose of as efficiently as possible. However, prompted in no small part by EU policy on waste, it is now regarded as a product which, if possible, should be converted into a usable form. It is essential, therefore, that provision is made for waste to be collected in such a manner which facilitates its being recycled. From 1 January 2014, a local authority must arrange for there to be provided to the occupier of every domestic property in its area, such receptacles as will enable the separate collection of dry recyclable waste from the property: s. 45C(2). From 1 January 2016, an authority is required to arrange for there to be provided to the occupier of every property in its area (apart from a property in a rural area) a receptacle which enables the separate collection of food waste from the property; or where an authority is satisfied that the amount of food waste that will be collected is not significantly less than would be collected in such a receptacle, a receptacle that enables the occupier to present food waste and other biodegradable waste for collection: s. 45C(5). Finally, from 1 January 2014, an authority has been required to take such steps as the authority considers reasonable to both promote the separate collection (including the making of arrangements for the provision of a food receptacle) and to promote recycling in any other manner: s. 45C(6).

In the above context, it should be observed that in September 2017 SEPA reported that Scotland's household waste recycling rate rose to 45.2 per cent in 2016. There was also a 1.6 per cent decrease in household waste which was disposed to landfill.

Finally, the EPA gives a local authority the power to recycle waste: s. 56.

THE DISPOSAL OF WASTE

A local authority, in its capacity as a waste disposal authority (a local authority in Scotland is constituted a waste disposal authority by virtue of s. 30(2)), is under a duty to arrange for the disposal of any waste which it collects: EPA, s. 53(1). Furthermore, in order to meet such a duty, the authority may provide, either within or outside its area, waste transfer stations, and also places at which to dispose of, or recycle, the waste and plant, and equipment for processing, recycling, or otherwise disposing of the waste.

THE REMOVAL OF UNLAWFULLY DEPOSITED WASTE

Unfortunately, waste is often disposed of unlawfully by being dumped on land. Since fly-tipping takes place surreptitiously, the unlawful deposit of waste is difficult to effectively regulate. However, the EPA makes provision for waste which has been deposited illegally. If any controlled waste is deposited on land, in contravention of s. 33(1), either SEPA or the relevant local authority may, by notice, require the occupier of the relevant land to do either, or both, of the following, namely, to:

(a) remove the waste from the land within a specified period, which is not less than twenty-one days, commencing from the date of the service of the notice;

(b) take, within such a period, specified steps with a view to eliminating or reducing the consequences of the deposit of the waste: s. 59(1).

In turn, a person on whom any requirements are imposed under s. 59(1) may, within the twenty-one period which is mentioned above, appeal to the sheriff by way of summary application: s. 59(2). On appeal, the sheriff is required to quash the requirement, if he or she is satisfied that either the appellant neither deposited, nor knowingly permitted the deposit of the waste, or that there is a material defect in the notice: s. 59(3). In any other case, the sheriff may either modify the notice or dismiss the appeal. If a person appeals against the notice, it has no effect pending the determination of the appeal: s. 59(4). Where the sheriff modifies the notice or dismisses the appeal, the sheriff may extend the period which is mentioned in the notice. If a person on whom a notice has been served fails, without reasonable excuse, to comply with a requirement in the notice, he or she is liable to pay a fine on summary conviction: s. 59(5). If the person on whom a notice has been served fails to comply with a requirement that has been imposed by the notice, either SEPA or the relevant local authority may do what the person was required to do, and recover any expenses which have been reasonably incurred by their so doing: s. 59(6). If it appears to SEPA, or a local authority, that waste has been deposited on, or in, land in contravention of s. 33(1) of the EPA, and that:

(a) in order to remove or prevent pollution of land, waste or air, or harm to human health, it is necessary that the waste be forthwith removed, or other steps be taken to eliminate, or reduce, the consequences of the deposit, or both; or

(b) there is no occupier of the land; or

(c) the occupier neither made, nor knowingly permitted, the deposit of the waste, the authority may remove the waste from the land, or take other steps to eliminate or reduce the consequence of the deposit, or, as the case may require, to remove the waste and take those steps: s. 59(7).

Subject to certain exceptions, the authority is entitled to recover costs from the relevant person for exercising such powers: s. 59(8). Finally, any waste which has been removed by an authority becomes vested in the authority, and can be dealt with accordingly: s. 59(9).

The reader's attention must be drawn at this juncture to the provisions of the Environmental Regulation (Enforcement Measures) 2015 (SSI 2015 No. 383), which empower SEPA to impose civil enforcement measures for failure to comply with a notice which requires the removal of waste.

CIVIL LIABILITY

It is unusual for any statute, which imposes a specific duty on an individual, to provide that a breach of that duty should confer a private right on any individual who sustains harm by virtue of that statutory provision being breached. That is to say, normally, the relevant statute is silent on this issue, leaving it up to the relevant court to decide if it is the intention of Parliament to confer such a private right of action on the part of the pursuer. However, under s. 73(6) of the EPA provision is made in respect of harm which has been caused by the unlawful deposit of waste. That section provides that any person who deposited such waste, or knowingly permitted it to be deposited in such a manner as to commit an offence under s. 33(1) (above) or s. 63(2) (which deals with the deposit of waste which is not controlled waste), is liable for the relevant harm except:

(a) where the damage was due wholly to the person who suffered it;
(b) or the harm was suffered by a person who voluntarily accepted the risk of the damage being caused.

For example, if inflammable waste was unlawfully deposited on land, the waste then ignites, and then the fire spreads to and damages the land of an adjoining proprietor, the person who deposited the waste, or the person who permitted the waste to be deposited, would be liable under s. 73(6).

WASTE CARRIERS AND WASTE BROKERS

It is almost a statement of the obvious that waste can easily be disposed of illegally (or fly-tipped) by those who transport waste. It has already been observed that those who transport waste are subject to a duty of care in terms of the EPA (p. 84, above). However, it is also important that the transport of waste is further regulated. The Control of Pollution (Amendment) Act 1989 makes provision for the registration of waste carriers. In Scotland, SEPA is the relevant regulatory authority for the purposes of the Act. It is made an offence, subject to certain exceptions, for any person who is not a registered carrier of controlled waste to transport to or from any place in Great Britain, in the course of any business of his or otherwise, with a view to profit: s. 1(1). The Controlled Waste (Registration of Carriers and Seizure of Vehicles) Regulations 1991

(SI 1991 No. 1624 as amended) make further provision relating to the registration of waste carriers and the seizure of vehicles.

The commercial transport of waste is further controlled by the Waste Management Licensing (Scotland) Regulations 2011 (SSI 2011 No. 228), which make provision for the registration of brokers and dealers of waste. Regulation 2(1) defines a broker as any undertaking arranging for the recovery or disposal of waste on behalf of others, whether or not such arrangements involve the broker taking physical possession of the waste. A dealer is defined as any undertaking which acts in the role of principal to purchase and subsequently sell waste, whether or not this involves the dealer taking possession of the waste. It is made an offence for an establishment, or undertaking, to arrange (as broker or dealer) for the recovery or disposal of controlled waste on behalf of another person, or to purchase or sell controlled waste, unless it is a registered broker or dealer in controlled waste: Reg. 30(1).

SPECIAL WASTE

Certain forms of waste may pose a risk to both human health and also to the environment. The EPA allows the Scottish ministers to make provision by regulations for controlled waste which is of a kind that is considered dangerous, or difficult to treat, keep or dispose of (i.e., special waste): s. 62(1). The Special Waste Regulations 1996 (SI 1996 No. 972) make provision for both the transport and disposal of special waste. The Regulations, *inter alia*, make detailed provision for special waste consignment notes, special waste registers and special waste site records.

WASTE RECOVERY: PRODUCER RESPONSIBILITY

Packaging waste now makes up a significant proportion of the total waste in the United Kingdom. During the early 1990s there was growing concern in Europe about the amount of packaging waste, and also the resultant negative impact such waste was having on the environment. Council Directive 94/62/EC, Art. 6(1), sets both recovery and recycling targets on packaging materials and packaging waste, in relation to which targets member states must meet. The Producer Responsibility Obligations (Packaging Waste) Regulations 2007 (SI 2007 No. 871) which currently implement the Directive, apply to the United Kingdom as a whole, and impose obligations on producers in order that the UK can meet these targets. The relevant recovery and recycling targets are confined to specific recyclable materials, namely, glass, aluminium, steel, paper board and wood: Reg. 2(2). However, producer responsibility obligations fall only on the larger producers. In order to meet the obligations under the Regulations, a producer can opt to join a scheme which is registered with the appropriate agency, namely, SEPA as far as Scotland is concerned.

END-OF-LIFE VEHICLES

Vehicles, as well as their components, can contaminate the environment unless the vehicles are suitably disposed of when they cease to be used. However, vehicle parts, can, of course, also be recovered and recycled. The End of Life Vehicles Directive (Directive 2000/53/EC) (the ELV Directive) addresses this. The main aim of the Directive is to prevent waste from vehicles, and also to make provision for the reuse, recycling and other forms of recycling and recovery of end-of-life vehicles: Art. 1. The Directive covers vehicles and end-of-life vehicles (the latter being defined by Art. 2 as 'waste' within the meaning of the WFD), including their components and materials: Art. 3. Member states are placed under an obligation to ensure that those who are involved in the manufacture of vehicles limit the use of hazardous substances in vehicles in order to protect the environment, facilitate recycling, and also to avoid the need to dispose of hazardous waste: Art. 4(1). Member states are also required to ensure that collection systems are introduced for end-of-life vehicles, and that such vehicles are transferred to authorised treatment facilities: Art. 5(1). The ELV Directive is transposed into UK law by the End of Life Vehicles Regulations 2003 (SI 2003 No. 2635) and also by the End of Life Vehicles (Storage and Treatment) (Scotland) Regulations 2003, which are discussed briefly below.

The ELV regulations apply to all vehicles, including their components and materials: Reg. 3(1). Any person who puts on the market materials and components of vehicles, is required to ensure that the vehicles do not contain heavy metals such as lead, mercury or cadmium or hexavalent chromium, subject to certain exceptions: Reg. 6. A producer is required to use material and component coding standards in order to facilitate the identification of those materials and components which are suitable for re-use and recovery: Reg. 14. A producer is also required to provide dismantling information in relation to each new vehicle that is put on the market within six months from the date that such vehicles are first put on the market: Reg. 18(1).

The storage and treatment of end-of-life vehicles is governed by the End of Life Vehicles (Storage and Treatment) (Scotland) Regulations 2003 (SSI 2003 No. 593). SEPA is required to include in any site licence which it grants for the keeping or treatment of waste motor vehicles, a condition to the effect that the keeping or treatment which is authorised by the site licence is in conformity with the obligations, and also the minimum requirements contained in the Regulations: Reg. 5(1).

WASTE ELECTRICAL AND ELECTRONIC EQUIPMENT

Waste from electrical and electronic equipment has become an increasing environmental problem in Europe, because such waste often contains dangerous contaminants. The Waste Electrical and Electronic Equipment Directive 2002 (Directive 2002/96/EC), which was re-cast and replaced by EU Directive 2012/19/EU (the WEEE Directive), makes provision for such waste. The WEEE Directive is implemented in the United Kingdom by the Waste and Electronic Equipment Regulations 2013 (the WEEE Regulations) (SI 2013 No. 3113). The WEEE Regulations apply to a range of electrical and electronic equipment, including large and small household appliances, IT and telecommunications equipment, lighting equipment, electric and electronic tools, toys, leisure and sports equipment, and medical devices. A producer of electrical and electronic equipment (EEE) is placed under an obligation to bear a proportion of the cost of the collection, treatment, recovery and environmentally sound disposal of waste electronic and electrical equipment (WEEE) from private households, which is deposited at a designated collection facility, or is returned, but is not deposited, at such a facility during the relevant compliance period (a period which is defined in Reg. 2(1)): Reg. 11(1). As far as waste from users (other than domestic users) is concerned, a producer is placed under an obligation to finance the costs of collection, treatment and recovery, and environmentally sound disposal of WEEE which is placed on the market in the United Kingdom on or after 13 August 2005 by the relevant producer: Reg. 12(1). With the exception of producers who are registered as small producers, a producer who is registered in the United Kingdom is required to join a compliance scheme in respect of any compliance period during which the producer puts EEE on the market in the UK: Reg. 14(1). If a producer is a member of a compliance scheme, the producer is exempt from complying with its obligations under the WEEE Regulations in respect of the relevant compliance period during which the producer's membership of that scheme subsists: Reg. 14(7)(8).

As far as distributors of EEE are concerned, a distributor who supplies new EEE to a person is required to ensure that WEEE from private households can be returned to the distributor, free of charge, on a one-to-one basis, by that person, provided that any such WEEE is of an equivalent type to, and has fulfilled the same function as the supplied equipment: Reg. 42(1). Distributors of retail premises EEE retailers with a sales area relating to EEE of at least 400 metres are placed under an obligation to provide for the collection of very small WEEE free of charge to the end user of the EEE, with no obligation to buy EEE of a similar type: Reg. 42(2). However, a distributor who is a member of a distributor take-back scheme is exempt from this requirement for the period during which its membership of the scheme subsists: Reg. 46.

ABANDONED MOTOR VEHICLES ETC.

The Refuse Disposal (Amenity) Act 1978 makes special provision for abandoned motor vehicles. Under s. 2(1) it is made an offence, which is subject to a penalty, for any person, without lawful authority:

(a) to abandon on any land in the open air, or on any other land forming part of a road, a motor vehicle, or anything which formed part of a motor vehicle, and was removed from it in the course of dismantling the vehicle on the land; or

(b) to abandon on any such land anything other than a motor vehicle, being a thing which he has brought on to the land for the purposes of abandoning it there.

A person is deemed to have abandoned (or brought to the land for the purposes of abandoning) a motor vehicle etc. if he or she leaves anything on land in such circumstances, or for such period, that he or she may reasonably be assumed to have abandoned it, or brought it there for purposes of abandoning it, unless the contrary is shown: s. 2(2).

A local authority is placed under a duty, subject to certain exceptions, to remove a vehicle where it appears that the motor vehicle has been abandoned without lawful authority on any land in the open air, or on any land which forms part of a road: s. 3(2). The Act also makes provision for the disposal of removed vehicles and the recovery of associated expenses: ss. 4, 5. Finally, the Act makes gives a local authority the power to remove and dispose of any other thing (i.e., refuse) other than a motor vehicle, which has been abandoned without lawful authority on any land in the open air or an any other land which forms part of a road: s. 6.

Essential Facts

- UK waste law has, since the 1970s, been heavily influenced by EU waste policy. The key principles in EU waste policy are proximity and self-sufficiency, the precautionary principle, and the polluter pays principle.
- Waste should be prevented, or re-used or recycled, or, finally, recovered in that order.
- The Environmental Protection Act 1990 (EPA) provides, *inter alia*, for the unlawful deposit of waste, and places individuals under a duty of care in relation to such waste.
- The meaning of 'waste' in terms of the EPA is derived from Directive 2008/98/EC (the Waste Framework Directive, WFD).
- The EPA places individuals under a duty of care in relation to the transport and disposal of waste.
- The EPA allows SEPA to regulate waste treatment facilities by means of a licensing system.
- The landfilling of waste represents the least acceptable form of waste disposal in terms of EU waste policy. SEPA regulates landfills by means of a licensing system.
- The EPA makes provision for the collection and disposal of waste and also the removal of waste which has been unlawfully deposited.

Essential Cases

- **Scottish Power Generation Ltd v Scottish Environment Protection Agency (2005):** waste-derived fuel which was used as fuel to produce electricity in a power station was 'waste' in terms of the WFD.
- **R (on the application of the OSS Group Ltd) v Environment Agency (2008):** concept of waste is not to be interpreted restrictively. Waste includes a substance that has been discarded by its owner even if the waste is capable of economic re-utilisation or has a commercial value and is collected on a commercial basis for recycling, reclamation or re-use. In deciding whether use of a substance for burning is to be regarded as 'discarding', it is irrelevant that it may be recovered as fuel in an environmentally responsible manner and without substantial treatment.

7 CONTAMINATED LAND

INTRODUCTION

In this chapter we address the issue of contaminated land in Scotland. Land may have become contaminated in a number of ways. For example, land may have become contaminated as a result of having been used in the past as a dumping ground for waste derived from chemical works or incinerators. However, land may also have become contaminated during the course of an industrial activity, for example, by the spillages and leaks from storage tanks and drums. The uses of land most commonly associated with contaminated land, include waste disposal sites. Most contamination of land in Scotland has occurred since the Industrial Revolution. Indeed, contaminated land is found mainly around the urban areas which were developed during the Industrial Revolution. However, contaminated land can be found anywhere. Unfortunately, the extent of the problem is unknown. Indeed, there has been no systematic survey to identify either the location of contaminated land or the seriousness of the problem. Such a lack of available information on contaminated sites in Scotland is similar to that in other European countries. Indeed, in a report that was published in 2014 by the European Environment Agency, it was estimated that there are 340,000 pieces of contaminated land in Europe, most of which remain to be identified.

CONTAMINATED LAND AND THE COMMON LAW

Land which has become contaminated, for example, by virtue of harmful chemicals (or other substances) escaping from tanks on the defender's premises, and then leaching through the defender's land into that of the of pursuer, thereby causing damage to the latter's property or unreasonably annoying him (by, for example, smell) can constitute a common law nuisance: see, e.g., *McKenna* v *O'Hare* [2017] SAC (Civ) 16.

Furthermore, those who carry out remedial operations on contaminated land owe a duty of care, in terms of the law of negligence, to those who may be foreseeably harmed by contaminating substances which are present on the land. For example, in *Corby Group Litigation* v *Corby DC* ([2010] Env LR D2; [2009] EWHC 1944), a local authority was held to have owed a duty to take reasonable care to prevent the dispersal of mud and dust (which contained a range of contaminants) during reclamation works which had been carried out on behalf of the defendants.

As a consequence of the breach of the defendant's duty of care, pregnant women in the local area had become exposed to the harmful substances, the upshot of which was that some children were born with birth defects: see also, *Esso Petroleum Co. Ltd* v *Scottish Ministers* [2016] CSOH 15.

CONTAMINATED LAND: THE STATUTORY REGIME

The current regime, which makes provision for contaminated land, is contained in Part II of the EPA 1990. That regime closely mirrors the statutory nuisance regime (see Ch. 3, above), which, it has already been observed, has been embedded in UK environmental law since the mid-nineteenth century. By way of a brief overview, local authorities are primarily responsible for dealing with contaminated land in Scotland. The main responsibility of the authority is to identify contaminated land, to decide what remediation is required, and to act as an enforcing authority for all contaminated land which is not designated as a special site; in which case, SEPA is responsible for enforcing the provisions of the EPA.

WHAT IS CONTAMINATED LAND?

The expression 'contaminated land' is a term of art, and is given a precise meaning under the EPA. Contaminated land is defined as being any land, which appears to the local authority in whose area it is situated, to be in such a condition, by reason of substances in or under the land that:

(a) significant harm is being caused, or there is a significant possibility of such harm being caused; or

(b) significant pollution of the water environment is being caused, or there is a significant possibility of such pollution being caused: s. 78A(2).

In determining whether any land appears to be such land, a local authority is required to act in accordance with guidance issued by the Scottish ministers.

The expression 'harm' is defined as harm to the health of living organisms, or other interference with the ecological systems of which they form part and, in the case of man, includes harm to his property: s. 78A(4). 'Harm' in relation to the water environment has the has the same meaning as in s. 20(6) of the Water Environment and Water Services (Scotland) Act 2003: s. 78A(4A). Furthermore, the question as to what harm or pollution of the water environment is to be regarded as significant, and whether the possibility of significant harm or of significant pollution of the water environment which is being caused is significant, is to be determined in accordance with the Scottish government's statutory guidance: s. 78A(5). The Statutory Guidance on Contaminated Land (Statutory Guidance) was published in 2006. (See Chapter A, 'Statutory Guidance on the Definition of Contaminated Land', *The Environmental Protection Act 1990: Part IIA. Contaminated Land. Statutory Guidance. Edition 2.* May 2006. SE /2006/44.)

CONTAMINATED LAND AND STATUTORY NUISANCE

In order to avoid duplication with the statutory nuisance regime (see Ch. 3, above), the EPA provides that no matter constitutes a statutory nuisance, to the extent that it consists of, or is caused by, any land being in a contaminated state: s. 79(1A). Land is deemed to be in a contaminated state if it is in such a condition, by reason of substances in, or under that land, that: (a) significant harm is being caused; or (b) significant pollution of the water environment is being caused or there is a significant possibility of such pollution being caused: s. 79(1B).

IDENTIFICATION OF CONTAMINATED LAND

The primary responsibility for regulating contaminated land falls to local authorities in Scotland. A local authority is placed under a duty to inspect its area, from time to time, in order to identify contaminated land, and also to enable the authority to decide whether any such land is to be designated as a special site: s. 78B(1). In performing this duty, a local authority is required to act in accordance with any guidance which is issued by the Scottish ministers: s. 78B(2). The Statutory Guidance (Chapter B, Part 3) requires a local authority to take a strategic approach in carrying out its duties under s. 78B(1).

If a local authority identifies any contaminated land in its area, the local authority is required to give notice of that fact to:

(a) SEPA;
(b) the owner of the land;
(c) any person who appears to the authority to be in occupation of the whole or part of the land; and
(d) each person who appears to the authority to be an appropriate person: s. 78B(3).

The expression, 'appropriate person' is defined as any person, determined in accordance with s. 78F of the EPA, to bear responsibility for anything which is to be done by way of remediation in any particular case: s. 78A(9).

If at any time after a local authority has given any person a notice, in terms of s. 78B (3)(d), that it appears to the enforcing authority that another person is the appropriate person, the enforcing authority is required to give notice to that other person:

(a) of the fact that the local authority has identified the land as contaminated land; and

(b) that person appears to the enforcing authority to be an appropriate person: s. 78B(4).

The expression 'enforcing authority' means:

(a) in relation to a special site, SEPA; and

(b) in relation to contaminated land (other than a special site) the local authority in whose area the land is situated: s. 78A(9).

SPECIAL SITES

The EPA makes special provision for the identification and designation of special sites. The expression 'special site' is defined as any contaminated land which has been designated as such under s. 78C(7) or s. 78D(6), and whose designation has not been terminated by SEPA under s. 78Q(4) of the EPA: s. 78A(3). If, at any time, it appears to a local authority that any contaminated land in its area might be land which is required to be designated as a special site, and, if the authority decides that the land is required to be so designated, the authority is required to give notice to the relevant persons: s. 78C(1). The 'relevant persons' are:

(a) SEPA;

(b) the owner of the land;

(c) any person who appears to the local authority to be concerned in the occupation of the whole, or part, of the land; and

(d) each person who appears to that authority to be an appropriate person: s. 78C(2).

Before making a decision to designate land as a special site, the local authority is required to request the advice of SEPA, and, in making its decision, the local authority is required to have regard to advice given by SEPA in response to that request: s. 78C(3). If, at any time, SEPA considers that any contaminated land is land which is required to be designated as a special site, SEPA may give notice of that fact to the local authority in whose area the land is situated: s. 78C(4). Where such notice is given to a local authority, the authority is required to decide whether the land in question is required to be designated as a special site, or does not require to be so designated: s. 78C(5). Notice of the decision is required to be given to the relevant persons.

Land is required to be designated as a special site if, and only if, the Scottish ministers so prescribe by Regulations: s. 78C(8). The Contaminated Land (Scotland) Regulations 2000 (SSI 2000 No. 178) (as amended) (the Regulations), Regs 2–3, require certain land to be designated as a special site. The Scottish ministers are required to determine any disputes between SEPA and a local authority as to whether any site should be designated a special site: s. 78D(1). The Scottish ministers have complete powers of review and can either confirm or reverse the decision in relation to the whole, or part, of the land to which it relates: s. 78D(4). The Scottish ministers are required to give notice of the decision to the relevant persons, and also to the local authority: s. 78D(4).

DUTY OF ENFORCING AUTHORITY TO REQUIRE REMEDIATION OF CONTAMINATED LAND

The EPA places both SEPA, in relation to special sites, and a local authority, in relation to other contaminated land, under a duty to serve a remediation notice on the appropriate person (defined in s. 78F, below): s. 78E(1). The notice is required to specify the measures which the appropriate person is required to carry out by way of remediation, and also the periods within which he or she is required to do such things. Different remediation notices, which require the carrying out of different things, may be served on different persons in consequence of the presence of different substances in, on or under any land, or the water environment: s. 78E(2). Where two or more persons are appropriate persons in relation to any particular thing which is to be done by way of remediation, the notice is required to state the proportion (which is determined under s. 78F(7)) of the cost of performing the activity that each of them is liable to bear: s. 78E(3). However, the relevant enforcing authority may only require to be done that which is reasonable, having regard to the cost which is likely to be involved, and also the seriousness of the harm or of the pollution of the water environment in question: s. 78E(4). In determining,

  (i) how the relevant land is to be remediated (either by the appropriate person, the enforcing authority or any other person) in any particular case,

(ii) the standard to which any land or the water environment is to be remediated, or

(iii) what is, or what is not, to be regarded as reasonable for the purposes of s. 78E(4), the enforcing authority is required to have regard to the Scottish ministers' guidance: s. 78E(5). (See Statutory Guidance, Chapter C, Part 4.)

The Regulations specify the contents of a remediation notice.

WHO IS THE APPROPRIATE PERSON?

For the purposes of determining the persons who should bear responsibility for remediating contaminated land, the EPA adopts a procedure that is analogous to that which is employed by the EPA to remedy statutory nuisances (see Ch. 3, above).

The EPA defines the appropriate person for the purposes of remediating contaminated land as:

> Any person, or any persons, who caused, or knowingly permitted the substances, or any of the substances, by reason of which the contaminated land in question is such land, to be in, on, or under that land: s. 78F(2).

However, a person is only an appropriate person, for the purposes of s. 78F(2), and is, therefore, liable to remediate the relevant land in relation to the substances which he caused, or knowingly permitted to be present in, on or under the contaminated land in question: s. 78F(3). Several cases illustrate this point.

In *R (National Grid Gas plc) v Environment Agency* [2007] 1 WLR 1780, coal tar residues from the production of coal gas were deposited underground at a gas works operated by a private gas company. The company was nationalised in 1948. All property of the company, together with relevant rights and liabilities, passed to a state-owned gas utility. Gas production was subsequently stopped at the works. In 1965, the site was sold for housing. In 1986, both the assets and the liabilities of the company passed to a public limited company, British Gas, part of whose undertaking later devolved upon National Grid Gas (NGG). In 2005, the site was designated as contaminated land by the Environment Agency, which notified NGG that it was an 'appropriate person' under s. 78F of the EPA in terms of the site. However, the House of Lords held that the liabilities, which were imposed on British Gas in 1986, were those which existed immediately before the transfer which took place on that date. Furthermore, such liabilities could not include liabilities which came into existence some nine years later, under the Environment Act 1995 (which amended the EPA). In short, it could not be plausibly argued that NGG had either caused, or knowingly permitted, the substances to be present on the land.

The Court of Appeal was required to decide the appropriate person who was responsible for the remediation of contaminated land, under s. 78F of the EPA, in *Powys County Council v Price* [2017] EWCA Civ 1133. In that case, the predecessor of Powys County Council (PCC) had operated a landfill site on a farm, which was owned by the respondents, the Prices (P). In 1996, local government reorganisation took place in Wales, under which PCC was established and its predecessor was abolished. In 2001, PCC entered into a tenancy agreement with P for the purposes of installing a treatment and filtration plant on the site. PCC carried out monitoring and treatment work on the assumption that it was bound by the remediation regime, under Part II of the EPA, which came into force in Wales in 2001. However, in 2015, PCC stopped all activity on the site and also terminated the agreement on the basis that PCC were not liable for any contamination on the site. P then sought a declaration to the effect that the transfer of liabilities from the predecessor local authority to PCC had included a contingent liability for contaminated land, under Part IIA of the EPA. The trial judge held that PCC was an 'appropriate person' under s. 78F(2) of the EPA, with the resultant responsibilities for remediation works, on the grounds that PCC had taken over the liabilities of its predecessor by virtue of Welsh local government legislation. This legislation made provision, *inter alia*, for the transfer of liabilities which existed on the date when the local authority was abolished. On appeal, the Court of Appeal held that PCC was not liable for the acts of its predecessor council(s). On the authority of *R (National Grid plc) (formerly) Transco v Environment Agency* [2007] 1 WLR 1780, there was nothing in the statutory scheme which was capable of transferring future liabilities, in terms of Part II of the EPA, which, as stated above, did not come into force until 2001. In short, the court held that, whereas Part IIA created liability in respect of past conduct, it did not establish that such liability existed before Part IIA came into force. That is to say, Part IIA did not operate retroactively in such a way as to deem a predecessor body to have been under liability, which only arose under legislation that came into force after the predecessor body ceased to exist. On the authority of *Transco*, very clear words would be needed if the Act were to be construed as intending to impose liabilities on a successor body that was non-existent at the time of succession, and only created later.

Again, in *R (Crest Nicholson Residential Ltd)* v *Secretary of State for the Environment, Food and Rural Affairs* [2011] Env LR 1, a site had been contaminated by chemicals which had been deposited on the site by a former owner, R. However, a subsequent owner, C, carried out demolition works on the site. These works exposed the site to rain, thereby accelerating the flushing-out of the contaminants into the soil. Remediation notices were served on both R and C. However, C sought judicial review of the notice. At first instance, it was held that C had caused the land to be contaminated.

However, if no person has, after reasonable enquiry, by virtue of s. 78F(2) been found to bear responsibility for the remediation of the relevant land, the owner or occupier of the land is deemed to be the appropriate person, and, as such, is responsible for the remediation of the land: s. 78F(4)(5). Where two or more persons would otherwise be appropriate persons who are required to remediate land, the enforcing authority is required to determine whether any, and, if so, which of them is to be treated as an appropriate person: s. 78F(6). (See Statutory Guidance Annex 3 Chapter D.) The relevant enforcing authority can also apportion costs of remediation between parties, in accordance with such guidance.

The EPA also provides that where a person has caused, or knowingly permitted there to be in, on or under any land, then that person is deemed to have caused, or knowingly permitted there to be in, on or under that land, any substance which is there as a result of a chemical reaction or biological process which affects that substance: s. 78F(9). In *Circular Facilities (London) Ltd* v *Sevenoaks DC* [2005] Env LR 35, it was held that the relevant person need only have knowledge of the substance in question. That is to say, that he or she need not have been aware of the possibility that a chemical reaction, or process, could lead to the land in question being contaminated.

Furthermore, the appropriate person may be required to carry out remediation simply because of the mere presence of a substance, notwithstanding the fact that the remediation in question would not be required to be carried out in consequence only of the presence of that substance, in any quantity; or, in consequence only of the quantity of that substance, which any particular person caused, or knowingly permitted to be present: s. 78F(10). For example, this provision would allow an enforcing authority to require remedial action where a watercourse could erode adjoining land, thereby exposing contaminants to the endangerment of the health of the public; see, e.g., *Clydebank District Council* v *Monaville Estates Ltd* 1982 SLT (Sh Ct) 2.

GRANT OF, AND COMPENSATION FOR, RIGHTS OF ENTRY ETC.

A remediation notice may require an appropriate person to do things by way of remediation, notwithstanding that he or she is not entitled to do those things: s. 78G(1). For example, the notice could require an appropriate person to enter the land of a neighbouring proprietor in order to carry out works which the enforcing authority requires to be done. Any person whose consent is required before the necessary works are carried out is required to grant, or join, in granting such rights, in relation to the relevant land or water environment as will enable the appropriate person to comply with any requirements which have been imposed by the remediation notice: s. 78G(2). However, before notice is served, the enforcing authority is required to attempt to consult every person who appears to the authority:

(a) to be the owner, or occupier, of the relevant land, or water environment, and

(b) to be a person who might be required by s. 78G(2) to grant, or join in granting, any rights, concerning the rights which that person may be so required to grant: s. 79G(3).

For the purposes of s. 78G 'relevant land' means:

(a) the contaminated land in question;
(b) the water environment affected by that land; or
(c) any land adjacent to that land or water environment: s. 78G(7).

However, there is no need to consult such persons if it appears to the enforcing authority that the contaminated land is in such a condition, by reason of substances in, on or under the land, that there is an imminent danger of serious harm, or serious pollution of the water environment being caused: s. 78G(4).

RESTRICTIONS AND PROHIBITIONS ON SERVING REMEDIATION NOTICES

The EPA makes certain restrictions in relation to the enforcing authority serving remediation notices. For example, the enforcing authority is required to make reasonable endeavour to consult:

(a) the person upon whom the notice is to be served;
(b) the owner of any land to which the notice relates;
(c) any person who appears to that authority to be in the occupation of the whole, or any part of the land; and

(d) any person of such other description, as may be prescribed, concerning what is to be done, by way of remediation: s78H(1).

The EPA also prohibits the service of a remediation notice during certain periods: s. 78H(3). However, the above restrictions do not apply in relation to the service of a remediation notice in any case where it appears to the enforcing authority that the land in question is in such a condition, by reason of substances in, on or under the land, that there is imminent danger of serious harm, or serious pollution of the water environment being caused: s. 78H(4).

Furthermore, an enforcing authority may not serve a remediation notice as long as one, or more, of the following conditions apply in the particular case, that is to say:

(a) the authority is satisfied that, in consequence of the provisions of s. 78E(4)(5) (which relate to the cost of remediation, and the seriousness of the harm, or of the pollution of the water environment) that there is nothing by way of remediation which could be specified in a remediation notice, which could be served on that person;

(b) the authority is satisfied that appropriate things are being, or will be, done by way of remediation without the service of a remediation notice on that person;

(c) it appears to the authority that the person on whom the notice would be served is the authority itself; or

(d) the authority is satisfied that the powers which are conferred on it by s. 79N (see below) to do what is appropriate by way of remediation are exercisable: s. 78H(5).

RESTRICTIONS ON LIABILITY FOR THE POLLUTION OF CONTROLLED WATERS

Section 79J of the EPA makes restrictions on liability in relation to land that is contaminated by reason of substances in, on or under the land, and that significant pollution of the water environment is being caused, or that there is significant possibility of such harm being caused: s. 79J(1)(2). No remediation notice may be served on the appropriate person, in such circumstances, insofar as that notice requires him or her to remediate either the land, or the water environment. Where s. 79J applies, a remediation notice may not be served in circumstances where a person permits, has permitted, or might permit water from an abandoned mine, or part of a mine:

(a) entering the water environment; or

(b) reaching a place from which it is, or as the case may be, was likely, in the opinion of the enforcing authority, to enter the water environment: s. 79J(3).

However, such a restriction does not apply to either the owner, or former operator, of any mine or part of a mine if the mine, or part of the mine, became abandoned after 31 December 1999: s. 79J(4). Where s. 79J precludes the service of a remediation notice on the appropriate person, the enforcing authority itself may carry out remedial work under the EPA: s. 78J(7). However, in such circumstances, the authority is not entitled to recover costs from any person in carrying out the work.

LIABILITY FOR CONTAMINATING SUBSTANCES WHICH ESCAPE TO OTHER LAND

The EPA makes provision for land that becomes contaminated by substances (as defined in s. 78A(7)) which are present on land and escape to other land.

A person who has either caused, or who has knowingly permitted, any substance to be in, on or under any land, is also to be taken for the purposes of Part IIA of the EPA to have caused, or, as the case may be, knowingly permitted, these substances to be in, on or under any land to which they appear to have escaped: s. 78K(1). Provision is made where it appears to the enforcing authority that any substances have been in, on or under any land (that is, land A) as a result of their escape (whether directly or indirectly) from other land which a person has caused, or knowingly permitted them to be: s. 78K(2). In such circumstances, no remediation notice may require a person who is the owner or occupier of land A (and has not caused, or knowingly permitted the substances in question to be in, on or under land A) to do anything by way of remediation to any land or the water environment (other than land, or the water environment, of which he or she is the owner or occupier) in consequence of land A appearing to be in such condition by reason of the presence of those substances in on or under it, that significant harm, or significant pollution to the water environment, is being caused, or there is significant possibility of such harm or pollution, being caused: s. 78K(3).

In the case of land (land B) on which the presence of substances has been caused as a result of their escape from land A to land B, no remediation notice may require the owner or occupier of land A (who has not caused or knowingly permitted the substances in question to be in, on or under that land) to do anything by way of remediation in consequence of further land (in, or under, which those substances, or any of them, either appear to be, or to have been present as a result of their escape from land A), land B, appearing to be in such condition by reason of the presence of those substances in, on or under it that significant harm, or significant pollution of the water environment, is being caused, or there is a significant possibility of such harm or pollution being caused, unless he or she is also the owner or occupier of land B: s. 78K(4).

In any case, where:

(a) one person (person A) has either caused, or knowingly permitted, any substances to be in, on or under any land;

(b) another person (person B) who has not caused, or knowingly permitted, those substances to be in, on or under that land becomes the owner or occupier of that land; and

(c) the substances, or any of the substances, mentioned in paragraph (a) appear to have escaped to other land, no remediation notice may require person B to do anything by way of remediation to that other land, in consequence of the apparent acts or omissions of person A, except to the extent that person B caused, or knowingly permitted the escape: s. 78K(5).

In circumstances where substances have escaped from one parcel of land to another, the enforcing authority may itself carry out the necessary remedial works, notwithstanding the fact that the authority is precluded, by the provisions of s. 78K, from requiring the relevant person to carry out such works: s. 78K(5). However, in such circumstances, the authority is precluded from recovering the relevant costs from any person.

APPEALS AGAINST REMEDIATION NOTICES

The EPA makes provision for appeals against a remediation notice which has been served by the relevant enforcement authority. A person on whom a remediation is served may, within a period of twenty-one days, which begins on the day on which the notice is served, appeal to the sheriff, by way of summary application, if the notice was served by a local authority or appeal may be made to the Scottish ministers, if the notice was served by SEPA: s. 78L(1). Both the sheriff and the Scottish ministers have complete powers of review, and are required to quash the notice on being satisfied that there is a material defect in the notice: s. 78L(2). Subject to such proviso, either the sheriff or Scottish ministers may confirm the notice (either with or without modification) or quash it. If the sheriff or the Scottish ministers confirm a remediation notice, either with or without modification, either can extend the period for doing what the notice requires to be done: s. 78L(3). The Contaminated Land (Scotland) 2000 (SSI 2000 No. 178) (Regs 7 and 8) which are made under s. 78L(4)(5), make provision for the grounds of appeal against a remediation notice, and also the procedure that governs the appeal.

Offences

It is made an offence, subject to a penalty, for any person on whom an enforcing authority serves a remediation notice to fail, without reasonable excuse, to comply with the requirements of the notice: s. 78M(1).

Powers of enforcement authority to carry out remediation

The enforcing authority has wide powers (subject to certain exceptions) to carry out works of remediation, in terms of the EPA: s. 79N(1). The enforcing authority is also entitled to recover reasonable costs in such circumstances: s. 79P(1).

Land no longer considered to be contaminated

The EPA makes provision for land that ceases to be contaminated land. In circumstances where a local authority has given notice that land (which has not been designated as a special site) in its area is contaminated, and the local authority is satisfied that the land is no longer contaminated land, the local authority may give notice (that is, a 'non-contamination notice') that the land is no longer contaminated: s. 78QA(1)(2). Such notice may be given (*inter alia*) to SEPA and the owner of the relevant land. However, these provisions do not prevent the land being designated as contaminated land on a subsequent occasion: s. 78QA(4).

Registers

Every enforcing authority is under a duty to maintain a register containing prescribed particulars of, or relating to, *inter alia*, remediation notices which have been served by that authority; appeals against such notices, and notices which designate the land as a special site: s. 78R(1). The EPA also makes provision for the exclusion of certain information from registers: ss. 78S and 78T. Finally, provision is also made to remove from the register information about land that has been designated as a special site: s. 78TA. If information has been so removed, any remediation notice that relates to the land ceases to have effect, and no proceedings may be begun against a person for an offence under s. 78M(1).

REPORTS BY SEPA ON CONTAMINATED LAND

SEPA is required periodically, and also if so requested by the Scottish ministers, to prepare and publish a report on the state of contaminated land in Scotland: s. 78U(1). SEPA may request a local authority to furnish SEPA with such information as it requires in order to enable it to perform this function: s. 78U(2).

Site-specific guidance by SEPA

SEPA is empowered to issue guidance to any local authority in relation to either the exercise or the performance of SEPA's powers or duties under Part IIA of the EPA in relation to any particular contaminated land: s. 78V(1). The relevant local authority is required to have regard to such guidance when it either exercises or performs those powers or duties in relation to that land. Furthermore, a local authority is required, at the written request of SEPA, to furnish it with such information as SEPA may require for the purpose of giving such guidance: s. 78V(3).

Power of Scottish ministers to issue guidance

The Scottish ministers may issue guidance to SEPA with respect to the exercise or performance of SEPA's powers and duties under Part IIA: s. 78W(1). In turn, SEPA is required to have regard to such guidance in exercising its powers or duties.

CONCLUSIONS

The regime that governs contaminated land in Scotland, and the UK as a whole, is relatively new. However, the provisions of the EPA which cover contaminated land are complex. Such complexity is compounded, in practical terms, by the fact that there are two quite separate regulatory bodies (namely, local authorities and SEPA) which have responsibility for contaminated land in Scotland. There is also a paucity of case law on the subject. Again, unlike waste and air pollution, there is no national strategy which deals with contaminated land. Furthermore, to date, there has been no comprehensive survey conducted in Scotland to ascertain both the nature and the extent of contaminated land. Such a state of uncertainty has ramifications in terms of public accountability, in that the public is unable to assess how effectively the relevant enforcing authority is adequately performing its duties in relation to contaminated land. Indeed, contaminated land, in this respect, resembles noise pollution where the nature and the extent of the problem remains uncertain.

Essential Facts

- Land may become contaminated in a variety of ways.
- Part IIA of the EPA which governs contaminated land, closely mirrors the statutory nuisance regime of the EPA.
- In practical terms, the provisions of the Statutory Guidance are perhaps of greater importance than the provisions of the EPA.
- The main responsibility for regulating contaminated land falls to local authorities in Scotland.
- SEPA is responsible for regulating special sites.
- Local authorities and SEPA are empowered to serve remediation notices on appropriate persons to remediate contaminated land.

Essential Cases

R (National Grid Gas plc) v Environment Agency [2007] 1 WLR 1780: coal tar residues from the production of coal gas were deposited underground at a gas works operated by a private gas company. The company was nationalised in 1948. All property, rights and liabilities of the company passed to a state-owned gas utility. Gas production was subsequently stopped at the works. In 1965, the site was sold for housing. In 1986, both the assets and the liabilities of the company passed to a public limited company, British Gas, part of whose undertaking later devolved upon the claimant. In 2005, the site was designated as contaminated land by the Environment Agency. The Environment Agency notified the claimant that it was an appropriate person in terms of the EPA. The House of Lords held that the liabilities which were imposed on British Gas in 1986 were those which existed immediately before the transfer that took place on that date. Such liabilities could not include liabilities which came into existence nine years later, under the Environment Act 1995 (which amended the EPA). In short, it could not be plausibly argued that the claimant had either caused, or knowingly permitted, the substances to be present on the land.

8 WATER

INTRODUCTION

In this chapter we discuss how water pollution is controlled. First, we look at the common law controls, and then we look at the relevant statutory controls.

LIABILITY FOR CAUSING POLLUTION BY ERECTING *OPERA MANUFACTA* (OR NEW WORKS)

The vast majority of cases which concern liability for harm caused by the erection of *opera manufacta* (or new works) relate to circumstances where the natural flow of a stream has been affected by the construction of a dam, embankment, etc., the upshot of which is that the property of the riparian proprietors downstream is flooded: see, e.g., *Potter* v *Hamilton and Strathaven Railway Co.* (1864) 3 M 83; *Kerr* v *Earl of Orkney* (1857) 20 D 298. However, there are instances of the doctrine of *opus manufactum* being successfully invoked by riparian proprietors against watercourse pollution.

For example, in *Montgomery* v *Buchanan's Trustees* (1853) 15 D 853, the defender erected dwelling houses on his land, and subsequently provided the houses with piped water and drainage. The sewage from the houses was conveyed to a nearby streamlet by drains. The streamlet passed through subjacent property. The water in the stream, which had formerly been fit for the use of cattle and also for domestic purposes (that is, the primary uses of the water), became polluted and, therefore, unfit for these purposes. The pursuer, a proprietor of land that adjoined the stream, raised an action in nuisance against the defendant. Whereas the decision, in the author's view, lacked clarity, the court, in finding in favour of the pursuer, set store by the fact that the adverse state of affairs was created by the erection of an *opus manufactum*.

Again, in the Inner House case of *Fleming* v *Gemmill* 1908 SC 340, the proprietors of workmen's houses erected earth closets and washhouses for the use of their tenants. Although the drains, which served the houses, were solely intended to receive waste water from washhouses and sinks in the premises, they were used by the tenants as a means of disposing of sewage. The result of this was that the stream into which the drains discharged became polluted. The stream flowed through an adjoining farm. Cattle, which watered at the stream, were injured as a consequence.

The pursuer, who was the tenant of the farm, raised an action against the proprietor of the houses. It was held that the defender was liable, on the basis that he had erected an *opus manufactum*, in the form of a drain, by means of which sewage would enter the stream.

LIABILITY IN NUISANCE

The introduction of polluting matter into a stream can constitute a nuisance. For example, in *Duke of Buccleuch* v *Cowan* (1866) 5 M 214, the River Esk had become polluted by waste from several paper mills which were situated on its banks. The defenders were proprietors of paper mills, which were situated at different places, on the banks of the stream. The pursuer owned land through which the river flowed. Before 1835, the water in the river had been pure in nature. However, with the passage of time, the river became polluted by refuse which was discharged from the mills. The Inner House held that whereas a riparian proprietor could use the water in the stream as he chose, he was required to send to proprietors down-stream water which was undiminished in quantity and also in quality. He could not pollute the stream by introducing impurities, especially artificial impurities, into the stream which would interfere with the primary use (which would vary with the particular stream) of the Esk, which was described as including bleaching, cooking and watering cattle. However, there was no absolute standard of water quality, in law. That is to say, what constituted polluting the river was a question of degree.

The House of Lords had the opportunity to discuss colliery waste and river pollution in *John Young and Co.* v *The Bankier Distillery Co.* [1893] AC 691. Here, the pursuers operated a distillery which used water from a burn for distilling. Whereas the water in the burn had been fit for distilling on account of its softness, the water had ceased to be so after the defenders began to discharge colliery waste water into the stream. The House of Lords held that the pursuers were entitled to an interdict, which prevented the defenders discharging the mine water into the stream. In the view of the author, *John Young* underscores the point that, at common law, whether the adverse state of affairs that is complained of ranks as a nuisance is often fact-sensitive. This is especially true in relation to water pollution. Indeed, Burn-Murdoch, *Interdict* (at 204) argued that, in the context of water pollution, that water in a river may be fit for the primary purposes of drinking and other domestic uses, or, on the other hand, the water may have ceased to possess such a degree of purity and simply be fit for 'secondary purposes', that is to say, for industrial use. Pollution which would be a nuisance in the former case may not be a nuisance in the latter. The learned author bases this view on the fact that, in determining whether a given state of affairs ranks as a nuisance, one is required to take into account, *inter alia*, the particular circumstances, the locality, and also the degree of the relevant pollution.

It should be added that to what extent, if any, interdicts were effective in securing the prevention of pollution of water courses in Scotland is uncertain. No relevant empirical research has been undertaken. It should also be added that during the nineteenth century, local authorities were, arguably, the greatest water polluters. For example, rivers such as the Water of Leith, in Edinburgh, were simply used as open sewers by municipal authorities as a means of disposing of sewage.

By way of conclusion, as was the case with air pollution, the law of nuisance was a rather ineffectual instrument in the battle against water pollution. Private law remedies, normally interdicts, in terms of the law of nuisance, simply scratched at the surface of the problem. What was really required was effective regulation.

THE EUROPEAN UNION

The EU has been the primary driver in the development of water policy and law in the United Kingdom. EU Directives, which relate to water pollution, can be categorised as Directives which either address the discharge of specific substances into surface water or groundwater; Directives which set quality standards for water in terms of a particular use, such as bathing; or Directives which regulate particular polluting activities, such as the discharge of urban waste and pollution by nitrates from agriculture. Currently, the most important directive, in terms of the regulation of water pollution in the EU is Directive 2000/60/EC, the Water Framework Directive (WFD). The WFD adopts a more holistic, and also revolutionary, approach to the regulation of water pollution and water management than previous EU Directives, and, indeed, than UK national law, in which the approach to water pollution regulation has largely been sectoral. The purpose of the WFD is to establish a framework for the protection and securement of good ecological status of inland surface waters, transitional waters, coastal waters and groundwater (these different types of water are defined in Article 2): Art. 1. Member states are required to ensure that a river basin management plan is produced for each river basin district (as defined in Article 2) lying entirely within their territory: Art. 13. In making operational the programmes and measures which are specified in the river basin management plans for surface waters, a member state is required (subject to certain exceptions) to prevent the deterioration of the status of all bodies of surface water: Art. 4. As far as groundwater is concerned, a member state is required (subject to certain exceptions) to prevent, or limit, the input of pollutants into the groundwater, and also to prevent (subject to certain exceptions) the deterioration of the status of all bodies of groundwater.

The WFD is implemented in Scotland by the Water Environment and Water Services (Scotland) Act 2003 (WEWSA).

WATER ENVIRONMENT AND WATER SERVICES (SCOTLAND) ACT 2003

River basin management planning

The WEWSA makes provision for the establishment of river basin districts in Scotland. The Scottish ministers are placed under a duty to designate, by order, one or more river basin districts (RBD) in Scotland. The Water Environment and Water Services (Scotland) Act 2003 (Designation of Scotland River Basin District Order 2003 (SSI 2003 No. 610, Art. 2), designates a single RBD which covers most of Scotland. There are also two cross-border RBD's with England. SEPA was required to carry out a 'characterisation' of each RBD by 22 December 2004: s. 5(1). The WEWSA defines a characterisation as an analysis of the characteristics of the water environment, a review of the impact of human activity on the status of the water environment, and an economic analysis of water use: s. 5(2). SEPA was required to review and, where necessary, update, each characterisation by December 2013, and by the end of every six years thereafter: s. 5(3). The Water Environment (River Basin Management Planning: Further Provision) (Scotland) Regulations 2013 (SSI 2013 No. 323) make further provision towards implementing the WFD, the environmental quality standards in the field of water policy (Directive 2008/105/EC, The Priority Substances Directive, amended by Directive 2013/39/EU) and also the requirements of Directive 2006/118/EC, the Groundwater Directive).

SEPA is placed under a duty to monitor the status of the water environment in the relevant RBD, and also the relevant territorial water which is adjacent to the RBD: s. 8(1). SEPA is also required to prepare a programme (a 'monitoring programme') for monitoring the status of the water environment and the relevant territorial water: s. 8(2). SEPA is required to set environmental objectives (as defined in s. 9(7)) for each body of water in a RBD, and also for each shellfish protected water within the RBD: s. 9(1). SEPA is also required to prepare a programme of measures which are to be applied in order to meet these objectives. SEPA must also prepare, and submit to the Scottish ministers, a RBD Management Plan for each RBD for such period as the Scottish ministers may direct: s. 10(1). The relevant RBD Management Plan is required to undergo a consultation process, and it is also required to be submitted to, and approved, by the Scottish ministers: ss. 11–13. The current RBD Management Plan for Scotland was published in 2015. The plan covers the period 2015–2027.

CONTROL OF WATER POLLUTION

The WEWSA makes specific provision for the control of water pollution. The Scottish ministers are empowered to make regulations for, or in connection with, regulating any activity, 'a controlled activity' for the purposes of protecting the water environment: s. 20(1). The Water Environment (Controlled Activities) (Scotland) Regulations 2011 (SSI 2011 No. 209 (as amended)) have been made under the WEWSA. The Regulations are wide-ranging and cover rivers, lochs, transitional waters (estuaries), coastal waters, groundwater and wetlands. The main provisions of the Regulations will now be briefly discussed.

THE WATER ENVIRONMENT (CONTROLLED ACTIVITIES) (SCOTLAND) REGULATIONS 2011

The Water Environment (Controlled Activities) (Scotland) Regulations 2011 (or Controlled Activities Regulations, CAR) apply, *inter alia*, to activities (that is, controlled activities) which are likely to cause pollution of the water environment, the direct, or indirect discharge, and any activity likely to cause a direct, or indirect discharge, into groundwater of any hazardous substance or other pollutant, and any other activity which, directly or indirectly, has, or is likely to have, a significant adverse impact on the water environment: Reg. 3(1).

A person is prohibited from carrying on, causing, or permitting others to carry on, a controlled activity, except insofar as that activity is authorised under CAR and is carried on in accordance with that authorisation: Reg. 4. A duty is imposed on any person carrying out a controlled activity which is authorised under CAR to take all reasonable steps to secure both efficient, and sustainable, water use: Reg. 5.

The authorisation system

General binding rules

The least onerous form of authorisation, in terms of CAR takes the form of the application of general binding rules. A controlled activity that is specified in column 1 of Schedule 3, Part 1 of CAR is automatically authorised if the activity is carried out in conformity with the general binding rules: Reg. 6(1). Controlled activities which fall to be regulated by general binding rules are activities which have a potentially less serious negative impact on the water environment. Such activities include the construction or extension of certain wells, and the dredging of certain rivers, burns and ditches.

Registration

A more onerous form of authorisation is that of registration. SEPA may authorise a controlled activity which falls within the scope of CAR by registering the controlled activity: Reg. 7(1). SEPA can effectively regulate the relevant controlled activity by imposing such conditions as it considers expedient for the purposes of protection of the water environment: s. 7(2). Registration is a form of authorisation that applies to controlled activities, which individually pose low environmental risk, but, cumulatively, can result in greater environmental risk.

Water use licence

The most onerous form of authorisation is that of a water use licence. SEPA may authorise a controlled activity by imposing appropriate conditions in the licence: Reg. 8(1). SEPA is required to impose such conditions, as it considers necessary, or expedient, for the purposes of the protection of the water environment; the enhancement of the water environment; or the protection of the interests of other users of the water environment: Reg. 8(2).

Power of SEPA to impose authorisation

SEPA may impose an authorisation in certain circumstances. For example, an authorisation can be imposed if it appears to SEPA that a person is carrying on a controlled activity which is not registered or licensed in terms of CAR: Reg. 10(1).

Applications for authorisation

An application for authorisation is required to be made in writing to SEPA: Reg. 11(1). If SEPA receives an application in respect of a controlled activity that SEPA considers likely to have a significant adverse effect on the environment, or on the interests of other users of the water environment, SEPA must consult any public authorities which appears to it to have an interest in the application: Reg. 12(1). SEPA is also required to advertise the application: Reg. 13.

Determination of application

Before SEPA determines an application, SEPA is required to assess the risk to the water environment which is posed by the carrying on of the relevant activity: Reg. 15(1).

Call-in powers of Scottish ministers

The Scottish ministers may call in for their determination applications of a class or description which is specified in the direction, or the Scottish ministers can call in a particular application or part of an application: Reg. 20(1).

Review of authorisations etc.

SEPA is placed under a duty to periodically review authorisations which have been granted by way of registration, or by way of a water use licence: Reg. 20(1).

Variation etc. of authorisations

The CAR makes provision for the variation of authorisations, either at the instance of SEPA itself, or at the request of the relevant responsible person, or operator: Regs 22–24.

The CAR also makes provision for the transfer of authorisation by a responsible person (Regs 25 and 26), and the surrender of authorisation by the relevant responsible person or operator (Regs 27 and 28).

Suspension and revocation of authorisation

SEPA may, at any time, suspend, or revoke, an authorisation (in whole or in part) by serving a notice on the responsible person, or operator, as the case may be: Reg. 29(1). Reasons are required to be given for the suspension or revocation of the authorisation: Reg. 29(2).

Monitoring and enforcement etc.

Monitoring

The overall duty to monitor compliance and enforce the provisions of the CAR regime falls on SEPA: Reg. 31(1). However, in relation to the Northumbria River Basin District and the Solway Tweed River Basin

District, SEPA must consult and collaborate, as is necessary, with the Environment Agency.

Enforcement

The CAR regime makes provision for the enforcement of the CAR by way of the service of enforcement notices by SEPA. SEPA may serve an enforcement notice on the relevant person where such a person has carried out, is carrying out, or is likely to carry out, a controlled activity, and SEPA is of the opinion that the activity, *inter alia*, has contravened, is contravening, or is likely to contravene, an authorisation under the CAR: Reg. 32(1).

SEPA is required to revoke an enforcement notice, *inter alia*, if the contravention, or likely contravention, of an authorisation has ceased and is unlikely to recur, and any remedial, mitigating or preventative steps which are required by SEPA have been carried out: Reg. 32(4).

Remedial action by SEPA

If SEPA considers that an enforcement notice should be served under Reg. 32(2), SEPA is entitled to take any steps which would be identified in that notice, or secure that those steps are taken, either if it considers that it is necessary to do so, forthwith, or, it appears to SEPA, after reasonable inquiry, that no person can be found on whom to serve that notice: Reg. 33(1). If SEPA has either carried out, or secured the carrying out of, any investigation in order to establish whether or not a notice under Reg. 32(2) is necessary, and, if necessary, on whom the notice should be served, or taken steps, or secured that steps were taken under Reg. 33(1), SEPA is entitled to recover the costs of doing so from the responsible person, or operator, who has carried out, or is likely to carry out, the activity in respect of which the notice would have been served: Reg. 33(2).

Enforcement by the courts

If SEPA is of the opinion that proceedings for an offence under the CAR for failing to comply with the requirements of an enforcement notice would afford an ineffectual remedy against any person, SEPA may take proceedings before any court of competent jurisdiction in order to secure compliance with the notice: Reg. 35.

Information and registers

The Scottish ministers may, by notice, require SEPA to furnish such information about the discharge of its functions in terms of the CAR as the former may require: Reg. 36(1). SEPA may itself serve a notice on any person, requiring that person to furnish the former, within the period which is specified in the notice, any information that SEPA reasonably considers is necessary for the purpose of any function that is conferred on SEPA by, *inter alia*, the WEWSA and the CAR: Reg. 36(2). SEPA is required to maintain a register, which contains the information specified in Sch. 8 to the CAR: Reg. 37(1). The CAR makes provision for the exclusion of commercially confidential information from the register: Regs 38–42.

Offences

The CAR makes provision for a number of offences, amongst which it is an offence for a person to:

(i) contravene Reg. 4;

(ii) fail to comply with or contravene a general binding rule;

(iii) fail to comply with or contravene a registration, including any condition which has been imposed;

(iv) fail to comply with or contravene a water use license, including any condition imposed; and

(v) fail to comply with an enforcement notice: Reg. 44(1).

Defences to principal offences

Provision is made for defences to the principal offences under the CAR. A person is not guilty of any such offence if:

(a) the contravention is the result of:

    (i) an accident that could not reasonably have been foreseen,

    (ii) natural causes, or *force majeure*, which are exceptional or could not reasonably have been foreseen,

    (iii) an act or omission by a category 1 or 2 responder (in terms of the Civil Contingencies Act 2004) that is reasonably necessary to protect people, property or the environment from imminent risk of serious harm,

(b) all practical steps are taken to prevent deterioration of the water environment;

(c) all practical steps are taken, as soon as is reasonably practical, to restore the water environment to its condition prior to the contravention; and

(d) particulars of the contravention are furnished to SEPA as soon as practical after it occurs: Reg. 48.

Power of court to order that offence be remedied

If a person is convicted of an offence under CAR which has had an adverse effect on the water environment, and it appears to the court that it is in the power of that person to mitigate, or remedy, such an impact, the court may, either, in addition to, or instead of imposing any punishment, order that person, within a specified period, to take such steps as are specified in the order to remedy those matters: Reg. 49(1). Before making such an order, the court is required to have regard to any representations of SEPA as to the steps which are required to mitigate or remedy the adverse impact: Reg. 49(2).

Appeals to the Scottish ministers

The following can appeal against certain decisions of SEPA, namely:

(a) a person who has been refused the grant of an authorisation of a controlled activity, or is deemed to have been refused the grant of such authorisation;

(b) a person who has been granted a form of authorisation which is different from the form of authorisation which that person believes ought to have been granted;

(c) a person who is aggrieved by the terms and conditions which are attached to an authorisation;

(d) a person who has been served with a variation notice, or a person who is aggrieved by the terms and conditions which are attached to such a notice;

(e) a person who has been refused the variation (in whole or in part) of an authorisation on request;

(f) a person who has been granted the variation of an authorisation on request, but that person is aggrieved by the removal, addition or amendment of any condition pursuant to that variation;

(g) a person whose application to SEPA to effect the transfer of an authorisation has been refused, or who is aggrieved by the conditions which are attached to that person's authorisation to take account of such a transfer;

(h) a person whose application to surrender an authorisation has been refused, or a person who is aggrieved by the conditions which are attached to that authorisation to take account of the surrender;

(i) a person whose authorisation has been suspended or revoked in whole or in part;

(j) a person on whom an enforcement notice has been served or who is aggrieved by the terms of that notice;

(k) if SEPA has determined that information is not commercially confidential, in terms of the CAR, the person to whom or to whose business that information relates: Reg. 50.

It should be noted, that the CAR are being replaced by the Environmental Authorisations (Scotland) Regulations 2018 (SSI 2018 No. 219), which in their current form are confined to radioactive substances, but will, in due course, include activities which are currently governed by CAR. The new regulations are based on the CAR. However, the detail is not always the same.

SEWERAGE

We now turn our attention to the important subject of sewerage, which is, of course, closely linked to that of water. One of the earliest functions that municipal authorities in Scotland were charged with performing was the provision of an adequate sewerage system for the community which the authorities served. An effective sewerage system, in common with the provision of municipal water supply, is required to be administered over a geographically large area, since often sewers may be required to collect sewage from a wide area, and then travelling a long distance to the point at which the sewage is treated. Therefore, increasingly, over the twentieth century larger local authority units were charged with the responsibility of providing adequate sewerage to their respective areas. At present, Scottish Water (SW) is the authority that is responsible for the provision of sewerage in Scotland. As far as the law relating to sewerage in Scotland is concerned, the principal statute is the Sewerage (Scotland) Act 1968 (as amended), which, in effect, radically reformed the law relating to sewerage and drainage (which had experienced little substantive change since 1897 with the passing of the Public Health (Scotland) Act 1897 (repealed)). The main provisions of the 1968 Act (the Act) are now discussed.

Duties and powers of Scottish Water to provide sewerage of its area

SW is placed under a duty to provide such public sewers and public sustainable urban drainage systems (SUDS) as may be necessary for effectually draining its area of domestic sewage, surface water and trade effluent, and to make such provision, by way of sewage treatment works or otherwise, as may be necessary for effectually dealing with the contents of its sewers and SUD systems: s. 1(1). The 1968 Act defines the following terms:

(1) 'domestic sewage' in relation to any area or premises, means sewage which is not surface water or trade effluent;

(2) a 'drain' in relation to premises, means any pipe or drain, within the curtilage of those premises, which is used solely for, or in connection with, the drainage of one building, or of any buildings or yards appurtenant to buildings within the same curtilage;

(3) a 'public sewer' is any sewer which is vested in Scottish Water;

(4) a 'public SUD' means any SUD system which is vested in Scottish Water;

(5) 'SUD' means a sustainable urban drainage system;

(6) 'sewage treatment works' means any works, apparatus or plant used for the treatment or disposal of sewage, and includes a septic tank but does not include a SUD system;

(7) 'sustainable urban drainage system' means a drainage system which:

(a) facilitates attenuation, settlement or treatment of surface water from two or more premises (whether or not together with road water), and

(b) includes one or more of the following: inlet structures, outlet structures, swales, constructed wetlands, ponds, filter trenches, attenuation tanks and detention basins (together with any associated pipes and equipment);

(8) a 'sewer' does not include a drain, as defined above, but includes all sewers, pipes or drains used for the drainage of buildings and yards;

(9) 'surface water' means the run-off of rainwater from roofs, and any paved ground surface within the curtilage of premises;

(10) 'trade effluent' means any liquid, with or without particles of matter in suspension therein, which is wholly, or in part, produced in the course of any trade or industry carried on at trade premises, including trade waste waters, or waters heated in the course of any trade or industry, and, in relation to any trade premises, means any such liquid, as aforesaid, which is so produced in the course of any trade or industry, carried on at those premises;

(11) 'trade or industry' for the purpose of definition of trade effluent, includes agriculture, horticulture and scientific research or

experiment, the carrying on of a hospital, and the provision of a care home service, and for the purpose of definition of 'trade premises' includes premises used, or intended to be used, in whole or in part, for carrying on agriculture, horticulture or scientific research or experiment, or as a hospital or accommodation provided by a care home service; and

(12) 'trade premises' means any premises used, or intended to be used, for the carrying on of any trade or industry: s. 59(1).

SW is under a duty to take its public sewers to such point, or points, as will enable the owners of premises which are to be served by the sewers to connect their drains, or private sewers, with the public sewers at a reasonable cost: s. 1(2). However, SW is under no such duty if it has agreed with a private provider that the provider will take a private sewer to such point, or points, as will enable owners to make such connection. The duty which is imposed on SW under s. 1(2) does not require SW to do anything which is not practicable at a reasonable cost: s. 1(3).

Mention should be made of the Provision of Water and Sewerage Services (Reasonable Cost) (Scotland) Regulations 2015 (SSI 2015 No. 79) (Regs 6–8), which make provision for the calculation of relevant costs in relation to the provision of such sewers.

Duty to maintain, construct public sewers etc.

SW has a duty to inspect, maintain, repair, cleanse, empty, ventilate and, where appropriate, renew all sewers, SUD systems, sewage treatment works, and other works which are vested in it by virtue of the Sewerage (Scotland) Act 1968, or the Water Industry (Scotland) Act 2002: s. 2. In the House of Lords case of *RHM Bakeries Ltd* v *Strathclyde Regional Council* 1985 SC (HL) 17, it was held that the duty to maintain a public sewer was not absolute.

SW may construct a public sewer or SUD system in, under or over any road, or under any cellar or vault below any road, or in, on or over any land not forming part of a road: s. 3(1). Furthermore, SW may construct a public sewage treatment works in or on any land which is held by it, or appropriated for that purpose. Before commencing construction of a sewer or a SUD system in, on or over any land not forming part of a road, SW is required to serve notice of its intention on the owner and occupier of the relevant land, together with a description of the proposed works and the right to object thereto: s. 3(2). However, if within a period of three months after the service of the notice, the owner or the occupier objects to the proposed works and that objection is not withdrawn, SW may not proceed to execute the works without such consent. In such circumstances, SW may refer the matter to the sheriff, by summary application. In turn, the sheriff may grant consent to the proposed works, either unconditionally or subject to such terms and conditions as he or she considers just. The sheriff may also withhold his or her consent. The decision of the sheriff is final. The sheriff has complete powers of review. In other words, the sheriff is not simply confined to considering whether SW has complied with the requisite statutory procedure: *Central Regional Council v Barbour European Ltd* 1982 SLT (Sh Ct) 49.

Without prejudice to its powers under s. 3 (including any power to authorise the construction on its behalf of a public sewer), SW may authorise a person to construct within its area, whether or not it connects with its sewers or sewage treatment works, a sewer:

(1) in under or over any road, or under any cellar or vault below any road; or

(2) in, on or over any land which does not form part of a road, and is not land in respect of which that person is the owner, lessee or occupier: s. 3A(1).

In such a case, the same notification procedure, as described above, applies to the relevant authorised person as it applies to SW. In giving its authorisation in terms of s. 3A(1), or in relation to any sewer or SUD system (not being a sewer or SUD system constructed by or on behalf of SW) the construction of which does not require such authorisation, may, in the case where a proposed sewer or SUD system will connect with its sewers or SUD systems, or sewage treatment works, determine (by written notice) that all, or part, of the sewer or SUD will not vest in SW under s. 16(1)(c) of the 1968 Act, but, rather in him or her: s. 3A(2). However, SW may either then, or at some later time, enter into an agreement under which the relevant sewer or SUD, or as the case may be, the part, is to vest in SW.

Scottish Water's power to close, alter, etc. public sewers

SW may close, alter or replace, or remove any sewer, SUD system, sewage treatment works or other works vested in it, either by virtue of the provisions of the Sewerage (Scotland) Act 1968 or those of the Water Industry (Scotland) Act 2002: s. 4. However, before any person, who is lawfully using the relevant sewer, is deprived of such use, SW is required to provide a sewer etc. that functions equally effectively as the sewer etc. that has been taken out of use. Furthermore, SW is required to carry out, at its own expense, any work that is necessary to connect his or her drain, private sewer or SUD with the sewer or works so provided.

Agreements between Scottish Water and local authorities

In order to provide coherence and overall efficiency of the sewerage system, a roads authority may enter into an agreement with SW as to the provision, management, maintenance or use of their sewers, SUD systems or drains for the conveyance of water from the surface of a road or surface water from premises: s. 7(1). However, neither the roads authority, nor SW, may unreasonably refuse to enter into such an agreement for such purposes, or unreasonably insist upon such terms and conditions which are unacceptable to the other party: s. 7(3). Any dispute as to whether either the relevant roads authority or SW are acting unreasonably is required to be determined by the Scottish ministers, whose decision is final.

Agreements to provide sewers etc.

If SW is satisfied that premises are to be constructed within its area, SW may enter into an agreement with that person as to the provision by that person or by SW of sewers, SUD systems and sewage treatment works which are to serve those premises: s. 8(1). The relevant agreement may specify both the terms, and conditions on which the work is to be carried out, including provision as to the taking over by SW of SUD systems and sewage treatment works so provided. Importantly, the agreement is enforceable against SW by the owner or occupier (for the time being) of premises which are to be served by the relevant sewers, SUD systems or works.

However, SW may enter into such an agreement only if it has no duty to provide public sewers to the premises under s. 1 of the 1968 Act: s. 8(2).

Rights of owners and occupiers of premises to connect with and drain into public sewers

The owner of any premises has the right to connect his or her drains, private sewers or private SUD systems with the sewers, SUD systems or sewage treatment works of SW: s. 12(1). In turn, the occupier of the relevant premises is entitled to use such drains or private sewers to discharge domestic sewage from the premises into SW's sewers or works from the relevant premises. The occupier is also entitled to use the relevant drain, private sewers or private SUD systems to discharge surface water from the premises into SW's sewers, SUD systems or works from the premises. However, the relevant owner is not entitled to connect his or her drains, sewers or SUD systems with the sewers, SUD systems or works of SW unless the intervening land is land through which the owner is entitled to construct a drain, sewer or SUD system. The owner of any premises who proposes to connect his or her drains, sewers or SUD systems with the sewers, SUD systems or works of SW, or to alter a drain, sewer or SUD system which is connected with such sewer, system or works in such a way as may interfere with them, is required to give SW notice of his or her proposals: s. 12(3). SW may refuse permission for the connection or alteration, or grant permission for the connection or alteration, subject to such conditions as it thinks fit. Any such permission may, in particular, specify the mode and point of connection, and where there are separate public sewers for foul water and surface water may prohibit the discharge of foul water into the sewer which is reserved for surface water and vice versa. If SW either refuses such permission or grants it subject to conditions, the owner must be informed of the reasons for the decision and also of his or her right of appeal: s. 12(4).

The Scottish ministers may confirm the decision and any such conditions either with or without modification, or they may refuse to confirm the decision: s. 12(5). In *Tayside Regional Council* v *Secretary of State for Scotland* 1996 SLT 473, it was held that in determining an appeal in terms of s. 12(5), provided that the rules of natural justice were complied with, the Secretary of State was not confined to considering matters which had been given as grounds for refusal of permission. That is to say, that he was entitled to consider other facts and circumstances.

Finally, it is an offence for a person to connect (or alter) a drain, sewer or SUD system to the sewers, SUD systems or works of SW without the necessary permission: s. 12(8).

Power of Scottish Water to direct manner of construction of works

Section 14 gives SW power to direct the owner of any premises who proposes to construct a drain, sewer, SUD system or sewage treatment works to construct the drain, sewer, SUD system or works in a different manner, if SW considers that the relevant drain, sewer SUD system or works are required to form part of a general sewerage system, which SW has either provided or proposes to provide. The section makes provision for an appeal against such a direction, and also payment of additional expense to the owner.

Remedy of defects in drains etc.

Power is given to both SW and a local authority to require, by notice, the owner or occupier of any premises to remedy any defect (which includes any obstruction in a drain, SUD system or sewage treatment works (s. 15(5)) in any drain, SUD system, or sewage treatment works (other than drains, SUD systems or works which are vested in SW) within a reasonable time, which is specified in the notice: s. 15(1). A person who is aggrieved by a notice can refer the matter, by summary application, to the sheriff, who may issue such directions as he or she thinks fit, and whose decision on the matter is final: s. 15(2).

In the face of the owner or occupier failing to comply with the terms of the notice, either in its original form or as modified under s. 15(2), the local authority can carry out the relevant works and recover the costs from the person on whom the notice was served: s. 15(3). Section 15(4) empowers SW or a local authority to take immediate action to remedy a defect.

Vesting of sewers etc. in Scottish Water

Prior to the advent of the Sewerage (Scotland) Act 1968, anecdotal evidence indicates (the subject is under-researched) that local authorities often encountered practical difficulties in ascertaining who was responsible for maintaining a private sewer or drain which was defective and causing a nuisance, and was therefore the author of the nuisance in terms of Part II of the Public Health (Scotland) Act 1897 (repealed). This state of affairs was rectified by the 1968 Act. One of the most important provisions of the 1968 Act relates to the vesting of sewers etc. in SW. Under the 1968 Act the following vest in SW:

(a) all sewers, SUD systems and sewage treatment works constructed by it, at its expense, in terms of SW's general duties to provide sewerage in its area;

(b) all junctions with its sewers, whether constructed at the expense of SW or otherwise;

(c) all private sewers and private SUD systems connecting with its sewers or sewage treatment works;

(d) all sewage treatment works and SUD systems which SW takes over by agreement or otherwise: s. 16(1).

Importantly, all sewers, junctions therewith, drains, SUD systems and sewage works which are vested in SW are the property of SW, which is solely responsible for their management, maintenance and renewal: s. 16(3).

Vesting of certain private sewers

The vesting of private sewers, the construction of which has been authorised by SW, has already been discussed (see p. 130, above).

Furthermore, there vests in the person whom SW authorises under s. 3A(1) to construct a sewer, which does not connect with SW's sewers or sewage treatment works, the sewer constructed: s. 16A(1). That sewer, and any sewer or SUD system, vested in him by virtue of a determination under s. 3A(2) above, remains his or her property and he or she is solely responsible for its management, maintenance and renewal. However, SW may enter into an agreement that the sewer, SUD system or any part of it will vest in it: s. 16A(2).

Power of Scottish Water to take over private sewage treatment works

SW may take over, either the whole or part, of any private sewage treatment works or private SUD system by agreement with the owner, or, failing such agreement, by compulsion: s. 17(1). Provision is made under the section for appeal to the Scottish ministers against such compulsory acquisition. All works which are taken over by SW then vest in it: s. 17(4).

Trade effluents

It is important that effluent, from industrial sources is controlled, in order to prevent the sewage treatment works into which the effluent flows being adversely affected. Another reason for the need to regulate such discharges is to protect sewer workers from harm. Part II of the 1968 Act allows SW to regulate the discharge of trade effluent (as defined in s. 59(1)) into public sewers.

Right to discharge into public sewers

The occupier of any trade premises (as defined in s. 59(1)) within the area of SW has the right to discharge any trade effluent from the premises into a sewer or sewage treatment works of SW: s. 24(1). However, the right of the occupier to discharge trade effluent into such sewer or works is circumscribed by the provision that that any occupier who discharges such effluent into the sewers or sewage treatment works of SW without the consent of SW (where such consent is required), or contrary to any direction or condition which is imposed under the 1968 Act, commits an offence which is subject to a penalty: s. 24(2).

Control of new discharges

The 1968 Act makes specific provision in relation to new discharges (as defined in s. 25) from trade premises into the sewers or sewage treatment works of SW. The occupier of trade premises who proposes to make a new discharge of trade effluent from those premises into the sewers or sewage treatment works of SW is required to obtain its consent: s. 26. SW may refuse its consent or may grant its consent, either unconditionally or subject to such conditions as SW thinks fit: s. 29(1). The applicant can appeal to the Scottish ministers against such a decision of SW: s. 31. The decision of the Scottish ministers is deemed to be that of SW from whose decision the appeal is made: s. 54(4). The decision of the Scottish ministers is final: s. 54(5).

SW may, and when requested to do so by the occupier of the relevant premises, review, by way of a direction, a decision which SW has made regarding consents, conditions and refusals in terms of s. 29: s. 32(1).

Existing discharges

The 1968 Act also makes provision for the control of existing discharges, which are discharges which were lawfully made within a period of two years ending 16 May 1973: s. 32(1). Except where SW and the person who is making the discharges agree otherwise, an existing discharge is allowed to continue: s. 34.

Review of existing discharges

SW may, and when requested by the person who is making the discharge, review the making of an existing discharge, and SW may direct that any continuation of the discharge is either unconditional or subject to such conditions as it thinks fit to impose: s. 36(1). Furthermore, SW may, by direction, from time to time, and when requested by the person making the discharge, review such a direction: s. 36(2). However, unless SW and the person who is making the direction agree in writing, reviews may not take place at intervals of less than two years. An appeal lies against a direction which is made by SW under s. 36: s. 36(3).

Under the Urban Waste Water Treatment (Scotland) Regulations 1994 (SI 1994 No. 2842), SW is under a general duty to ensure that, as far as its functions under the Act which relate to trade effluents with respect to the discharge of industrial waste water (as defined in Reg. 2(1)), the provisions of the Regulations are met in relation to the discharge: Reg. 7(1). Furthermore, SW is required to review and, if necessary, for the purposes of complying with the Regulations, modify any consent which has been granted under the Act: Reg. 7(5). Furthermore, any directions which have been made under the Part II of the Act must also be reviewed for the same purposes.

It should be mentioned that, in determining an application for consent in terms of CAR, SEPA is required to have regard to the provisions of the 1994 Regulations: SSI 2011 209, Reg. 15(1), Sch. 4, Pt 2.

Public register

SW is required to maintain a register for the purposes of the Act: s. 37A(1). The register is required to contain certain prescribed information: s. 37A(2). The Trade Effluent (Registers) (Scotland) Regulations 1998 (SI 1998 No. 2533) prescribe the particulars which are required to be entered in the register. The Act makes provision for the exclusion from the register of information which affects national security: s. 37B.

Essential Facts

- At common law pollution of a watercourse can rank as a nuisance.
- Law and policy relating to water pollution is currently EU-driven.
- The most important Directive relating to the pollution of water is the Water Framework Directive (WFD).
- The Water Environment and Water Services (Scotland) Act 2003 (WEWSA) implements the WFD.
- The WEWSA makes special provision for the prevention of water pollution.
- Activities which could potentially threaten the purity of watercourses, that is 'controlled activities', are regulated under the CAR regulations by SEPA through a system of binding rules, registration and licensing.
- The CAR regime is enforced by enforcement notices.
- Scottish Water (SW) is placed under a duty to effectively drain its area.
- SW has special control over trade effluents.

9 INTEGRATED POLLUTION, PREVENTION AND CONTROL AND ENVIRONMENTAL PERMITTING

INTRODUCTION

In this chapter we discuss integrated pollution prevention and control and permitting. The regulation of pollution was traditionally piecemeal in the United Kingdom as a whole. This situation was a legacy of its Victorian origins. Not only were a variety of different agencies involved in regulating pollution, from both industrial and other sources, but often different agencies would regulate different forms of pollution from the same premises. For example, local authorities were, and still are, responsible for enforcing the provisions of the Clean Air Act 1956 in relation to grit and dust emanating from certain industrial premises into the atmosphere, whereas the regulation of river pollution from the same premises fell to be regulated by the relevant rivers purification authority. That is to say, the relevant agency simply possessed the power to regulate pollution which was being discharged into one medium. The obvious disadvantage of such a fragmented approach to the control of pollution is that effective enforcement action by one agency may simply cause another environmental problem, which falls to be addressed by another agency. For example, if a local authority required the occupier of the factory to provide adequate drainage to the relevant site, and the drainage which was installed discharged into a nearby watercourse, pollution of that watercourse would fall to be regulated by another agency.

The first attempt which was made by Parliament to deal with environmental pollution in an integrated and holistic manner was the Control of Pollution Act 1974 (COPA). Part 1 of COPA required a waste disposal authority, when it was considering whether to grant a waste licence, to refer the proposal to the relevant river purification authority. Furthermore, the former was also required to take into account the representations of the latter in deciding whether to grant a licence. We see here an example of what can be described as 'substantive integration', in that the waste disposal authority had not only to consider the potential impact of the proposed landfill on the relevant surrounding land, but also (albeit, simply in terms of the representations which were made by the river purification authority) the potential impact on water.

The move to a more integrated approach to pollution control came with the Environmental Protection Act 1990 (EPA). In essence, Part I of the EPA introduced an entirely new legal regime as far as regulating environmental pollution was concerned. The EPA made provision for the regulation of 'prescribed processes'. It was the intention of the EPA to make industries which posed a substantial threat to the general environment (essentially, air, water and land), such as petrochemical works and cement works, subject to integrated pollution control (Part A processes), and industries which possessed the capacity to simply pollute the air (Part B processes) to be made subject to local air pollution control. However, the Environment Act 1995 made provision for the creation of a new regulatory agency, namely, SEPA, which made SEPA solely responsible for regulating both Part A and Part B processes under the EPA.

The Pollution Prevention and Control (Scotland) Regulations 2000 (SSI 2000 No. 323), which were made chiefly in order to implement the Integrated Pollution and Prevention Control Directive (Directive 96/61/EC), were repealed and replaced by the Pollution Prevention and Control Regulations 2012 (SSI 2012 No. 360) (the Regulations), which (as were the 2000 Regulations) are made under the Pollution Prevention and Control Act 1999. The Regulations make provision for an integrated pollution control regime in Scotland. Other environmentally polluting activities are also covered by the Regulations.

By way of a brief overview, the regime established by the Regulations requires that a person who operates an installation or mobile plant which falls within the scope of the Regulations is authorised to do so by a permit which is granted by SEPA. SEPA can also attach conditions to a permit in order to ensure that the installation does not present a significant threat to the environment. Provision is also made for both the transfer and the variation of permits. Finally, the Regulations give SEPA the power to serve enforcement and suspension notices on the holder of a permit in order to secure compliance with the Regulations.

THE POLLUTION PREVENTION AND CONTROL (SCOTLAND) REGULATIONS 2012

The Pollution Prevention and Control (Scotland) Regulations (the Regulations) implement the Industrial Emissions Directive (Directive 2010/75/EU (the Industrial Emissions Directive, the IED). The Regulations also make provision for the regulation of other environmentally polluting activities which are not covered by the Directive. The Regulations apply to all installations and also mobile plant (as defined in Reg. 2(1)) which carry out an activity which is listed in Annex 1 to the Directive, which is transposed by Schedule 1 of the Regulations. However, it should be pointed out the Regulations also cover some domestic activities which are not covered by the IED.

The Regulations divide installations into Part A and Part B processes. Part A processes have the capacity to pollute the atmosphere, water and also land, whereas Part B processes simply have the capacity to pollute the atmosphere. Part A installations are subject to integrated pollution prevention and control, whilst Part B installations are subject to local air pollution control. SEPA is the relevant enforcing authority for both Part A and Part B installations in Scotland.

APPLICATION FOR A PERMIT

The Regulations provide that no person may operate a Part A or Part B installation, or mobile plant or solvents installation, without a permit: Reg. 11. SEPA must, on receiving an application for a permit, either grant a permit, subject to the conditions which are required or authorised to be imposed by, or under the Regulations, or Reg. 10 of the Landfill Regulations or SEPA may refuse the application: Reg. 13(1). However, SEPA is required to refuse an application if it considers that the applicant will not be a person who will have control over the operation of the installation or mobile plant after the grant of the permit, or that the applicant will not ensure that the installation or mobile plant is operated so as to comply with the conditions which would be included in the permit: Reg. 13(2). A permit may authorise the operation of more than one Part A or Part B installation, mobile plant or solvents installation on the same site, if operated by the same operator: Reg. 14(1).

SEPA may include a condition in a permit that imposes a limit on the amount or composition of any substance which is produced or utilised during the operation of the installation or mobile plant in any period, or which is supplemented, or incidental to other conditions which are contained in the permit: Reg. 15(1). SEPA may exercise such a power separately from any requirement or power to include a condition in a permit which is provided for elsewhere in the Regulations: Reg. 15(2). However, in order to avoid duplication, SEPA may not include any condition in a permit for the purpose only of securing the health of persons at work within the meaning of Part I of the Health and Safety at Work etc. Act 1974.

SEPA may grant a permit in respect of a specified waste management activity only if SEPA is satisfied that the applicant is a fit and proper person to carry out the activity, and that planning permission is in force under the Town and Country Planning (Scotland) Act 1997 where such permission is required: Reg. 18(1). In determining whether a person is a fit and proper person, SEPA is required to do so by reference to the ability of the person concerned to fulfil the conditions of the permit which either apply, or will apply, to the carrying out of that activity: Reg. 18(3). A person is not a fit and proper person if, in particular, it appears to SEPA, *inter alia*, that the person or a relevant person has been convicted of a relevant offence: Reg. 18(4) (the expressions 'relevant person' and 'relevant offence' are defined in Reg. 18(7)). However, this provision does not apply where SEPA considers it appropriate to treat the person as being a fit and proper person: Reg. 18(5).

Permits may only be transferred, and also cease to have effect, in accordance with the provisions of the Regulations: Reg. 19(1)(2).

Schedule 1: general principles and conditions

The Regulations require SEPA, on determining the conditions of all permits, to take into account certain general principles. SEPA is also required to take into account additional general principles in relation to Part A operations: Reg. 21(1). In determining the conditions which apply to a permit which relate to both Part A and Part B installations and mobile plant, the general principles which SEPA is required to take into account are that they should be operated in such a way that all appropriate preventative measures are taken against pollution, in particular, through application of the best available techniques (as defined in Reg. 4) and that no significant pollution is caused: Reg. 21(2). The additional general principles which apply to Part A processes include the principle that waste generation is prevented and that energy is used efficiently.

The Regulations go on to require general conditions which are to be included in permits. SEPA is required to include a condition in a permit for a Part A or a Part B installation (subject to certain exceptions) or any mobile plant that the operator must use the best available techniques for preventing or, where that is not practicable, reducing emissions from an installation or mobile plant: Reg. 22(1)(3). However, in order to avoid duplication, this requirement does not apply to the extent that any other condition of a permit, or a standard rule, which has effect as a standard condition has the same effect: Reg. 22(2).

As far as general conditions which apply to Part A installations are concerned, SEPA is required to include in a permit conditions which it considers appropriate to comply with the provisions of Reg. 23(2) (below) and also to ensure that, by means of the principles which are enshrined in Reg. 22, a high level of protection for the environment as a whole, taking particular account for that purpose of the general principles in Reg. 21: Reg. 23(2) requires a permit for a Part A installation to include, *inter alia*, conditions:

(i) aimed at minimising long-distance or transboundary pollution;

(ii) ensuring, where necessary, appropriate protection of the soil and groundwater, including requirements for the regular maintenance and surveillance of measures taken to prevent emissions to soil and groundwater; and

(iii) ensuring, where appropriate, monitoring and management of waste produced by the installation.

As far as conditions which apply to Part B installations and mobile plant are concerned, SEPA is required to include in the relevant permit the conditions which SEPA considers appropriate, when taken with Reg. 22, for the purpose of preventing or, where that is not practicable, reducing emissions into the air, taking particular account for that purpose of the general principles set out in Reg. 21(2).

As far as both Part A and Part B installations are concerned, SEPA may include in a permit a condition which requires an operator to carry out works, or do other things in relation to land, which do not form part of the site of the installation, an 'off-site' condition, whether or not the operator is entitled to carry out such works, or do that thing in relation to the land: Reg. 24(1). The person whose consent would be required to carry out such works etc. must either grant, or join in granting, the operator in relation to land, as will enable the operator to comply with an off-site condition: Reg. 24(2). Regulation 24 (Sch. 6) makes provision for the payment of compensation to the person who has granted such an off-site right.

Schedule 1: emission limit values and environmental quality standards

SEPA is required to ensure that a permit for either a Part A or a Part B installation or a mobile plant includes certain conditions which relate to emissions (as defined in Reg. 2(1)) from the installation, as SEPA considers appropriate to comply with the provisions which are contained in Reg. 25: Reg. 25(1). In summary, a permit is required to include emission limit values (as defined in Reg. 2(1)) for the polluting substances which are listed in Sch. 5, and also other polluting substances which are likely to be emitted in significant quantities from an installation or any mobile plant, having regard, for that purpose, to the nature of the pollutant, and in the case of a Part A installation, the potential for emissions to transfer pollution from one environmental medium to another: Reg. 25(2). SEPA may supplement or replace an emission limit value by an equivalent parameter, or technical measure, ensuring an equivalent level of protection for the environment: Reg. 25(3). An emission limit value must apply at the point at which the emissions leave the installation or mobile plant, any dilution before that point being disregarded for the purpose of determining the value: Reg. 25(4). An emission limit value may apply to groups of pollutants, rather than to individual pollutants: Reg. 25(5).

The Regulations also make specific provision for the implementation of certain EU Directives, including that part of the Industrial Emissions Directive which relates to large combustion plants and installations which produce solvents: Regs 26–35.

Standard rules

The Regulations make provision for the rule-making authority (namely, SEPA or the Scottish ministers) to make standard rules which apply generally to an installation or mobile plant which are described in the rules: Reg. 36(1). A rule-making authority is required when making or revising standard rules to ensure that the rules give effect to the best available techniques for preventing, or where that is not practicable, reducing emissions from an installation or any mobile plant: Reg. 36(2). However, a rule-making authority may only make, or revise, standard rules if it is satisfied that the operation of an installation or any mobile plant will, to the extent that it is covered by the standard rules condition, result in the same level of environmental protection, and, in the case of Part A installations, the same high level of integrated pollution prevention and control, as would result were 'tailor-made' conditions made applicable under the Regulations: Reg. 36(3). A rule-making authority is required to keep standard rules which are made by the authority under review, and revise any such rules whenever it considers it necessary to do so, in order to follow developments in best available techniques or to ensure compliance with the Industrial Emissions Directive: Reg. 36(4). The rule-making authority is required before making, revising or revoking standard rules to consult those whom it considers representative of the interests of those communities which are likely to be affected by the proposed rules, revision or revocation; the operators appearing to the authority to be likely to be so affected; and such other persons as appear to the authority to be likely to be affected by, or otherwise have an interest in the proposed rules, revision or revocation: Reg. 38(1).

Review of permits

The Regulations make provision for the review of permits by SEPA. SEPA is required to review the conditions of a permit, *inter alia*:

(i) if the pollution which is caused by an installation or mobile plant is of such significance that the emission limit values in the permit need to be revised, or new emission limit values need to be included;

(ii) if the operational safety of the activities which are carried out in the installation or mobile plant requires other techniques to be used;

(iii) where it is necessary to comply with a new or revised environmental standard in accordance with Article 18 of the Industrial Emissions Directive: Reg. 44(1).

Notwithstanding the above, SEPA is under a general duty to periodically review the conditions of a permit, and may also review the conditions of a permit at any other time: Reg. 44(3)(4).

Variation of permits

SEPA is required to vary a permit if it considers it necessary to do so in order to ensure that the permit complies with the Regulations or the Landfill Regulations: Reg. 46(1). However, SEPA may vary the conditions of a permit at any other time: Reg. 46(2). Furthermore, the operator of an installation or mobile plant may apply to SEPA for a variation of the permit: Reg. 46(3).

Transfer of permit

The Regulations make provision for the transfer of a permit from the current holder of the permit to another: Reg. 46(1). Such a transfer can only take place where the existing permit-holder and the proposed permit-holder make a joint application to SEPA to approve the transfer of either all or part of a permit: Reg. 46(3).

SURRENDER OF PERMIT

The operator of a Part A installation may apply to SEPA to surrender all or part of a permit for the installation: Reg. 48(1). SEPA is required to approve such an application if SEPA is satisfied that all appropriate measures have been taken to:

(a) avoid pollution risk (as defined in Reg. 48(13)) which results from the operation of the installation;

(b) return the site to a satisfactory state, taking into account the technical feasibility of the measures;

(c) remove, control, contain or reduce any relevant hazardous substance in soil or groundwater, so that the site, taking into account its current or approved future use, ceases to pose a significant risk to human health or the environment: Reg. 48(8).

As far as the surrender of a permit, other than a Part A permit, is concerned, the relevant operator may give notice (that is, a surrender notice) to SEPA of the surrender of all or part of a permit: Reg. 48(2). The permit-holder can give such notice if he or she ceases, or intends to cease, the operation of all or part of the installation or mobile plant: Reg. 49(1).

REVOCATION OF PERMIT

SEPA may at any time revoke either all or part of a permit by serving a of revocation notice on the relevant operator: Reg. 50(1). In particular, SEPA may serve a revocation notice where a permit authorises the carrying out of a specified waste management activity, and it appears to SEPA that the operator has ceased to be a fit and proper person by reason of:

(i) the operator or a relevant person having been convicted of a relevant offence, within the meaning of Reg. 18 of the Regulations, or

(ii) the management of the activity has ceased to be in the hands of a technically competent person: Reg. 50(2).

SEPA may also serve a revocation notice where the holder of the permit has ceased to be the operator of the installation or plant which is covered by the permit. The power which SEPA possesses to revoke a permit is wide. SEPA may revoke a permit, either entirely or only to the extent that it authorises the operation of some of the installations or mobile plant to which it applies, or SEPA may revoke a permit only to the extent that it authorises the carrying out of some of the activities which may be carried out in an installation or by means of a mobile plant to which it applies: Reg. 50(3).

Where a permit for a Part A installation is revoked, either entirely or only to the extent that it authorises the operation of some of the installations or mobile plant to which it applies, and SEPA considers that the operator must take steps in respect of the installation when once no longer operating to:

(a) avoid any pollution risk resulting from the operation of the installation on the site;

(b) return the site to a satisfactory state, taking into account the technical feasibility of the steps; or

(c) remove, control, contain or reduce any relevant hazardous substance in soil or groundwater so that the site, taking into account its current or approved future use, ceases to pose a significant risk to human health or the environment, the revocation notice is required to specify any steps which are required to be taken in respect of the site (or part of the site) that are further to those which are required by the permit: Reg. 50(5). The permit continues to have effect, insofar as it requires the above steps to be taken, until SEPA issues a certificate of completion which states that SEPA is satisfied that such steps have been taken, those steps falling to be treated (as well as those which are contained in the relevant permit) as conditions which require steps to be taken, until SEPA issues a certificate of completion: Reg. 50(7).

Subject to certain exceptions, a permit ceases to have effect, in whole or in part, from the date which is specified in the notice: Reg. 50(6).

ENFORCEMENT NOTICES

SEPA may serve an enforcement notice on the operator of an installation or mobile plant in respect of which a permit is granted, if it considers that:

(a) the operator has contravened, is contravening, or is likely to contravene any condition of a permit; or

(b) an incident or accident which significantly affects the environment has occurred as a result of the operation of the installation or mobile plant: Reg. 55(1).

The enforcement notice is required to:

(a) state why SEPA considers that there is, or is likely to be, such a contravention;

(b) specify the matter which constitutes the contravention, or the matter which makes it likely, that the contravention will arise (as the case may be); and

(c) specify the steps which the operator must take in order to remedy the contravention, or to remedy the matter which makes it likely that the contravention will arise (as the case may be): Reg. 55(2).

An enforcement notice which is served under Reg. 55(1)(b) must specify the steps which the operator must take:

(a) to limit the environmental consequences of the incident or accident; and

(b) to prevent further possible incidents or accidents: Reg. 55(3).

The enforcement notice is required to specify the period within which the relevant steps must to be taken: Reg. 55(4).

The steps which may be specified in an enforcement notice may, without prejudice to the generality of Reg. 55(3), include steps which must be taken to remedy the effects of any pollution which is caused by the contravention: Reg. 55(5). The operator of the relevant installation or mobile plant is required to comply with an enforcement notice: Reg. 55(6). SEPA may withdraw an enforcement notice at any time: Reg. 55(7).

SUSPENSION NOTICES

The Regulations also make provision for the issuing of suspension notices by SEPA. SEPA must issue a suspension notice if it considers that any aspect of the operation of the installation or mobile plant:

(a) poses an immediate danger to human health;

(b) threatens to create an immediate significant adverse effect upon the environment; or

(c) involves some other risk of serious pollution: Reg. 56(1).

However, SEPA may not issue a suspension notice where SEPA intends to arrange for steps to be taken under Reg. 57(1) in relation to such operation of the installation or mobile plant: Reg. 56(2). The obligation which is placed on SEPA to issue a suspension notice applies whether or not the particular manner of operation is regulated by, or contravenes, a condition of the permit: Reg. 56(3). SEPA may also issue a suspension notice to an operator who is carrying on specified waste management facilities if SEPA considers that the operator has ceased to be a fit and proper person, in relation to those activities, by reason of the management of those activities having ceased to be in the hands of a technically competent person: Reg. 56(4). A suspension notice is required to state why SEPA considers that the notice is required and, in the case of a suspension notice which is served under Reg. 56(1), the notice is required to specify:

(i) the nature of the harm which is being (or may be) caused by the operation of the installation or mobile plant; and

(ii) the steps that must be taken to remedy the harm, or remove a risk, and the period within which those steps must be taken: Reg. 56(5).

The suspension notice is also required to state the extent to which the permit ceases to have effect to authorise the operation of the installations or mobile plant, or the carrying-out of an activity in the installation or by means of the mobile plant, and, where the permit is to continue to have effect to authorise an activity, any steps which are in addition to those which are already required under the permit which are to be taken in carrying out that activity: Reg. 56(5). The operator of the installation or mobile plant must comply with a suspension notice: Reg. 56(6). A permit ceases to have effect, to the extent which is stated in the suspension notice, on the service of the notice: Reg. 56(7). SEPA may withdraw a suspension notice at any time, and SEPA must withdraw a notice if it is satisfied that, in the case of a suspension notice which has been served under Reg. 56(1), the steps which are required by the notice to remove the risk of pollution have been taken, and, in the case of a notice which has been served under Reg. 56(4), that the management of the activities is in the hands of a technically competent person: Reg. 56(8).

It should be noted at this juncture that in 2016 SEPA published a statement relating to its enforcement policy. At the same time, SEPA issued guidance on how it would use enforcement action.

SEPA is empowered to arrange for steps to be taken, in order to remove an imminent risk of serious pollution if SEPA considers that the operation of any installation or mobile plant which is regulated by a permit, or the operation in a particular manner, involves such a risk: Reg. 57(1). SEPA may also arrange for steps to be taken towards remedying the effects of pollution which is caused by the commission of an offence which comprises the failure to comply with the requirement for a permit; the failure to comply with or contravene a condition of the permit; or the failure to comply with the requirements of an enforcement notice, suspension notice or a closure notice in terms of the Landfill Regulations: Reg. 57(2). In such circumstances, SEPA is required to give at least seven days' notice to the relevant operator before such steps are taken: Reg. 57(3). SEPA may recover the cost of taking such remedial action from the operator of the installation or mobile plant concerned: Reg. 57(4). However, no costs fall to be recovered if, in relation to steps which are taken in order to remove the imminent risk of serious pollution, the operator shows that there was no imminent risk of serious pollution which required such steps to be taken: Reg. 57(5). Furthermore, no costs can be recovered if the operator can show that such costs have been unnecessarily incurred by SEPA: Reg. 57(5).

APPEALS

The Regulations make provision for appeals to the Scottish ministers and to the sheriff. A person may appeal against the relevant decision of SEPA to the Scottish ministers in the following circumstances, namely, where:

(a) an application for a permit has been refused;

(b) an application for the variation of a permit has been refused;

(c) conditions have been attached to a permit after an application has been made under Reg. 13, or, by way of a variation notice, following an application under Reg. 46;

(d) an application for a transfer of a permit has been refused, or conditions have been attached to a permit, in order to take account of such transfer;

(e) an application to surrender a permit has been refused, or conditions have been attached to a permit, in order to take account of the surrender; and

(f) a request to begin closure procedure is not approved under the Landfill (Scotland) Regulations 2003: Reg. 58(1).

Furthermore, a person who is served with:

(a) variation notice;

(b) a revocation notice;

(c) an enforcement notice;

(d) a suspension notice; or

(e) a closure notice under the Landfill (Scotland) Regulations, may appeal against the notice to the Scottish ministers: Reg. 56(2).

However, there is no right of appeal where SEPA's decision gives effect to directions which are given to SEPA by either the Scottish ministers or the sheriff: Reg. 58(3).

On determining an appeal against a decision of SEPA under Reg. 58(1), the Scottish ministers may:

(a) affirm the decision;
(b) where the decision was a refusal to grant a permit, or to vary the conditions of a permit, direct SEPA to grant the permit or to vary the conditions of the permit;
(c) where the decision was as to the conditions which were attached to a permit, quash all or any of the conditions of the permit;
(d) where the decision was a refusal to effect the transfer, or to accept the surrender of a permit, direct SEPA to effect the transfer or to accept the surrender: Reg. 58(4).

On determining an appeal under Reg. 58(1)(b) or (c) above, the Scottish ministers may give SEPA directions as to the conditions which are to be attached to the permit. In giving such directions, the Scottish ministers possess identical powers to those of SEPA: Reg. 58(13).

On determining an appeal against a notice in terms of Reg. 58(2), the Scottish ministers may either quash or affirm the notice, and, if affirming it, may do so either in its original form or with such modifications as they think fit: Reg. 58(5). Both SEPA and any person who is affected by the relevant determination of the Scottish ministers may appeal to the sheriff: Reg. 58(6). The appeal is required to be made by summary application, within twenty-one days from the date of the decision of the Scottish ministers: Reg. 58(7). The sheriff may, in disposing of an appeal, take any step which is open to the Scottish ministers under Reg. 58(4) and (5): Reg. 58(8). The determination of an appeal by the Scottish ministers, or the disposal of an appeal by the sheriff, in relation to a decision to include a standard rules condition in a permit, does not affect the continued validity of the relevant standard rules: Reg. 58(9). Furthermore, the bringing of an appeal in relation to the conditions which are attached to a permit does not suspend the operation of the condition: Reg. 58(10). Again, the bringing of an appeal does not suspend the operation of either an enforcement notice, a suspension notice or a variation notice. In an appeal against a revocation notice, the notice, if affirmed, does not take effect until the expiry of a period of twenty-one days or the withdrawal of the appeal: Reg. 58(11).

DIRECTIONS ETC. BY THE SCOTTISH MINISTERS

The Scottish ministers may give SEPA a direction, which may be either of a general or a specific character in relation to the carrying out of the functions of the latter, either under the Regulations or under the Landfill Regulations: Reg. 60(1). SEPA may be directed to either exercise, or refrain from exercising, any functions under the Regulations or the Landfill Regulations, or to exercise, or refrain from exercising, any function in such circumstances, or in such manner, as may be specified, or as to the objectives which are to be achieved by any condition of a permit: Reg. 60(2). SEPA is placed under a duty to comply with any such direction: Reg. 60(5). The Scottish ministers may also issue guidance to SEPA in relation to the carrying out of its functions under the Regulations or the Landfill Regulations: Reg. 61(1). SEPA is required to have regard to such guidance in carrying out its functions under the Regulations or the Landfill Regulations: Reg. 61(2).

PUBLIC REGISTERS

SEPA is required to maintain a public register which contains a variety of particulars, including particulars relating to applications for a permit, particulars of permits, particulars which relate to the variation, transfer and surrender of permits, as well as particulars relating to appeals, enforcement notices and closure notices under the Landfill Regulations: Reg. 64(1). SEPA is required ensure that the register is available at all reasonable times for public inspection free of charge: Reg. 64(3). The register may be kept in any form, for example, in electronic form. The Regulations make provision for the exclusion from the register of information which affects national security, and also confidential information: Regs 65 and 66.

OFFENCES

The regulations make provision for a variety of offences, including:

(i) operating an installation without a permit;
(ii) failing to comply with or contravene a condition of a permit;
(iii) failing to comply with an enforcement notice, a suspension notice or a closure notice under the Landfill Regulations: Reg. 67(1).

By way of concluding remarks, brief mention should be made of the intention of the Scottish government to introduce an integrated authorisation framework which will integrate the authorisation, procedural and enforcement arrangements relating to water, waste, radioactive substances and pollution prevention and control. New regulations will be made under s. 18 of the Regulatory Reform (Scotland) Act 2014. At the time of writing (March 2019) regulations have been made only in relation to radioactive substances.

Essential Facts

- The Pollution Prevention and Control Act 1999 creates a single unified pollution control regime. The Act is a framework Act which is 'fleshed-out' by the Pollution Prevention and Control (Scotland) Regulations 2012.
- The Regulations institute a system of permitting of installations.
- SEPA has sole responsibility for regulating both Part A and Part B processes in terms of the Regulations.

10 PLANNING AND POLLUTION CONTROL

INTRODUCTION

In this chapter, we turn our attention to the role played by town and country planning in regulating pollution. As far the control of the development of land is concerned, since 1947, under the Town and Country Planning (Scotland) Act, and its English counterpart, one has required planning permission from the state in order to develop land. Whereas these Acts vested overall responsibility for planning in central government, local planning authorities were given the responsibility of granting planning permission for particular projects. Indeed, this remains the current position. Town and country planning is a devolved function under the Scotland Act 1998. The role of both the Scottish government and also planning authorities is now discussed, with special reference to pollution control.

SCOTTISH GOVERNMENT PLANNING POLICY

The main function performed by the Scottish government in relation to planning, is the formulation of national planning policy. The Scottish government sets out its planning policies in the National Planning Framework and also in Scottish Planning Policy. The former sets out a special plan for Scotland, and sets out, in broad terms, how the Scottish ministers consider that the development of land could, and should, occur. The latter relates to national planning policy. The Scottish government also prepares circulars on planning. Circulars may give guidance on relevant legislation and the implications of court decisions. Planning advice notes give advice on good planning practice.

THE CONTROL OF DEVELOPMENT

When a planning authority is determining a planning application, the Town and Country Planning (Scotland) Act 1997 (the Act) (s, 37(2)) requires a planning authority to take into account the relevant development plan, insofar as that application is relevant to the plan and also to any other material considerations. However, the Act does not define the expression 'material considerations'. In the context of the relationship between planning and pollution control, first, one needs to consider whether a planning authority can legitimately take into account the potential negative impact of pollution from a proposed development? Secondly, if pollution from a proposed development is, indeed, a material consideration, to what extent, if any, can a planning authority take into account that the activity will be regulated by a different regulatory body (such as SEPA) under a separate regulatory regime?

These issues were discussed in the English Court of Appeal case of *Gateshead Metropolitan BC* v *Secretary of State for the Environment* [1995] Env LR 37. In that case, first, the court was required to decide whether the potential pollution from a proposed development ranked as a material consideration, and, secondly, what significance should be accorded to the regulatory regime which would come into effect after the plant became operational.

The Northumbrian Water Group (NWG) had submitted an outline planning application to Gateshead Metropolitan Borough Council (GMBC) for the construction and operation of a clinical waste incineration plant. Since the plant was a prescribed process in terms of the Environmental Protection Act 1990 (EPA), it was necessary for the prospective operators of the plant to obtain authorisation to carry on the process of incineration from HM Inspectorate of Pollution (HMIP) (now the Environment Agency), in addition to planning permission. Planning permission was refused by the planning authority on the ground that potential pollution from the incinerator would have a negative impact on the environment. NWG appealed to the Secretary of State against the decision. An enquiry into the appeal was heard. The inspector recommended that planning permission be refused. However, the Secretary of State disagreed with the inspector's recommendation. The Secretary of State took the view that concerns about atmospheric pollution could be satisfactorily addressed by HMIP (now the Environment Agency) in terms of the EPA regulatory regime. The former, therefore, granted outline planning permission, subject to conditions. GMBC applied to the High Court, under s. 288 of the Town and Country Planning Act 1990, for an order that the decision of the Secretary of State be quashed. However, the application was dismissed. GMBC then appealed to the Court of Appeal.

The key issue that the court was required to determine was whether the Secretary of State was entitled to decide that the controls under the EPA were adequate to deal with the concerns about air pollution from the plant, which had been raised by the Inspector. In dismissing the appeal, in a judgment which, with respect, lacks clarity, Glidewell LJ held (at [49]) that when the Secretary of State was determining the planning application, he could legitimately take into account the powers which the HMIP possessed under the EPA. His Lordship went on to conclude (at [50]) that the Secretary of State was justified in deciding that the issues which had been raised at the planning inquiry in relation to the atmospheric pollution from the plant could be addressed by the HMIP, and, furthermore, could also be dealt with adequately by that body. In the last analysis, the decision of the Secretary of State could not be impugned.

The inter-relationship between pollution, planning controls and the relevant regulatory pollution regime came to be discussed again in *R v Bolton MBC ex p Kirkman* [1998] JPL 787. In that case, the claimant (K) was a local resident. He applied for the judicial review of a decision by the defendant planning authority, namely, Bolton Metropolitan Borough Council (BMBC) to grant planning permission for the installation of a waste incinerator. K contended, *inter alia*, that when BMBC was determining the planning application it had failed to address potential pollution from the incinerator. At first instance, Carnwath J (as he then was) held (at [795]) that the impact of discharges from the incinerator ranked as a material consideration in terms of planning law. Furthermore, in considering that issue, BMBC was entitled to take into account the system of controls under the integrated pollution control regime (IPC) of the EPA, unless it appeared to the planning authority that the discharges in question would, or would probably be, unacceptable to the Environment Agency. It was, therefore, legitimate for BMBC to leave potential pollution from the waste incinerator to the Environment Agency.

Again, in *Hopkins Development Ltd v First Secretary of State and North Wiltshire DC* [2007] Env LR 14, the claimant (H) applied to the second defendant (NWDC) for planning permission in relation to the construction of a concrete plant. However, the second defendant failed to determine the application within the requisite period. H, therefore, appealed to the first defendant (FSS). NWDC argued that the proposed development would be contrary to existing planning policy, in that it would have a serious effect on the amenities of the area. The inspector refused the appeal on the basis that the development would have a detrimental effect on the amenity of local residencies and businesses due to a significant increase in dust, noise and visual intrusion. H challenged the decision under s. 288 of the Town and Country Planning Act 1990 on the ground, *inter alia*, that the relevant controls under the pollution prevention control regime would provide sufficient protection for those who might be affected by pollution from the plant.

In dismissing the appeal, the court endorsed the approach taken in both the *Gateshead* and *Bolton* cases (above) to the effect that the impact of air emissions from a proposed development could rank as a material consideration in terms of the Act. Furthermore, a planning authority could take into account the pollution control regime. However, in considering the issue of pollution, whereas the relevant planning authority could leave pollution control to the pollution control authorities, the planning authority was not, as a matter of law, obliged to do so. In the last analysis, the inspector was correct in focusing on whether the development itself was an acceptable use of the land and the impacts which it would have, rather than on the control of the processes or emissions themselves. He, therefore, acted in accordance with the law.

The above cases, of course, concern the relationship between the control of development and relevant pollution control regimes. However, to what extent, if any, do the legal duties which relate to the protection of the environment, on a more 'macro' level, which fall on central government, influence the manner in which such duties are exercised in terms of the planning regime? This question fell to be answered in *Shirley* v *Secretary of State for Communities and Local Government, Canterbury City Council and Corinthian Mountfield Ltd* [2018] EWCA Civ 22.

Here, a planning application had been made for the construction of 4,000 dwelling houses on a site that was situated within an air quality management area for which an air quality plan (AQP) had been established under Directive 2008/50/EU, Art. 23, and the Air Quality Standards Regulations 2010. Article 13 of the Directive required member states to ensure certain limit values in relation to ambient air for the protection of human health. The planning committee were advised that there were potential adverse impacts on local air quality during the construction phase of the proposed development. However, these effects would be temporary, and capable of mitigation.

In short, it was claimed on behalf of S that the requirements of the AQD mandated the Secretary of State to call in the planning application, for his own determination, under s. 77 of the Town and Country Planning Act 1990, on the ground that the issues which were raised were of national importance, and also concerned conflicts with the National Planning Framework.

However, this argument was rejected by Dove J, at first instance, who held that the scheme which was set out in the AQD did not impose any free-standing responsibility on the Secretary of State to take specific actions in relation to either permit or development consents. In short, the AQD did not require any additional action to be taken by the Secretary of State, apart from the preparation and implementation of an AQP. It followed, therefore, that there was no wider duty on the part of the Secretary of State, either under the AQD or under the 2010 Regulations, which required him to exercise his discretion under s. 77 of the 1990 Act to call-in the planning application for his own determination. In the last analysis, the decision on the part of the Secretary of State not to call in the application was, therefore, neither unlawful nor irrational.

Dove J's decision was upheld on appeal (see [2019] EWCA Civ 22).

PLANNING CONDITIONS

On granting planning permission, a planning authority can, *inter alia*, attach such conditions as it thinks fit: s. 37(1). Such powers can be used to reduce the potential negative impact of a proposed development, including reducing pollution from the relevant premises. Whilst a planning authority has fairly wide discretion as to both the nature and the content of a condition which it may impose on the grant of planning permission, such discretion is not unfettered. The limits of the powers of planning authorities in imposing planning conditions were delineated by the House of Lords in *Newbury DC* v *Secretary of State for the Environment* [1981] AC 578. The House held that for a planning condition to be *intra vires* and, therefore, valid, the relevant condition was required to be for a planning purpose, and not for any ulterior one; secondly, the condition was required to fairly and reasonably relate to the relevant development; and, finally, the condition was required not to be so unreasonable that no reasonable planning authority could have imposed the condition.

The requirements which were set out in *Newbury* were applied by the Inner House in *British Airports Authority* v *Secretary of State for Scotland* 1979 SC 200. In that case, the British Airports Authority (BAA) applied to the planning authority, namely, Aberdeen County Council (ACC) to carry out certain developments at Aberdeen Airport. The developments included the erection of a new terminal building, and also a new aircraft apron. The Secretary of State confirmed the grant of planning permission by the planning authority, subject to two conditions, which were designed to restrict the operational hours at the airport, and also to regulate the direction of both take-offs and landings of aircraft at the airport. Both conditions were imposed in order to reduce the potential noise impact from the premises.

An application for planning permission had also been made by British Airways Helicopters Ltd (BAHL) for the erection of a one-storey building, in order to provide an office for its flight operations at the terminal. In that case, planning permission had been granted to BAHL, subject, *inter alia*, to a condition which was designed to restrict its operational hours at the terminal.

Bristow Helicopters Ltd (BH) had also applied for planning permission to build an extension to its terminal building at the airport, in order to provide freight-handling facilities and additional office accommodation. Again, ACC had attached a condition to the grant of planning permission which restricted BH's operational hours at the terminal.

As far as the appeal by BAA was concerned, the Lord President (Emslie) held (at [212]) that there was a close relationship between the permitted development and future noise levels. It, therefore, followed that the conditions which ACC had imposed in order to control the potential noise impact from the future use of the runway, were fairly and reasonably related to that development.

However, as far as the conditions which sought to regulate the direction of take-offs and landings from the airport were concerned, the power to regulate both the take-offs and landings from the airport fell to be regulated not by the Secretary of State but, rather, by the Civil Aviation Authority. It, therefore, automatically followed that the conditions were incapable of enforcement, and also were *ultra vires*.

As far as the appeal by BAHL was concerned, the Inner House held that the condition which related to its operational hours was *ultra vires* on two grounds; first, that the permitted development had no connection with the helicopter operations at the airport, on the basis that no flying of helicopters took place on land which was occupied by BAHL. That is to say, that the flying of all aircraft took place from any land which was occupied by the BAA. Secondly, it followed that the imposition of the condition was unnecessary, that is to say, operational hours at the airport fell to be regulated by the relevant valid planning condition which had been imposed on BAA.

In the case of the BH appeal, it was held that BH's proposed development had no connection with BH's helicopter operations at the airport. It, therefore, followed that any conditions, the aim of which were to restrict operational hours from the proposed development, were *ultra vires*.

PLANNING CONTROL AND HAZARDOUS SUBSTANCES

Because of their very nature, substances which are hazardous require special controls in order to ensure that the presence of such substances on land does not pose a potential danger to either human health or the environment. However, in a work of this nature, these controls can only be briefly discussed.

The Planning (Hazardous Substances) (Scotland) Act 1997 (the Act) places a duty on a planning authority to control hazardous substances:

s. 1. Subject to certain exceptions, the presence of a hazardous substance, which is either on, over or under any land, requires the consent of the planning authority (that is, hazardous substances consent). The Town and Country Planning (Hazardous Substances) (Scotland) Regulations 2015 (SSI 2015 No. 181) specify which substances rank as hazardous for the purposes of the Act, and also the relevant quantity which falls to be controlled: Reg. 3(1)(2).

ENVIRONMENTAL IMPACT ASSESSMENT

We now turn our attention to the subject of environmental impact assessment (EIA), which is a key legal mechanism that has emerged in the last thirty years. EIA enables decision-makers (which are mainly planning authorities, as far as Scotland is concerned) to take account of the environmental impact of their decisions which relate to development control. In essence, the importance of EIA is that information concerning the likely environmental impacts of certain projects or developments, is fully considered before a decision is taken as to whether or not the relevant project or development should proceed. However, the importance of EIA is not simply confined to the benefit of the developer and the relevant planning authority. That is to say, the EIA process conduces to transparency on the part of actions which are taken by decision-makers, and also increases the opportunity for the public to participate in the planning process.

EIA DIRECTIVE AND ITS IMPLEMENTATION IN SCOTLAND

As far as Scotland (and indeed the UK as a whole) is concerned, EIA is largely driven, and also shaped, by EU policy. Directive 85/337/EEC (which had a relatively long period of gestation) was amended several times, and was codified in 2011 by Directive 2011/92/EU, which, in turn, was amended by Directive 2014/52/EU. The preamble to the 2011 Directive (the Directive) states that EU environmental policy is based on the precautionary principle, and also on the principle that environmental damage should, as a priority, be rectified at source, and also that the polluter should pay. The preamble further provides that the effects on the environment should be taken account, at the earliest possible stage, in all technical planning decision-making processes.

Article 2 requires that member states adopt all measures which are necessary to ensure that before consent (that is, development consent) is given, projects which are likely to have significant effects on the environment by virtue, *inter alia*, of their nature, size or location are made subject to both a requirement for development consent and also an assessment with regard to their effects on the environment. Importantly, Article 2 goes on to provide that EIA may be integrated into the existing procedures for development consent to projects in member states.

What is a project?

Article 1 of the Directive defines a project as either the execution of construction works, or other installations or schemes, or other interventions in the natural surroundings and landscape, including those involving the extraction of mineral resources. Normally, to be classed as a project, some form of construction or physical intervention is required: *Brussels Hoofdstedilijk Gewest* v *Vlaams Gewest* [2011] Env LR 26.

A potential difficulty that arises when determining whether any proposal for the development consent of a project requires an environmental impact assessment is whether the project is simply part of a larger project. For example, whereas a relatively small project, when viewed in isolation, may not require an environmental impact assessment, the project may, however, when considered, *in toto*, would, indeed, constitute a project which falls within the scope of the Directive, and therefore require an EIA. In essence, what is at issue here is what has been (rather infelicitously, in the author's view) described as 'salami-slicing', that is to say, the splitting of a large development project into smaller units which, if considered individually, would not fall within the thresholds which would require an EIA. For example, in *Commission* v *Spain* Case C-227/01; [2005] Env LR 20, the Court of Justice held that a relatively short section of a long-distance railway line was simply part of a larger project and, therefore, the former fell within Annex 1 of the Directive (see below). Therefore, an EIA was required to be carried out.

Generally, a project that falls within the scope of the Directive will fall within the definition of 'development' in terms of the Town and Country Planning (Scotland) Act 1997 and, therefore, be subject to planning control. In such cases, the EIA process is governed by the regulations which we now discuss. However, projects which do not fall within the scope of the 1997 Act fall to be regulated by separate legislation which incorporates EIA procedure. However, lack of space precludes discussion of such legislation.

THE TOWN AND COUNTRY PLANNING (ENVIRONMENTAL IMPACT ASSESSMENT) (SCOTLAND) REGULATIONS 2017 (SSI 2017 NO. 102)

Directive 2011/92/EU (as amended) is implemented in Scotland by the Town and Country Planning (Environmental Impact Assessment)

PLANNING AND POLLUTION CONTROL 161

(Scotland) Regulations 2017 (SSI 2017 No. 102) (the Regulations). It should be observed at the outset that, in contrast to the Directive, the Regulations do not employ the expression 'project' in terms of environmental impact assessment. In contrast, the Regulations use the term 'development' in terms of what falls to be regulated by the planning regime.

The Regulations prohibit either a planning authority or the Scottish ministers from granting planning permission for an EIA development unless an environmental impact assessment has been carried out in respect of that development, and, in carrying out such assessment, the planning authority (or the Scottish ministers, as the case may be) are required to take environmental information (as defined in Reg. 2(1)) into account: Reg. 3. An EIA development is defined as a development which is either a Schedule 1 development, or a Schedule 2 development which is likely to have a significant effect on the environment by virtue of factors such as its nature, size or location: Reg. 2(1).

The expression 'environmental impact assessment' is a term of art (a technical term) which is defined in the Regulations, as a process consisting of, *inter alia*:

(i) the preparation of an EIA report by the developer;

(ii) the carrying out of relevant consultation and notification;

(iii) the examination by the planning authority or the Scottish ministers of the information which is presented in the EIA report, and any other environmental information;

(iv) the reasoned conclusion by the planning authority (or the Scottish ministers, as the case may be) on the significant effects of the development on the environment, taking into account the results of the examination; and

(v) the integration of that reasoned conclusion in the relevant decision notice that is given to the developer.

The EIA is required to identify, describe and assess both the direct and also indirect significant effects of the proposed development on certain factors, and also the interaction between those factors: Reg. 4(2). Such factors include population and human health, biodiversity, protected habitats and species, land, soil, water, air and climate: Reg. 4(3). Subject to certain exceptions, the EIA, which is to be carried out in relation to the determination of an application for planning permission for an EIA development, must identify the significant effects of the proposed development on the environment before a decision to grant planning permission is made for that development: Reg. 4(5).

Schedule 1 development

Schedule 1 of the Regulations implements Annex 1 of the Directive. Schedule 1 includes twenty-three different categories of development, including airports, nuclear power stations and steelworks. For such developments, an EIA is mandatory unless the development ranks as an exempt development (that is, exempted by the Scottish ministers under Reg. 6 (4)(6)) in terms of the Regulations: Regs 2(1) and 3. Almost exclusively, each category in Schedule 1 has its own threshold by means of which one determines whether the development ranks as a Schedule 1. Whereas some thresholds take the form of the size of the development, other thresholds are 'triggered' by the output of the relevant development. Furthermore, any change to a Schedule 1 development also ranks as such a development, provided that such a change, in itself, meets the relevant threshold, if any, of the development: Sch. 1, para. 24.

Schedule 2 development

Generally speaking, a Schedule 2 development is one that is likely to have a lesser environmental impact than a Schedule 1 development. Examples of Schedule 2 developments include intensive fish farming, drilling for water supplies, brewing and malting. In determining whether any development is to be classified as a Schedule 2 development, the planning authority or the Scottish ministers are required to take into account relevant criteria (which are specified in Sch. 3), which consist of the characteristics and the location of the development, the characteristics of the potential impact of the development, in addition to the information which is provided by the developer in terms of the Regulations: Reg. 7(1). However, a planning authority has wide discretion as to whether or not a Schedule 2 development is an EIA development. In effect, the courts will only intervene and quash a decision taken by a planning authority whether an EIA is required, if no reasonable planning authority could have made that decision. In other words, the relevant decision can only be overturned on *Wednesbury* grounds: *R (Malster)* v *Ipswich BC* [2002] Env LR D7. The rationale for this approach is that planning authorities are more suited than judges to evaluate the potential environmental impact of a project: *R (Jones)* v *Mansfield District Council* [2004] Env LR 21 (*per* Carnwath LJ at [61]). Again, in *R (Loader)* v *Secretary of State for Communities and Local Government* [2012] Env LR 8 at [37], Lloyd J stated that the question as to whether a development would have significant effects on the environment was pre-eminently a matter for expert judgement in the context of the particular case.

However, it should be stressed at this juncture that neither the EIA Directive nor the Regulations define the term 'environment'. In *Malster* it was held that in determining whether a particular proposed development had a significant effect on the environment, the planning authority was not obliged to set store by the 'shadowing' effect of the development on nearby houses. The court held that there might be significant impact on a particular dwelling, or dwellings, without any likely significant effect on the environment for the purposes of the EIA Regulations. *Malster* is also authority for the proposition that a planning authority has wide discretion as to the meaning of 'environment' in the terms of the Regulations.

To what extent, if any, can a planning authority, in determining whether any proposed development is likely to have a significant effect on the environment, legitimately take into account mitigation measures which the developer proposes? In the Court of Appeal case of *Gillespie v First Secretary of State* [2003] Env LR 30, which concerned a proposed redevelopment of a former gasworks, it was held that when a planning authority was considering whether a development would have a significant effect on the environment (at [36]) the authority was not obliged to ignore remedial measures which were submitted as part of the relevant planning application. Again, in *R (Treagus) v Suffolk CC* [2013] Env LR 36, it was held lawful for a planning authority, in determining if the relevant development would have a significant effect on the environment, to take into account the fact that any pollution from the proposed development could be effectively controlled by the Environment Agency, in terms of the relevant pollution permitting regime.

Screening opinion

A developer may request a planning authority to adopt what is termed a 'screening opinion' as to whether an EIA is required for the relevant development: Reg. 8(1). The request must be accompanied by information that includes a description of the aspects of the environment which are likely to be significantly affected by the proposed development: Reg. 8(2)(c). A planning authority that receives such a request is required (unless a screening direction is made by the Scottish ministers) to adopt a screening opinion within three weeks (or such longer period, not exceeding ninety days, as is agreed between the parties): Reg. 9(1).

Where it appears to the planning authority that a planning application relates either to a Schedule 1 or a Schedule 2 development, and that the development in question has not been subject to either a screening opinion or a screening direction, and that application is not accompanied by an EIA report, the application falls to be treated as a request for a screening opinion: Reg. 11.

The screening process takes place at a relatively early stage of the planning process, the upshot of which is that there may be some uncertainty about the full possible potential environmental impact of the development. However, the screening opinion must be based on sufficient information to allow the planning authority to make an informed decision as to whether the development will have a significant effect on the environment: *R (Cooperative Group Ltd) v Northumberland CC* [2010] Env LR 40. However, a planning authority can adopt a screening opinion, notwithstanding the fact that its decision is based on less than complete information: *R (Bateman) v Cambridgeshire DC* [2011] EWCA Civ 157. In that case, Bick-Moore LJ stated (at [20]) that a screening assessment was not intended to involve a detailed assessment of the factors which were relevant to the grant of planning permission. This came later in the planning process. Screening assessment did not, therefore, involve a full assessment of any identifiable environmental effects. His Lordship added that the screening decision was often, inevitably, based on less than complete information. Furthermore, in *R (Thakeham Village Action Ltd) v Horsham DC* [2014] Env LR 21 (*per* Lindblom J at [29]) it was stated that a planning authority was not bound to require an EIA, notwithstanding that there was some uncertainty about the likely effects of the development at the time the authority adopted the relevant screening opinion. The point that a screening decision need not involve a rigorous assessment by the planning authority was succinctly expressed by Beatson J in *Zeb v Birmingham City Council* [2010] Env LR 30, at [25], where his Lordship stated that detailed reports were not required. What was required was an initial assessment of an intended proposal.

In *R (Birchall Gardens LLP) v Hertfordshire CC* [2017] Env LR 17, at [66], Dove J reiterated the point that had been made in *Bateman* to the effect that, in determining whether a planning authority had sufficient information before it to lawfully make a screening decision, the court should not impose too high a burden on planning authorities. His Lordship went on to add (at [67]) that whether there was sufficient information before the planning authority for them to issue a screening opinion, and whether a development was likely to have significant environmental effects, were both matters of judgement for the planning authority, and such decisions could be challenged only on the grounds of irrationality or other public law error.

Where a planning authority fails to adopt a screening opinion within the relevant period, or to adopt an opinion that the development is an

EIA development, the developer may request the Scottish ministers to make a screening direction: Reg. 9(5).

Where a planning authority adopts a screening opinion, or the Scottish ministers make a screening direction, the relevant opinion or direction is required to be accompanied by a written statement giving, with reference to Schedule 3, the main reasons for their conclusions that the development is, or is not, an EIA development: Reg. 7(2). Where the screening opinion or the screening direction is to the effect that the development is not an EIA development, the statement is required to state any features of the proposed development or proposed measures which are envisaged to avoid or prevent significant adverse effects on the environment.

In the Court of Appeal case of *R (Bateman)* v *South Cambridgeshire DC* [2011] EWCA Civ 157 (*per* Moore-Bick LJ, at [21]), it was held that when adopting a screening opinion, the planning authority must provide sufficient information to enable anyone who is interested in the decision to see that proper consideration has been given to the possible environmental effects of the development, and to understand the reasons for the decision.

Whereas the planning authority is not required to set out at length in its screening opinion the considerations which it has taken into account, the essence of its reasoning must be plain: *R (Thakeham Village Action Ltd)* v *Horsham DC* [2014] Env LR 21 (*per* Lindblom J, at [28]). In the Court of Appeal case of *R (Friends of Basildon Golf Course)* v *Basildon DC* [2011] Env LR 16 (*per* Pill LJ, at [62]), it was held that a screening opinion is required to be based on information that is both sufficient and accurate. Whereas the opinion need not be elaborate, the opinion is required to demonstrate that the relevant issues have been understood and considered. Finally, in *Birchall Gardens* (at [84]), Dove J held that the level of detail that was required in a screening opinion depended on the complexity, or otherwise, of the relevant issues which fell to be considered. His Lordship went on to emphasise that, in issuing a screening opinion, the planning authority was not issuing a decision letter in a planning appeal. Rather, in issuing a screening opinion, the planning authority was issuing a screening opinion for a narrower purpose.

The planning authority is required to send a copy of the screening opinion and the written statement to the developer as soon as possible after the former has adopted a screening opinion: Reg. 7(3).

Environmental impact assessment report

An application for an EIA development must be accompanied by an environmental impact assessment report (EIA report): Reg. 5(1). An EIA report is simply a report that is prepared by the developer by means of which one can assess the environmental effects of a project. Whereas the Regulations do not prescribe the precise form which the EIA report should take, it is required to contain certain information, including a description of the likely significant effects of the development on the environment; a description of the features of the development; any relevant mitigation measures; a description of reasonable alternatives; a non-technical summary of the information which the developer has collated; and any other information specified in Schedule 4 that is relevant to the specific characteristics of the development, and also to the environmental features which are likely to be affected: Reg. 5(2). Where a scoping opinion or scoping direction (see below) has been issued, the EIA report must be based on that scoping opinion or scoping direction: Reg. 5(3). With a view to avoiding the duplication of assessments, account is to be taken of the available results of other assessments in preparing the EIA report: Reg. 5(4). The developer is also required to ensure that the EIA report is prepared by competent experts: Reg. 5(5).

In *Berkeley* v *Secretary of State for the Environment* [2001] 2 AC 603, Lord Hoffmann stated (at 617) that an environmental statement (as it was then known) must comprise a single and accessible compilation (as opposed to a number of separate documents) which is produced by the applicant at the very start of the application process. However, the EIA is not required to contain detailed and exhaustive information of the potential environmental impact of a development. Moreover, the courts are prepared to allow any inadequacies and omissions (including apposite remedial or mitigation measures which may be required to be adopted in the future) in the EIA report to be addressed by the planning authority in the publicity and consultation process which is incorporated in the EIA Regulations as a whole. In *R (Blewett)* v *Derbyshire CC* [2004] Env LR 29, Sullivan J emphasised (at [68]) that the EIA process was designed to identify any deficiencies in the EIA report, so that the planning authority has the 'full picture' when it comes to consider the 'environmental information' of which the environmental statement will be but a part.

The courts accord planning authorities wide discretion as to the content of an EIA report. In *Kent* v *First Secretary of State* 2005 Env LR 30, the claimant was an objector to a proposed waste development. The First Secretary had called in the relevant planning application, and had granted planning permission for the development. The claimant claimed, *inter alia*, that the hazardous waste which was to be dumped on the site was not described with sufficient particularity in the relevant environmental statement. It was further claimed that the environmental statement was defective, in that it had not included a quantitative risk assessment. However, it was held (at [76]) that, whereas an environmental statement was required to contain sufficient information to allow a planning authority to make an informed judgement as to whether a development would have a significant effect on the environment, it fell to the relevant planning authority to decide if the information in the environmental statement was sufficient for this purpose, subject to review on *Wednesbury* grounds.

Scoping opinion

A developer who intends to make an EIA application can request that the planning authority adopts a scoping opinion: Reg. 17(1). A scoping opinion is defined as an opinion of the planning authority as to the scope and level of detail of information which is to be provided in an EIA report: Reg. 2(1). The planning authority has five weeks to adopt a scoping opinion, or such longer time as may be agreed with the developer: Reg. 17(7). Where a planning authority fails to adopt a scoping opinion, the developer may request the Scottish ministers to make a scoping direction: Reg. 17(8).

Environmental impact reports and publicity, consultation, etc.

Where an EIA report is submitted to either a planning authority or the Scottish ministers, either are required to publish a notice in accordance with the Regulations: Reg. 21(1). The notice is required to give details, *inter alia*, as to how representations may be made, and also details for the arrangements for public participation: Reg. 21(2). Furthermore, copies of the EIA report are required to be made available for inspection on the planning authority application website: Reg. 21(5). The planning authority is required to send copies of the EIA report to both the Scottish ministers and also to the bodies with whom the former is required to consult: Reg. 21(1).

STRATEGIC ENVIRONMENTAL ASSESSMENT

Essentially, a strategic environmental assessment (SEA) is an assessment of the potential environmental impacts of plans and programmes on the environment by competent authorities. Speaking generally, whereas environmental impact assessment (EIA) operates at a micro level, a SEA operates at a macro level. In common with the EIA, the SEA is purely procedural in nature. However, both regimes are largely complimentary.

The purpose of an SEA is to prevent major effects on the environment being predetermined by earlier planning measures before the EIA stage is reached.

THE SEA DIRECTIVE 2001/42/EC

In common with the EIA, SEA is EU-driven. An important feature of the SEA Directive 2001/42/EC (the Directive) is the precautionary principle: Preamble. A principal objective of the Directive is to contribute to the integration of environmental considerations into the preparation and adoption of plans and programmes, with a view to promoting sustainable development by ensuring that an environmental assessment is carried out in respect of plans and programmes which are likely to have significant effects on the environment. In essence, the purpose of the SEA is to prevent major effects on the environment being predetermined by earlier planning measures before the EIA stage is reached: *R (Buckinghamshire CC)* v *Secretary of State for Transport* [2014] 1 WLR 324, at 339 (*per* Lord Carnwath).

Scope of the SEA

It is mandatory for an environmental assessment (EA) to be carried out for all plans and programmes which are prepared for agriculture, forestry, fisheries, energy, industry, transport, waste management, water management, telecommunications, tourism, town and country planning or land use, and which set the framework for projects for which an EIA is required or, which in view of the likely effect on sites, is likely to require an assessment in terms of Articles 6 or 7 of the Habitats Directive: Art. 3. The SEA Directive, therefore, makes an important link between SEA and EIA. The criteria which are required to be taken into account in determining whether the plan or programme will have a significant effect on the environment are set out in Annex II to the Directive, and include having regard, in particular, to the probability, duration, frequency and reversibility of the effects, the risks to human health or the environment, and special natural characteristics or cultural heritage. However, plans and programmes which determine the use of small areas at local level, and minor modifications to plans and programmes, require an EA only if they are likely to have significant environmental effects.

The SEA is required to be carried out during the preparation of the plan or programme, and before its adoption or submission to the relevant legislative procedure: Art. 4.

Meaning of 'plans and programmes'

'Plans and programmes' (as well as any modifications to them) are defined as those which are prepared and/or adopted by an authority at both national, regional or local level, or which are prepared for adoption through a legislative procedure by Parliament or government, and are required by legislative, regulatory or administrative provisions: Art. 2. In *Inter-Environment Bruxelles ASBL* v *Region de Bruxelles-Capitale* Case 567/10; [2012] Env LR 30, it was held that for a plan or programme to fall within the scope of the Directive, the relevant plan was not required to be either mandatory or compulsory. Furthermore, a procedure for the partial or total repeal of a programme also fell within the scope of the Directive. An example of a plan or programme that would fall within the scope of the Directive would be the National Planning Framework, which the Scottish ministers are required to prepare under the Town and Country Planning (Scotland) Act 1997: s. 3A. In *Cala Homes (South) Ltd* v *Secretary of State for Communities and Local Government* [2010] EWHC 97, it was held that the revocation of regional strategies, which were development plans set at a regional level, in order to assist in the implementation of planning policies and in the taking of planning decisions fell within the scope of the Directive.

The issue as to what constitutes a plan or programme which falls within the scope of the Directive was considered by the Supreme Court in *Walton* v *The Scottish Ministers* 2013 SC (UKSC) 67. The case concerned a challenge to the Aberdeen Western Peripheral Route (AWPR). Proposals for a western peripheral route around Aberdeen had been in existence since the 1950s. The factual background to the case was that in 2001 a non-statutory regional transport partnership, known as the North East Scotland Transport Partnership (NESTRANS), was established with support from the Scottish ministers. Its remit was to develop a regional transport strategy for the northeast of Scotland. NESTRANS membership included relevant local authorities and also Scottish Enterprise. The regional transport strategy, which was developed to cover the period to 2011, was described in a NESTRANS report published in 2003. That strategy was described as the Modern Transport System (or MTS). It comprised the local transport strategies which had been adopted by the two relevant roads authorities. Numerous schemes were described and costed in the report. One scheme included the AWPR. In 2003, the Minister for Transport announced that the AWPR would be promoted by the Scottish ministers as a trunk road. However, in 2004, in the face of a campaign against the routing of the AWPR along a certain 'corridor', the minister instructed that work on that corridor should be reviewed, and also that four other options should be re-examined. In 2005, the minister announced that the route would comprise a 'hybrid route' (the Fastlink), that is to say, a route that differed from the options that had previously been considered in the earlier consultation exercise in that it broadly comprised the whole of one option and part of another. In 2006, draft trunk road schemes, *inter alia*, under s. 7 of the Roads (Scotland) Act 1984, together with an EIA, were published. Objections were made to the proposed Fastlink. One objection included a letter from Walton (W), the pursuer. A public inquiry was held. However, its remit was confined to technical and environmental issues. W argued that the Fastlink element of the scheme had been adopted without the public consultation which was required by the SEA Directive.

The Supreme Court reserved its opinion as to whether the MTS or its associated strategies constituted a plan or programme which fell within the scope of the Directive. However, the court held that the decision to construct Fastlink was not the modification of a plan or programme, since the decision was taken by the Scottish ministers in the course of executing a specific project and related solely to that project. In the view of the Court, the ministers did not take the decision to modify the MTS, or otherwise set a legal or administrative framework, for the future development consent of projects. Furthermore, the relevant decision was implemented in accordance with the procedures which were laid down for specific road projects in the 1984 Act. Lord Carnwath stated *obiter* (at [99]) that, given the relatively informal character of the NESTRANS exercise, the MTS lacked the requisite formality to rank as a plan or programme that fell within the scope of the Directive. See also *R (Berks, Bucks and Oxon Wildlife Trust) v SoS for Transport* [2019] EWHC 1786.

The Supreme Court had another opportunity to determine the meaning of the expression 'plan or programme' in terms of the Directive in *R (Buckinghamshire CC) v Secretary of State for Transport* [2014] 1 WLR 324. In 2012, the Secretary of State for Transport published a Command Paper, titled 'High Speed Rail: Investing in Britain's Future – Decisions and Next Steps' (Cmnd. 8274) (DNS), which set out the government's strategy for the development of High Speed Two (HS2) – a high-speed national rail network from London to Birmingham, Manchester and Leeds. One of the issues which fell to be decided by the Court was whether the DNS constituted a plan or programme within the meaning of the Directive.

Lord Carnwath, who gave the main judgment, was prepared to accept, *obiter* (at 334), the proposition that the DNS could rank as a plan or programme which fell within the scope of the Directive. However, his Lordship concluded (at 339) that, since the DNS did not constrain the decision-making process of the authority responsible (that is, Parliament), the DNS fell out-with the scope of the Directive.

For Lord Sumption (who tacitly accepted (at 360) that the DNS was a plan or programme which fell within the scope of the Directive), the DNS was 'simply a proposal' which did not constrain the discretion of Parliament (at 361).

In *Friends of the Earth Ltd* v *Secretary of State for Housing, Communities and Local Government* [2019] EWHC 518, the court was required to determine whether the revised National Planning Policy Framework (NPPF), which was published in 2018, required a strategic environmental assessment, on the ground that it constituted a plan or programme which fell within the scope of the Directive. Dove J held that, given that the fact that the NPPF is a voluntary measure, which was not produced as a result of any legislative or administrative provisions which regulate or determine the procedure for preparing or adopting it, the NPPF did not fall within the scope of the Directive.

Environmental Report

Where a SEA is required, an environmental report must be prepared: Art. 5. The environmental report is required to identify, describe and evaluate the likely significant effects on the environment of implementing the plan or programme (together with reasonable alternatives), taking into account the objectives and geographical scope of the plan and programme. In *R (Friends of the Earth, England, Wales and Northern Ireland Ltd)* v *The Welsh Ministers* [2016] Env LR 1, at [88] (*per* Hickinbottom J), it was held that the expression 'reasonable alternatives' did not include all possible alternatives. It required an evaluative judgement as to which alternatives should be included. That was a matter for the decision-maker, which was subject to challenge only on public law grounds.

The report is also required to include the information which may be reasonably required, taking into account current knowledge and methods of assessment, the contents and level of detail in the plan or programme, its stage in the decision-making process, and the extent to which certain matters are more appropriately assessed at different levels in that process, in order to avoid duplication of the assessment. The information required to be provided in the report is contained in Annex 1 to the Directive. The environmental report must include a non-technical summary. In the recent case of *Spurrier* v *Secretary of State for Transport* [2019] EWHC 1070, at [433], it was held that the information which was required to be included in the report was a matter for the judgement of the authority preparing the plan or programme. Such a judgement was a matter for evaluative assessment of the authority subject only to review on normal public law principles, including *Wednesbury* unreasonableness.

SEA and Scotland

The 2001 Directive is implemented in Scotland by the Environmental Assessment (Scotland) Act 2005 (the Act). The SEA regime is similar to the EIA regime, which has already been discussed in this chapter. The Act requires a 'responsible authority' to conduct an environmental assessment during the preparation of a new qualifying plan or programme: s. 1(1). The expression, 'responsible authority' is defined as any person, body or office-holder exercising functions of a public character: s. 2(1). The Act applies to plans and programmes, which are subject to preparation or adoption by a public body, (whether at national, regional or local level), and includes modifications to such plans or programmes: s. 4(1)(2). However, a qualifying plan or programme is only such, to the extent that it relates to matters of a public character: s. 5(2). A qualifying plan or programme is a plan or programme that is required by a legislative, regulatory or legislative provision, and that is prepared for agriculture, forestry, fisheries, energy, industry, transport, waste management, water management, telecommunications, tourism, town and county planning or land use, and, importantly, sets the framework for future development consent in relation to projects which are listed in Schedule 1 of the Act: s. 5(3). Schedule 1 contains a list of activities, including crude oil refineries, thermal power stations, nuclear power stations, lines for long-distance railway traffic and waste disposal installations. A SEA is also required if, in view of the likely effect on sites, an assessment under the Habitats Directive is necessary, or it does not fall within the aforementioned categories but, nonetheless, sets the framework for future development consents of projects: s. 5(3)(c). The Act also makes provision for the inclusion of additional plans and programmes within the meaning of 'qualifying plan or programme': s. 5(4). The Act gives the Scottish ministers the power to modify Schedule 1: s. 5(5).

The Act makes provision for the exclusion of certain plans and programmes: ss. 5(4), 6(1). A plan or programme that relates to an individual school is exempt from the requirement to have an EA. The Scottish ministers may, by order, also exempt a plan or programme from the requirement to have an EA if it is considered that the plan or programme will have no, or minimal, effect on the environment: s. 6(3).

Exemptions: pre-screening

A plan and programme that falls out-with the scope of the SEA Directive is required to be pre-screened by the responsible authority, in order to ascertain whether the plan or programme will either have no, or minimal, impact on the environment: s. 7(1). In making such a determination, the responsible authority is required to apply the criteria which are set out in Schedule 2: s. 7(2). If it is determined that the plan or programme will have no such impact, the responsible authority is required to inform the consultation authorities of that fact: s. 7(3). The Scottish ministers are required to keep a register of any such notifications: s. 7(5). The register must be available for public inspection: s. 7(6).

Exemptions: screening

A responsible authority is required to determine whether or not:

(a) a plan or programme of a description set out in s. 5(3) that determines the use of small areas at local levels;

(b) a minor modification to a plan or programme of a description set out in s. 5(3);

(c) a plan or programme of a description set out in s. 5(3)(c);

(d) a plan or programme of the description set out in s. 5(4) which is not exempt by virtue of s7(1), is likely to have significant environmental effects: s. 8(1).

In making such a determination, the responsible authority is required to apply the criteria specified in Schedule 2: s. 8(3). If the responsible authority decides that a plan or programme is unlikely to have significant environmental effects, and, therefore, that the relevant plan or programme is exempt from the requirement to be subject to an EA, the responsible authority is required to prepare a statement of the reasons for its decision: s. 8(2).

Screening procedure

Before making a decision under s. 8(1), the responsible authority is required to prepare a summary of its views as to whether or not the plan or programme is likely to have significant environmental effects: s. 9(1). The summary is required to be sent to each consultation authority for its consideration: s. 9(2). If the responsible authority and the consultation authorities agree that the plan or programme is unlikely to have significant environmental effects or, alternately, that the plan or programme is likely to have environmental effects, the responsible authority is required to make a determination to that effect: s. 9(4)(5). In the event of the responsible authority and consultation authorities failing to reach an agreement, the responsible authority is required to refer the matter to the Scottish ministers: s. 9(6). In such circumstances, the Scottish ministers make the relevant determination. A determination by the Scottish ministers has similar effect to a determination made by a responsible authority: s. 9(7).

Screening publicity

The Act makes provision for the determination to be given publicity: s. 10.

Preparation of environmental report

The responsible authority is required to prepare an environmental report for any qualifying plan or programme: s. 14(1). The report is required to identify, describe, and evaluate, the likely significant effects on the environment of implementing the plan or programme, and also to identify reasonable alternatives to the plan or programme: s. 14(2). Schedule 3 specifies the information which is required to be included in the report: s. 14(3).

Scoping

Before deciding, *inter alia*, on the level of detail of the information which is to be included in an environmental report, the responsible authority is required to send each consultation authority such sufficient details of the qualifying plan or programme that will to allow the latter to form a view on those matters: s. 15(1). The responsible authority is required to take into account the views which the consultation authorities make: s. 15(3).

Consultation procedures etc.

The responsible authority is required to send a copy of the environmental report, and the plan or programme to which it relates, to each consultation authority and also invite comments on the relevant documents: s. 16(1). The responsible authority is also under a duty to publicise the relevant documents and also to invite comments on the documents: s. 16(2).

In preparation of the relevant plan or programme, the responsible authority is required to take account of the relevant environmental report, every opinion that is expressed on the environmental report, and the outcome of any relevant consultation under Regulation 14 of the Environmental Assessment of Plans and Programmes Regulations 2014 (SI 2014 No. 1633): s. 17.

After the relevant plan or programme has been adopted, the responsible authority is required to make the plan or programme and the environmental report available for public inspection, and also to publicise the plan or programme: s. 18(1).

Importantly, the responsible authority is placed under a duty to monitor the significant environmental effects of every qualifying plan or programme for which it has carried out an environmental assessment: s. 19.

Essential Facts

- A planning authority is required to treat the potential pollution from a proposed development as a material consideration when the planning authority is determining the relevant planning application.
- In granting planning permission for a proposed development, a planning authority can attach conditions to regulate pollution from the proposed development.
- The Town and Country Planning (Environmental Impact Assessment) (Scotland) Regulations 2017 (SSI 2017 No. 102) make provision for the EIA of certain developments which may have a negative impact on the environment.
- The Environmental Assessment (Scotland) Act 2005 makes provision for the strategic assessment of plans and programmes of a public character.

INDEX

abatement notices
  appeals, 30
  best practical means defence, 31
  clarity, 27
  conditions, 26
  construction sites, 31
  contents, 27–28
  failure to comply, 25, 30
  fixed penalties, 30
  local authority abatement
    proceedings, 31–32
  mandatory nature, 26
  persons on whom served, 28–29
    defaulters, 28
    failure to act, 29
    owners, 29
    structural defects, 29
  specification of measures, 27
  statutory nuisance, 26–33
  time for compliance, 28
  validity, 27–28
accumulations, 22, 23
acquiescence, 17–18
agriculture, SEAs, 168, 172
air pollution
  1993 Clean Air Act, 56–61
  ambient air quality, 62–71
    air quality plans, 64–68, 156
    Air Quality Strategy, 68
    clean air zones, 65–68
    EU regulation, 62–68, 156
    local authority review, 69
    local plans, 69
    SEPA powers, 70–71
  aviation, 72–73
  chimneys, 59
  development of regulation,
    55–56
  dust, 57–58
  EU regulation
    2005 Strategy, 62
    2008 Ambient Air Quality
      Directive, 63–68
    ambient air quality, 62–68
    NECD (2016), 63
  grit, 57–58
  history, 1
  investigation, 61
  major public health risk, 55
  overview, 55–75
  ozone depletion, 73–74
  planning control and, 154–156
  road vehicles, 71–72
  shipping, 73
  smoke *see* **smoke**
  sources, 1–2, 55, 62
aircraft *see* **aviation**
alkali, 1–2
Alkali Inspectorate, 55–56
animals
  noise, 39–40
  statutory nuisance, 24
anti-social behaviour, noise,
  40–43
appeals
  abatement notices, 27, 30
  chimney notices, 59
  construction site notices, 38, 39
  contaminated land remediation
    notices, 112–113

appeals *(cont.)*
  grit arrestment plants, 58
  integrated pollution, prevention and control, 148–149, 150
  Scottish Water directions, 132
  sewers
    compulsory acquisition, 134
    construction directions, 132
  trade effluent discharges, 135
  waste management licences, 87, 88, 89
  waste notices, 94
  water decisions, 126–127
aviation
  air pollution, 72–73
  noise
    airport noise, 51, 157–158
    EU regulation, 50–51
    flight noise, 50–51
    military aircraft, 51
    regulation, 49–51
  planning control, 157–158

best available techniques, 140, 142
best practical means defence
  abatement notices, 31
  grit and dust, 57
  statutory nuisance, 33
  water offences, 125
BREXIT, 5–6
bye-laws, 25, 84

cables, 61
cadmium, 97
Carson, Rachel, 4
Chicago Convention on International Civil Aviation (1944), 50
chimneys, 59
cholera, 3

civil aviation *see* **aviation**
Civil Aviation Authority, 50
clean air zones, 65–68
colliery spoil-banks, 61
common law nuisance
  defences, 7, 16–18
    acquiescence, 17–18
    prescription, 17
    statutory authority, 16, 52
  duration/intensity, 10–11
  fault requirement, 13
  liable persons, 14–15
    authors of nuisance, 14
    licensors, 15
    occupiers, 14–15
  limitations, 21
  locality and, 9–10
  motivation of defenders, 8–9
  negligence, 19–20
  noise, 35–36
  outside premises, 23
  oversensitivity and, 11–12
  overview, 7–19
  planning permissions and, 10
  preventive measures, 12
  proprietary interest requirement, 14, 21
  remedies, 18–19
  social utility and, 8, 12
  statutory nuisance and, 23
  time of day and, 11
  unreasonable conduct, 8–13
  water, 118–119
construction sites, noise, 31, 37–39
contaminated land
  common law, 101–102
  definition, 102–103
  duty of care, 101–102
  enforcing authorities, 104
  identification, 103–104

ministerial guidance, 114
negligence, 19
non-contamination notices, 113
notification, 103–104
   appropriate persons, 103–104
overview, 101–115
pollution of neighbouring land, 111–112
registration, 113
remediation, 105–106
   appeal against notices, 112–113
   appropriate persons, 106–108
   compensation, 109
   consents, 109
   consultation, 109
   by local authorities, 111
   neighbouring land, 111–112
   non-compliance, 113
   notice restrictions, 109–110
SEPA guidance, 114
SEPA reports, 114
sources of contamination, 101
special sites, 104–105
statutory nuisance, 25, 103
statutory regime, 102–114
   assessment, 114
surveying, 101
water pollution, liability, 110–111
culpa, 13, 19

damages, nuisance, 18
deposits, statutory nuisance, 23
devolution
   air quality policy, 68
   environmental issues, 6
diseases, history, 3
drains, meaning, 128
dust, 23, 57

end-of-life vehicles, 97–98
energy, SEAs, 168, 172
enforcement issues, 5
entry powers, noise, 40, 42–43
environmental impact assessments
   2017 Regulations, 160–167
   contents, 161
   definition, 161
   EIA Directive, 159–160
   importance, 159
   overview, 159–167
   projects, 160, 161
   publicity, 167
   reports, 161, 165–167
   Schedule 1 developments, 161, 162
   Schedule 2 developments, 161, 162–163
   scoping directions, 166, 167
   scoping opinions, 166, 167
   screening directions, 165
   screening opinions, 163–165
   SEAs and, 167–168
   transparency, 159
environmental legislation
   see also specific areas of regulation
   development, 1–6
   piece-meal development, 137
European Aviation Safety Agency (EASA), 50–51, 72
European Convention on Human Rights
   family and privacy rights, 43–48
   margins of appreciation, 44
   noise and, 43–48
   property rights, 43–44
European Environment Agency, 5

European Union
air pollution
2005 Strategy, 62
2008 Ambient Air Quality Directive, 63–68, 156
ambient air quality, 62–68, 156
NECD (2016), 63
regulatory model, 61
BREXIT, 5–6
Clean Air Programme (2013), 62
Environmental Action Programme (2001), 49
environmental impact assessments, 159–160, 162
environmental regulation, 5
Habitats Directive, 172
Industrial Emissions Directive, 138, 142, 143
institutions, 5
IPPC Directive, 138
Montreal Protocol and, 73
noise law, 48–49
civil aviation, 50–51
END Directive, 49
strategic environmental assessments, 168, 170, 171, 172
waste
definition, 77–82
electrical/electronic equipment, 98
end-of-life vehicles, 97
landfill, 89–90, 91
recycling, 96
Water Framework Directive, 119–120

family and privacy rights, noise and, 43–48
fault, nuisance and, 13, 19
fisheries, SEAs, 168, 172
fly-tipping, 82–84, 93–95
***force majeure* defence**, 125
forestry, SEAs, 168, 172
furnace smoke, 57–59

greenhouse gases, 71
grit, 57–58

Habitats Directive, 172
hazardous substances
planning control, 158–159
waste, 89, 90, 166–167
human rights, noise and ECHR, 43–48

Industrial Pollution Inspectorate, 5
Industrial Revolution, 1, 3, 55, 101
influenza, 3
insects, statutory nuisance, 24
integrated pollution, prevention and control
2012 Regulations, 138–151
appeals, 148–149
closure notices, 147, 148, 150
development, 138
enforcement notices, 145–146, 148
EU Directive, 138
ministerial directions, 148, 149–150
offences, 150–151
overview, 137–151
permits, 139–145
applications, 139–143
conditions, 140–141, 143, 150
emission limits, 141, 143
fits and proper persons, 139–140, 144

INDEX

principles, 140–141
review, 143
revocation, 144–145, 148
standard rules, 142–143
surrender, 143–144
transfers, 140, 143
variation, 143, 148
public registers, 150
substantive integration, 137
suspension notices, 146–148
interdicts, nuisance, 18–19
International Civil Aviation Organisation (ICAO), 50

landfill
allowance schemes, 91–92
classification, 89, 90–91
closure notices, 147, 148, 150
hazardous waste, 89, 90
inert waste, 89, 90
offences, 91
permits, 89–90
prior treatment, 90
regulation, 89–92
landlords, liability for nuisance, 15
lead, 97
licensing
licensors' liability in nuisance, 15
noise and, 43
waste management, 85–89
water use, 122
light pollution, 24
Lister, Joseph, 3
loudspeakers, noise, 39

measles, 3
mercury, 97
migration, 1
Montreal Protocol (1987), 73

motor vehicles *see* **road vehicles**
music, 40, 43

negligence
fault and, 13
nuisance and, 19–20
noise
abatement notices, 27, 30, 31
animals, 39–40
anti-social behaviour, 40–43
aviation, 49–51
  airports, 51
  EU law, 50–51
  flight noise, 50–51
  military aircraft, 51
common law nuisance, 35–36
construction sites, 31, 37–39
entry powers, 40, 42–43
EU law, 48–49
  civil aviation, 50–51
  END Directive, 49
health impact, 35
human rights law and, 43–48, 51
investigation, 41–42
landlords' liability, 15
loudspeakers, 39
musical entertainment, 43
musical instruments, 40
neighbourhood, 36–37
nuisance, 35
offences, 42
overview, 35–53
penalties, 42
planning and, 43, 157–158
pollution, 35
railways, 52
road traffic, 51–52
seizure of equipment, 42
sources, 48

noise (*cont.*)
  statutory nuisance, 24, 35, 36–43
  warning notices, 42
nuisance
  common law *see* **common law nuisance**
  statutory *see* **statutory nuisance**

occupiers
  liability for nuisance, 14–15
  statutory nuisance powers, 32
opus manufactum, 117–118
owners, abatement notices to, 29
ozone depletion, 73–74

packaging waste, 96–97
partnerships, offences, 91
Pasteur, Louis, 3
planning
  advice notes, 153
  circulars, 153
  conditions, 157–158
  development plans, 153
  EIAs *see* **environmental impact assessments**
  hazardous substances, 158–159
  IPPC permits and, 140
  material considerations, 153, 155
  noise and, 43
  nuisance and, 10
  policy, 153, 155, 156, 171
  pollution control and, 153–157
  SEAs *see* **strategic environmental assessments**
prescription, 17
privacy rights, 43–48
property rights, noise and, 43–44

radioactive substances, 5, 127, 150–151
radioactive waste, 78
railways, noise, 52
recycling waste, 96–97
remedies, nuisance, 18–19
rivers, 2–3, 117–121
road traffic, noise, 51–52
road vehicles
  abandoned vehicles, 99
  air pollution, 71–72
  end-of-life vehicles, 97–98
  fuel use, 61

scarlet fever, 3
scoping directions, 166, 167
scoping opinions, 166, 167
Scottish Environmental Protection Agency *see* **SEPA**
Scottish Water
  local authority agreements, 131
  private agreements, 131
  sewerage powers, 127–136
  vesting of sewers in, 133–134
screening
  directions, 165
  opinions, 163–165
  SEAs, 173–174
seizure powers
  noise, 42
  waste vehicles, 96
SEPA
  air pollution control, 68, 70–71
  contaminated land control, 102, 104, 105, 114
  creation, 5, 56
  functions, 5
  integrated pollution control, 138–151
  public registers, 150
  smoke control, 60

INDEX

waste control powers, 77, 86–89, 90
water management and, 120–127

sewerage
control, 127–136
costs, 129
defects, 133
domestic sewage, 128
drains, 128
private sewers, 134
private treatment works, 134
provision duties, 127–129
public sewers
  closure, 130
  connection rights, 131–132
  construction, 129–130, 134
  construction directions, 132
  discharge of trade effluents into, 134–135
  maintenance, 129
  meaning, 128
  vesting in Scottish Water, 133–134
Scottish Water powers, 127–136
  local authority agreements, 131
  private agreements, 131
  vesting of sewers, 133–134
sewage treatment works, 128
sewers, meaning, 128
SUDS, 127–129
trade effluents, 128, 134–136
  discharge into public sewers, 134–135
  existing discharges, 135–136
  new discharges, 135
  registration, 136

shipping, air pollution, 71, 73
smallpox, 3
smell, statutory nuisance, 23
smog, 3–4, 56, 62

smoke
colliery spoil-banks, 61
dark smoke, 56–57
furnace smoke, 57–59
investigation, 61
statutory nuisance, 23

smoke control areas, 59–61

statutory authority defence, 16, 52

statutory nuisance
see also specific nuisances
abatement notices *see* **abatement notices**
best practical means defence, 31, 33
common law nuisance and, 23
complaint-driven regime, 26
contaminated land and, 25, 103
enforcement powers, 32–33
  private individuals, 32–33
health prejudice, 21–22
local authority abatement proceedings, 31–32
local authority inspection duties, 26
meaning of nuisance, 23–25
noise, 35, 36–43
overview, 21–34
PPCA 1999 and, 25
premises, 21–23

steam, statutory nuisance, 23

strategic environmental assessments
consultation, 174–175
EIAs and, 167–168
EU Directive, 168, 170, 171
  Scottish implementation, 172
objectives, 168
overview, 167–175
plans and programmes
  exemptions, 172–173
  meaning, 168, 169–171, 172

strategic environmental assessments (*cont.*)
  publicity, 174
  reports, 171–172, 174
  responsible authorities, 172
  scope, 168
  scoping, 174
  screening, 173–174
structural defects, 29
surface water, meaning, 128
sustainable urban drainage systems (SUDSs), 127–128

telecommunications, SEAs, 168, 172
tourism, SEAs, 168
trade effluents, 128, 134–136
transport
  air pollution, 71–73
  SEAs, 168, 169–171, 172
typhus, 3

Vienna Convention for the Protection of the Ozone Layer (1985), 73

waste
  1990 EPA, 77–89
  abandoned vehicles, 99
  approaches, 77, 84
  brokers, 96
  carriers, registration, 95–96
  collection, 92–93
  command and control enforcement, 84
  contaminated land and, 101
  controlled waste, 78
  definition, 77–82
  duty of care, 84–85, 95
  electrical/electronic equipment, 98–99
  end-of-life vehicles, 97–98
  fly-tipping, 82–84
    civil liability, 95
    defences, 83
    penalties, 83
    removal, 93–95
  hazardous waste, 89, 166–167
  incineration, 78, 80, 101, 154–155
  inert waste, 89, 90
  landfill, 89–92
  licences, 85–89
    appeals, 88, 89
    fit and proper persons, 86–87, 88
    revocation, 88
    surrender, 88
    suspension, 88
    transfer, 88–89
    variation, 87–88
  local authority duties, 83–84
  municipal waste, 90
  overview, 77–100
  packaging, 96–97
  producer responsibility, 96–97
  radioactive waste, 78
  recycling, 96–97
  SEAs, 168, 172
  self-regulation, 84
  separation, 92–93
  special waste, 96
  transport, 95–96
  unlawfully deposited waste removal, 93–95
  Zero Waste Plan, 77
water
  authorisations
    appeals, 126–127

applications, 122–123
determination, 123
general rules, 122
ministerial powers, 123
monitoring, 123–124
registration, 122
revocation, 123, 126
SEPA powers, 122–124
suspension, 123, 126
system, 122–124
transfers, 126
variations, 123, 126
water use licences, 122
common law, 117–119
contaminated land and, 102–103
liability, 110–111
enforcement
appeals, 126–127
defences, 125
information, 124–125, 127
judicial actions, 124, 126
notices, 124, 127
offences, 125
registration, 125
remedial orders, 126
SEPA remediation, 124
system, 124–127
EU regulation, 119–120
history, 2–3
new works, 117–118
nuisance, 118–119
overview, 117–136
pollution control
2011 Controlled Activities Regulations, 121–127
authorisation system, 122–124
river basin management planning, 120–121
SEAs, 168, 172
Sewerage *see* **sewerage**
statutory nuisance, 23–24
surface water, meaning, 128
WEWSA (2003), 120–121
World Health Organization (WHO), 35, 45, 48

Zero Waste Plan, 77